CONCISE CATALOGUE OF FOREIGN PAINTINGS

Manchester City Art Gallery

1980

Manchester City Council Cultural Committee 1979/80

The Right Worshipful The Lord Mayor
Councillor Gerard W. G. Fitzsimons

Chairman
Councillor R. W. Ford

Deputy Chairman
Councillor Mrs. S. V. Shaw

Councillor D. Barker
Councillor H. Conway, JP
Councillor Mrs. M. I. Crawford
Councillor N. I. Finley
Councillor K. McKeon
Councillor C. McLaren
Councillor Mrs. B. Moore
Councillor H. Platt
Councillor L. Sanders
Councillor R. E. Talbot
Councillor M. J. Taylor
Councillor Miss M. A. Vince, JP
Professor B. Deane, BA, PHD
Professor C. R. Dodwell, MA, PHD
Mr. H. M. Fairhurst, MA, FRIBA
Mr. C. Paine, BSC, FRIC, FSDC
Dr. F. W. Ratcliffe, MA, PHD, JP
Professor K. R. Richards, MA
Mr. C. G. H. Simon, MA, JP

Director of Cultural Services
L. G. Lovell, FLA

Director of Art Galleries
T. P. P. Clifford, BA, AMA

Published by the City of Manchester Cultural Services
Printed in Great Britain by Revell and George Limited

ISBN 0 901673 16 1

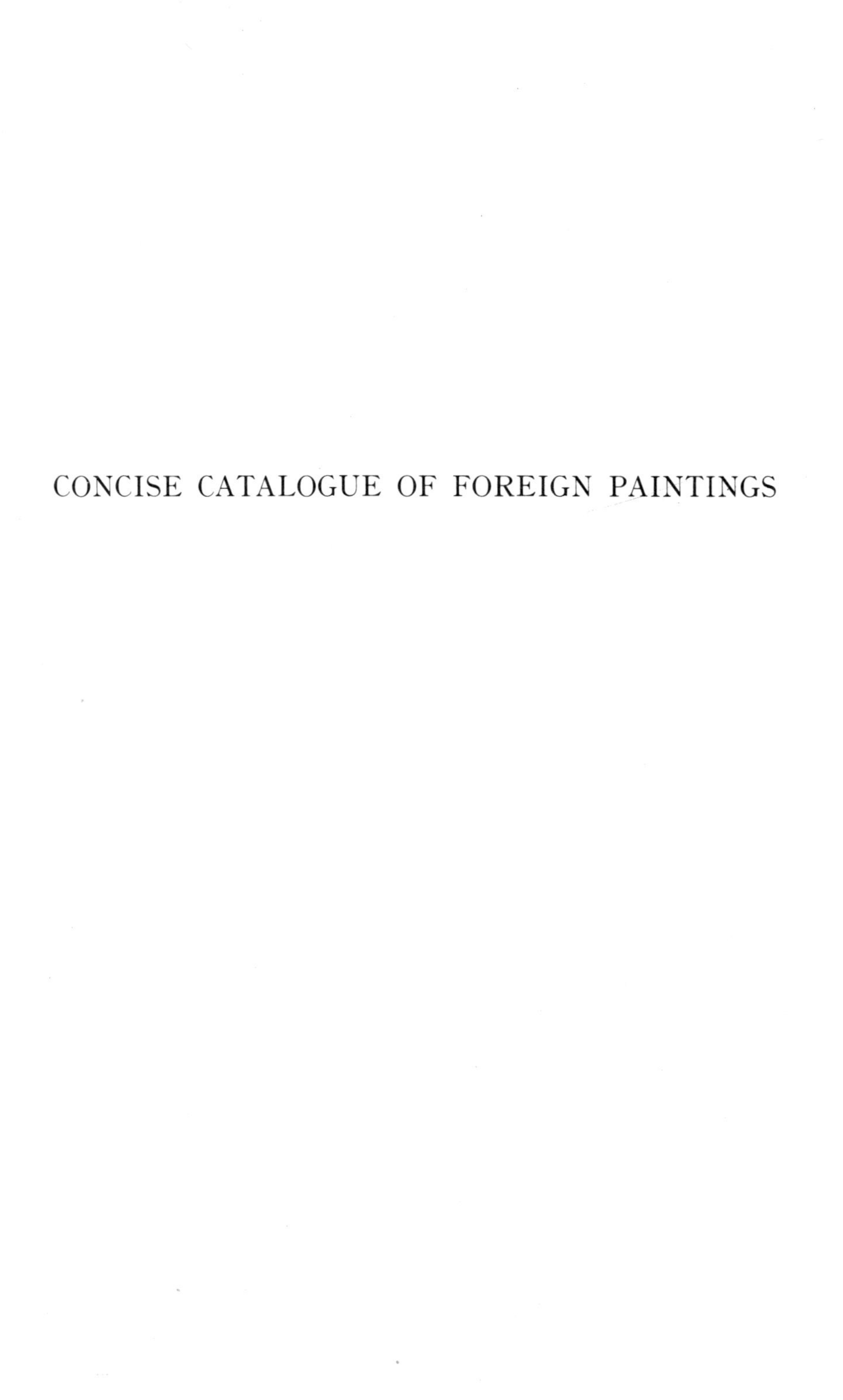

CONCISE CATALOGUE OF FOREIGN PAINTINGS

NOTES

The present catalogue is the companion to the two volumes already published covering all the British school paintings in the permament collection. All works in oil or tempera are included, except for loans.

Arrangement of entries

Works are arranged by artist, in alphabetical order. Where there are several works by one artist these are given in accession order for each artist. Unattributed works are listed under their national schools if they cannot clearly be related to a particular master.

Attributions

Artist's name
The work is by the artist in question. This judgment is based on firm documentation or on style. Traditional attributions are adhered to where no reasonable alternative has been put forward.

Attributed to
The work may be by the artist, but doubts have been expressed about the attribution.

School or Studio of
The work is not by the artist, but is executed by one of the pupils or assistants working in the master's studio.

Follower of
The work is not by the artist in question, but is by an artist working at roughly the same period, in a style close to that of the master.

Manner of
The work is not by the artist in question, nor necessarily of the period, but is in the artist's generic style.

After
The work is a specific copy of a painting by the artist in question, but could be of any date.

Former attributions
These are given in every case to aid identification.

Unattributed works
These will be found under their respective schools, i.e. German, Netherlandish, etc.

Titles

Wherever possible works are given their traditional titles, or the titles under which they have already been published. In some cases more precise titles have been given to replace vague ones, such as 'Landscape'. Paintings acquired through the Assheton-Bennett bequest are given the titles which appear in Frits Grossmann, *Catalogue of Paintings and Drawings from the Assheton Bennett Collection*, Manchester, 1965.

Dates

The date of the work, where known, is given on a separate line. The following abbreviations are used:

c. *circa*, for approximate dating on stylistic or other grounds

b. born

d. died

Dimensions

Works have been remeasured for this catalogue. Sizes are given in centimetres, and followed in brackets by inches to the nearest sixteenth. Height precedes width. Dimensions given are those of the original painted surface, not of any additional supporting canvas, panel or mount.

Signature and Inscriptions

These are recorded in full:

s. signed

inscr: inscribed, for insciptions in the artist's hand

(blc): bottom left corner

(tr): top right, etc.

(mon) following a signature, denotes that the initials form an artist's monogram

Signatures and inscriptions are given in italics. An oblique stroke is used to indicate the beginning of a fresh line in an inscription.

Provenance

Only the immediate source of each work is given. The date of accession to the Gallery forms in most cases the first part of the accession number given in brackets at the end of the entry. If the date of accession is different it is given separately.

Illustrations

All works are illustrated.

Appendices

A number of paintings by British school artists have been acquired or accessioned since the publication of Volume II of the Concise Catalogue of British Paintings in 1978. These have been listed in Appendix I, with illustrations. Appendix 2 relates to those works transferred from the Royal Manchester Institution in 1882, and Appendix 3 lists works no longer in the collection which were included in the 1910 'Handbook'. Appendices 4 and 5 are indices of portraits and donors. Finally, there is an index of artists by schools.

FOREWORD

The collection of Foreign Schools paintings in the Manchester City Art Galleries has never been the subject of a published catalogue and as, regrettably, much of Manchester's collections are still in store, some of our more important works have been overlooked in the standard monographs and *oeuvre* catalogues. The Old Master paintings are admittedly uneven in quality and the pattern of the collection lacks coherence but it does contain works of fine quality by artists of excellence – like the *Adoration* attributed to Ridolfo Ghirlandaio, an exquisite *Madonna* by the Master of the Magdalen Legend, Stanzioni's *Salome with the head of St. John the Baptist*, Reni's *St. Catherine*, Batoni's *Portrait of Sir Gregory Page-Turner*. Several of these paintings were acquired recently by my predecessor, Loraine Conran, who was also responsible for creating the Art Fund, which merits the Gallery's undying gratitude. His deputy, Dr. F. G. Grossmann, had earlier purchased for lesser sums a modest group of oil sketches, some of special significance like the Charles de la Fosse for the staircase ceiling of Montagu House, London, and the Anton Raphael Mengs of the *Apotheosis of S. Eusebio*, for the church of that name in Rome. But these were elegant, sophisticated additions to a nucleus of foreign paintings given or bequeathed by Mancunians largely in the late 19th and early 20th centuries.

The existing holding was transformed last year by the most generous bequest of the late Mr. and Mrs. Edgar Assheton-Bennett of 100 oil paintings principally of the Dutch School. These Dutch 17th century cabinet pieces, which had been loaned to Manchester from 1965, added to our existing Netherlandish collection, put Manchester City Art Galleries in a class quite by itself outside London. As can be seen from this *Concise Catalogue* we now have small masterpieces by Ter Borch, van de Cappelle, van Goyen, van der Heyden, Koninck, van der Neer and Paulus Potter, not forgetting the superb flowerpieces and still lifes by Kalf, van Huysum and van Os.

Later foreign paintings consist mainly of examples by Salon painters like Bouguereau, Ary Scheffer, Prof. Wagner and Adolphe Yvon acquired in Manchester's hey-day, and works by the Barbizon and Impressionist Schools. In this connection should be mentioned works by Boudin, Corot, Courbet, Harpignies, Troyon, a large group by Fantin-Latour; and pictures by Blanche, Cazin, Derain, Forain, Gauguin, Léger, Marcoussis, Camille Pissarro, Renoir, Sisley and Vlaminck. The painting of other European countries is represented by the Dutchmen, Jacob and Willem Maris, the Franco-Italian Monticelli, and the Surrealist, Max Ernst.

This summary catalogue is the third in a series initiated several years ago to make a useful pictorial inventory of the collection. Its completion, following on from the two volumes on British paintings, means that now all the oils belonging to the Gallery have been published in this concise format. It will be noticed that further British paintings acquired after the publication of Volume II appear in this volume's appendix. The next stage, already in hand, is the publication of the full catalogue.

The City of Manchester's British 19th century paintings are known to be one of the greatest collections in the country, coinciding with the city's huge wealth at that time. Considering the city's important position in world commerce then, it is curious that Manchester did not build up an equally distinguished collection of foreign paintings. Regrettably, unlike Liverpool, Manchester has, as yet, no precious early panel paintings comparable to, say, their Ecole de'Roberti or Simone Martini, nor do we boast a Bellini and Botticelli like Birmingham. However with the financial assistance of our newly formed *Friends*, which already number over 700 members, and our new business organisation, the *Patrons and Associates*, it is intended to improve greatly our Foreign Schools holdings. Although the City gives us a generous purchase grant, Titians and Rembrandts will remain forever beyond our purse unless the Government allocates to us such fine paintings through the present 'in lieu' capital transfer tax arrangements. It will be noticed that by this scheme we have recently received a superb Turner oil (see Appendix), for which we are most grateful. Let us hope that other great treasures of the foreign schools will follow in its wake, to render Manchester one of the greatest collections outside London.

Much important spade work was done on Manchester's foreign paintings by Dr. F. G. Grossmann, Dr. Michael Kauffmann and myself. More recently most helpful suggestions and assistance have been received from Mr. Christopher Brown of the National Gallery, Mrs. Elizabeth Conran of the Bowes Museum, Barnard Castle, Mr. M. S. Robinson, formerly of the National Maritime Museum, Greenwich, Mr. W. van der Watering of the Rijksbureau voor Kunsthistorische Documentatie, The Hague, and Mr. Christopher Wright, formerly of the Witt Library, Courtauld Institute of Art. Many others have contributed information and they will be fully acknowledged in the forthcoming catalogue.

Preparatory work on this volume has been undertaken by the staff of the Gallery over many years but my especial thanks are due to Martin Royalton-Kisch, Assistant Keeper in the Paintings Department, by whom the entries in this volume have been most speedily and assiduously collated.

Timothy Clifford
Director

Josef van Aken
1709–1749 Flemish

A TEA PARTY

Oil on canvas
37·4 × 45·7 (19½ × 17¾)
Unsigned
Assheton-Bennett bequest (1979.537)

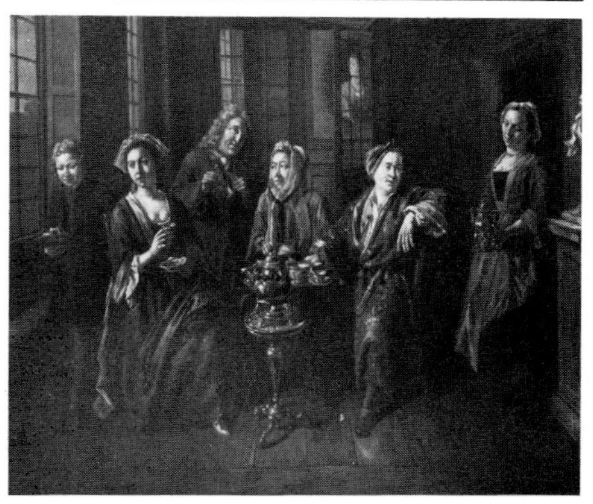

Alexandrian
See Egyptian

Antwerp School, 16th century

THE JUDGEMENT OF SOLOMON
1526

Oil on panel
110·2 × 95·3 (43⅜ × 37½)
inscr(bl): *1526*
Purchased (1960.331)

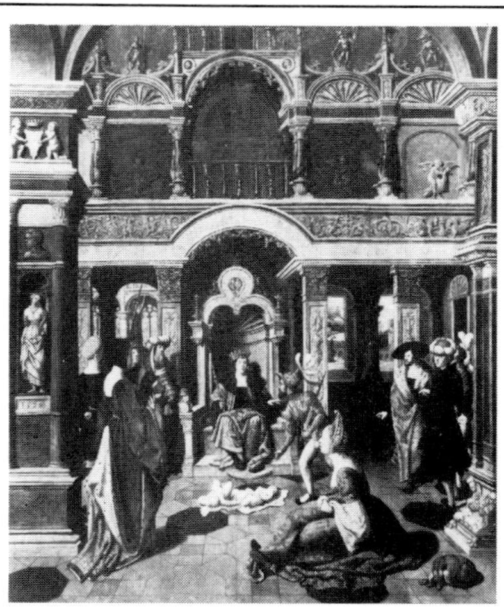

Arent Arentz., called Cabel
1585/86–1635 Dutch

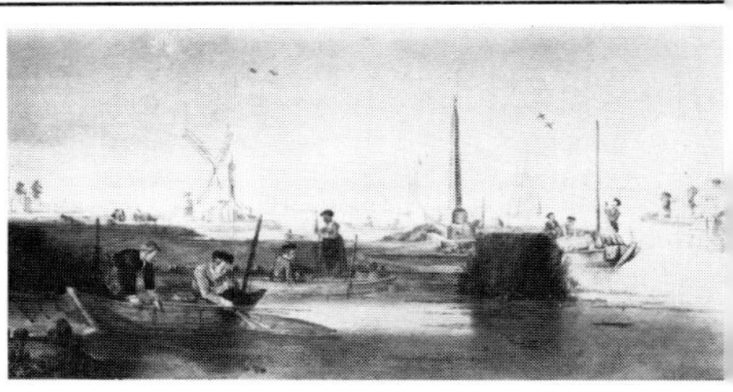

RIVER SCENE WITH FISHERMEN IN A ROWING BOAT IN THE FOREGROUND

Oil on panel
28·7 × 58·8 (11¼ × 23⅛)
s (centre to r, on base of obelisk): *AA* (mon)
Assheton-Bennett bequest (1979.439)

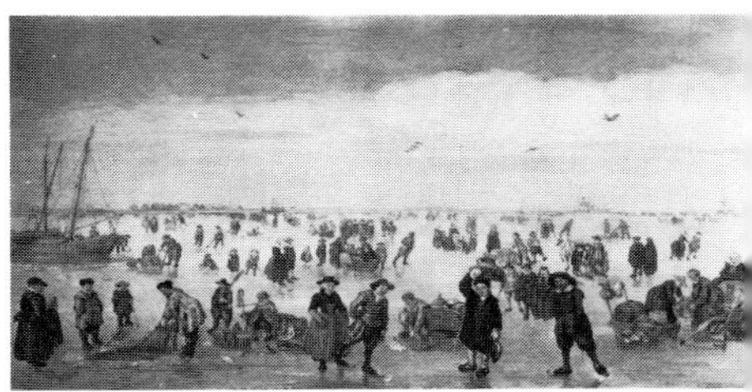

WINTER SCENE WITH NUMEROUS FIGURES ON THE ICE

Oil on panel
25·7 × 50·8 (10⅛ × 20)
s(br, on barrel): *AA* (mon)
Assheton-Bennett bequest (1979.440)

?Austrian or South German, 18th century
(formerly attributed to Matteo Bonechi)

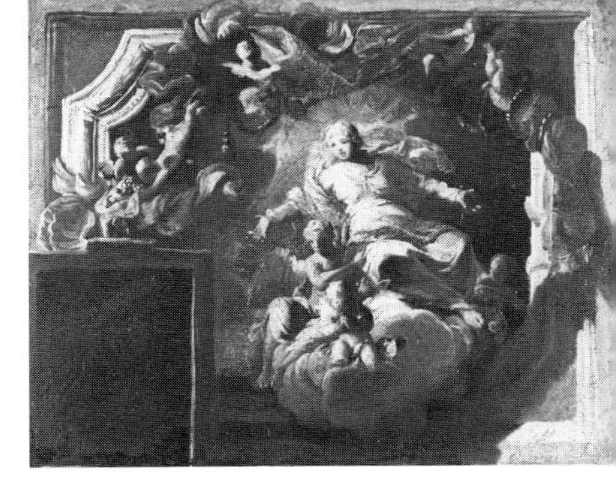

THE ASSUMPTION OF THE VIRGIN: STUDY FOR A WALL DECORATION

Oil on paper stuck down on canvas
23·2 × 30·2 (9⅛ × 11⅞)
Unsigned
Purchased (1966.181)

A CONCERT OF ANGELS:
STUDY FOR A WALL DECORATION

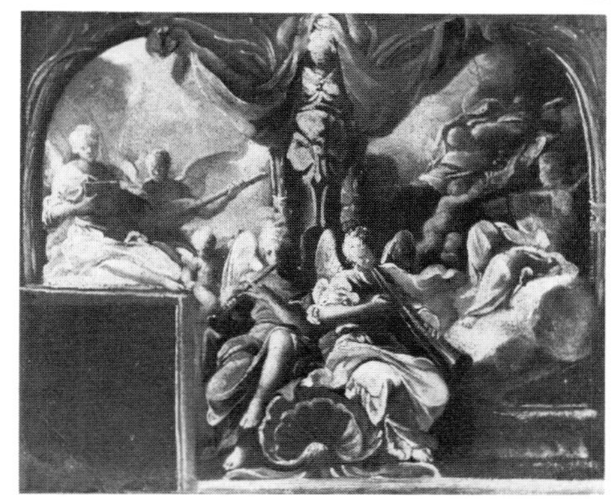

Oil on paper stuck down on canvas
23·2 × 30·4 (9⅛ × 11 15/16)
Unsigned
Purchased (1966.182)

Jacques-André-Joseph Aved
1702–1766 French

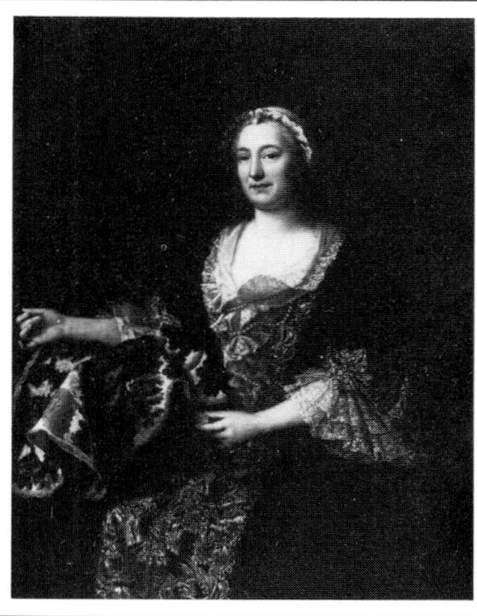

A LADY WITH EMBROIDERY

Oil on canvas
127·5 × 101·9 (50 3/16 × 40⅛)
Unsigned
Purchased (1904.1)

Barent Avercamp
1612–1679 Dutch

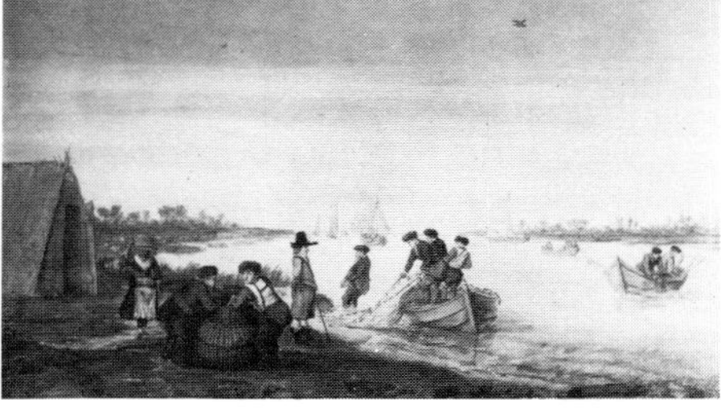

RIVER SCENE WITH FISHERMEN
DRAWING NETS
1650

Oil on panel
33·4 × 52·4 (13⅛ × 20⅝)
s(br on piece of wood):
B. Avercamp / 1650.
Assheton-Bennett bequest (1979.441)

Baciccio
See Giovanni Battista Gaulli

Ludolf Backhuysen
1631–1708 Dutch

COAST SCENE: FIGURES ON A QUAY IN THE FOREGROUND AND SAILING BOATS ON A WINDSWEPT SEA

Oil on canvas pasted onto panel
44.2 × 54.5 ($17\frac{7}{16} \times 21\frac{1}{2}$)
s(bl on piece of wood beneath figure with outstretched arm): *L.B.*
Assheton-Bennett bequest (1979.442)

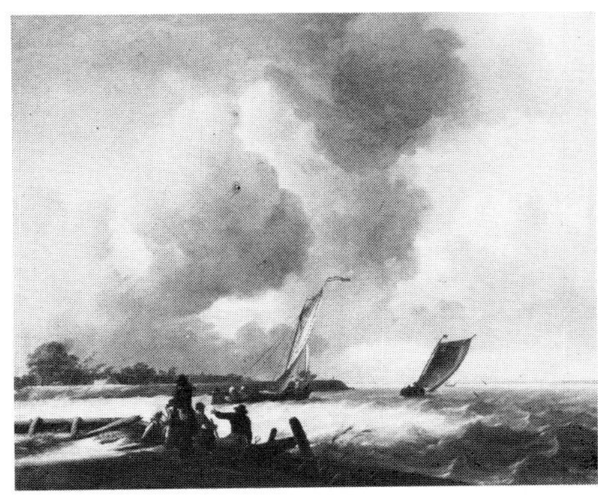

SEASCAPE WITH MEN OF WAR AND SMALLER VESSELS; JETTY, LEFT

Oil on canvas
46·5 × 58·8 ($18\frac{1}{4} \times 23\frac{1}{8}$)
s(centre to l on rowing boat):
L. Backhui . . . (illegible)
Assheton-Bennett bequest (1979.443)

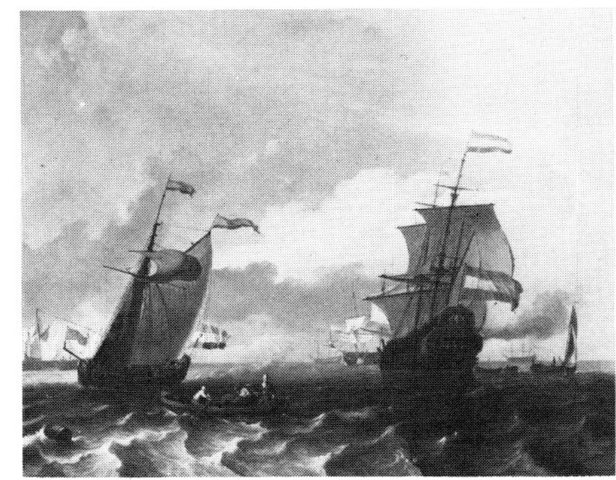

Attributed to
Cornelis de Baellieur the Elder
1607–1671 Flemish
(formerly attributed to Ambrosius Francken I)

MARTYRDOM OF ST. CATHERINE

Oil on panel
43·1 × 34 ($16\frac{15}{16} \times 13\frac{3}{8}$)
Unsigned
Purchased (1931.50)

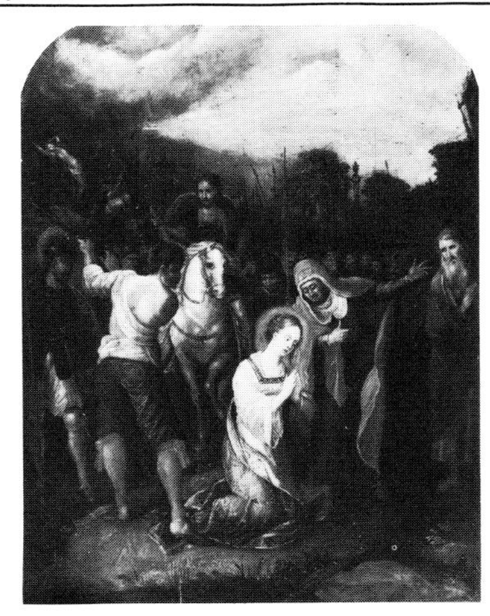

Matteo Balducci
fl. 1509–55 Italian
(formerly attributed to Lo Spagna)

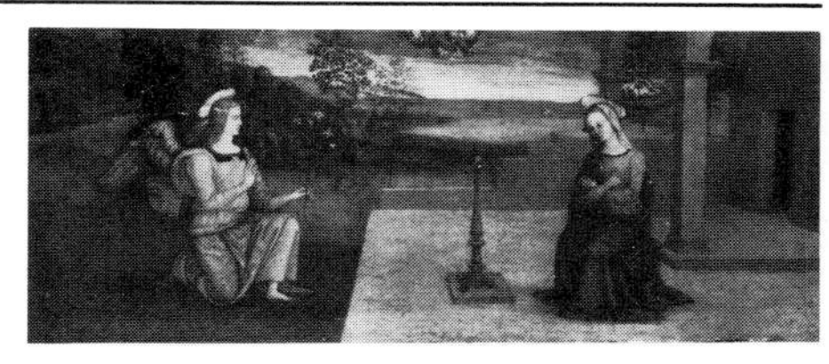

THE ANNUNCIATION

Tempera on panel
23·6 × 57·6 ($9\frac{5}{16} \times 22\frac{11}{16}$)
Unsigned
Henry Whitehead bequest through the National Art-Collections Fund
(1947.184)

(formerly attributed to Lo Spagna)

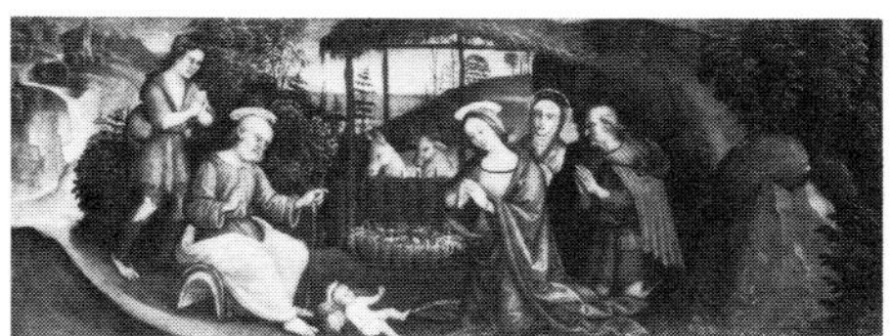

THE NATIVITY WITH ST. BRIDGET

Tempera on panel
23·1 × 59·8 ($9\frac{1}{8} \times 23\frac{9}{16}$)
Unsigned
Henry Whitehead bequest through the National Art-Collections Fund
(1947.185)

(formerly attributed to Lo Spagna)

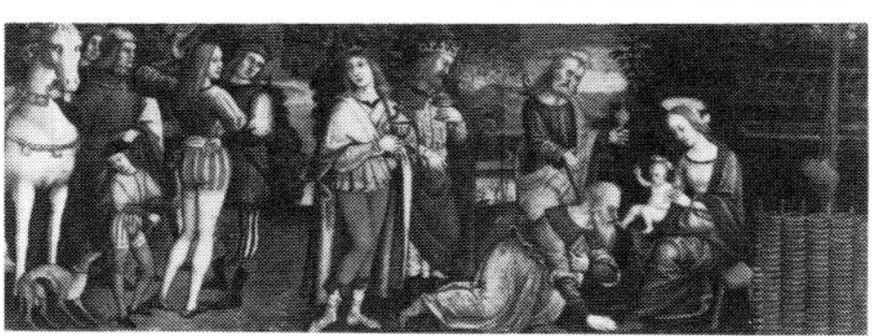

THE ADORATION OF THE MAGI

Tempera on panel
22·5 × 59·3 ($8\frac{7}{8} \times 23\frac{3}{8}$)
Unsigned
Henry Whitehead bequest through the National Art-Collections Fund
(1947.186)

(formerly attributed to Lo Spagna)

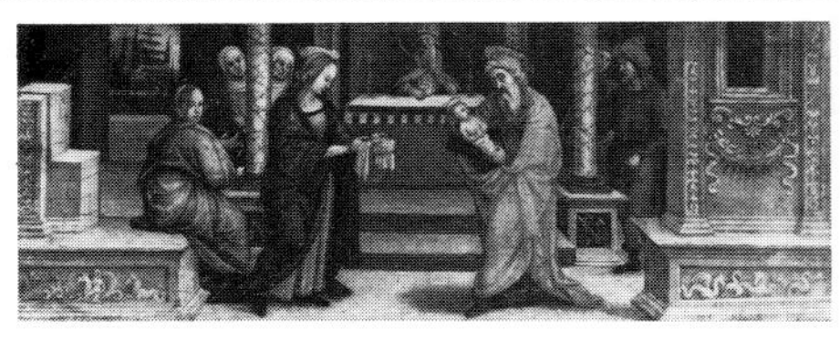

THE PRESENTATION IN THE TEMPLE

Tempera on panel
22·4 × 59.1 ($8\frac{13}{16} \times 23\frac{1}{4}$)
Unsigned
Henry Whitehead bequest through the National Art-Collections Fund (1947.187)

Johannes Antonius van der Baren
1616–1686 Flemish

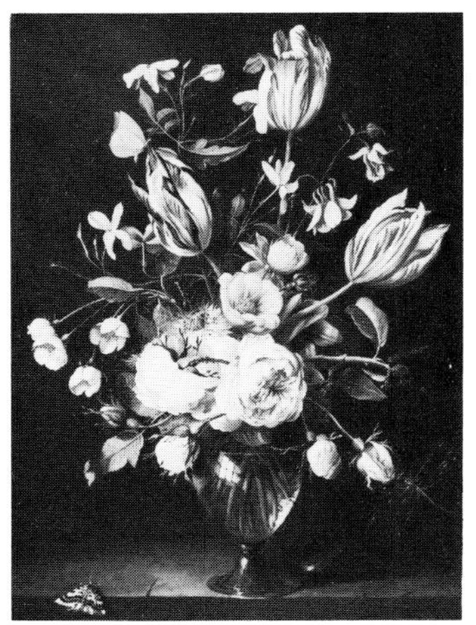

ROSES, TULIPS, TOBACCO PLANTS AND OTHER FLOWERS IN A GLASS VASE
1663

Oil on canvas
56·4 × 41·4 ($22\frac{1}{4} \times 16\frac{1}{4}$)
s(b, centre): *16JVB63* (mon)
Assheton-Bennett bequest (1979.535)

Bassano
See South Netherlandish

Pompeo Batoni
1708–1787 Italian

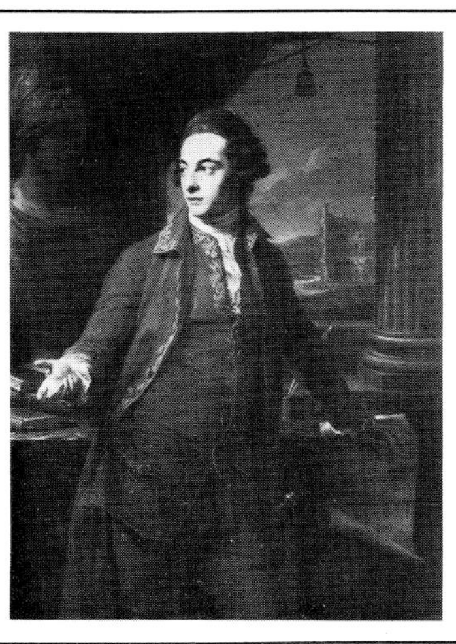

SIR GREGORY PAGE-TURNER (1740–1805)
1768

Oil on canvas
134·5 × 99·5 ($52\frac{15}{16} \times 39\frac{3}{16}$)
s(r, on base of column): *P. BATONI PINXIT ROMAE / ANNO 1768.*
Purchased (1976.79)

Frederick Bauhof
active 19th century, Austrian?

A CATTLE MARKET IN PONT CROIX, BRITTANY

Oil on canvas
107 × 153·5 ($42\frac{1}{8} \times 60\frac{7}{16}$)
s(brc): *Bauhof*
W. Pownall gift (1911.28)

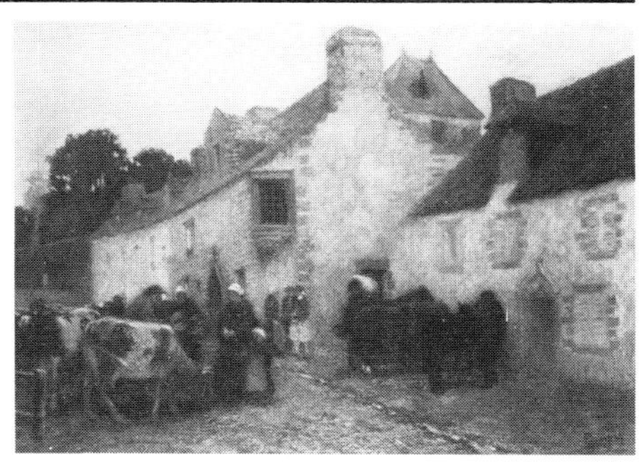

Cornelius Bega
c. 1632–1664 Dutch

THREE PEASANTS SEATED TOGETHER

Oil on panel
28·5 × 22·4 ($11\frac{1}{4} \times 8\frac{13}{16}$)
s(brc): *C. Bega.*
Assheton-Bennett bequest (1979.444)

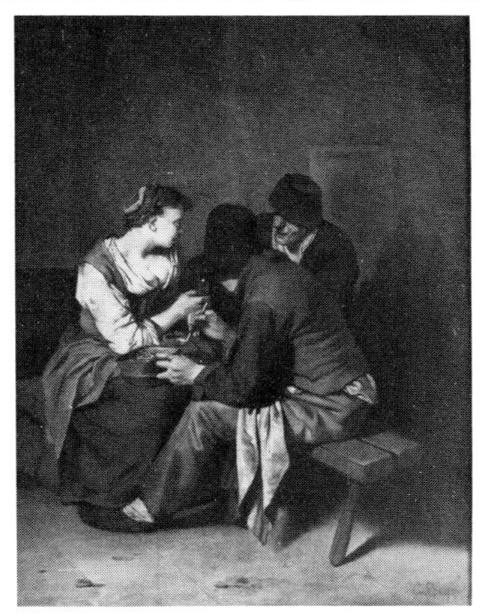

Follower of Pietro Berrettini da Cortona
1596–1669 Italian

THE FINDING OF MOSES

Oil on canvas
34 × 54·5 ($13\frac{3}{8} \times 21\frac{7}{16}$)
Unsigned
T. Gough gift (1928.12)

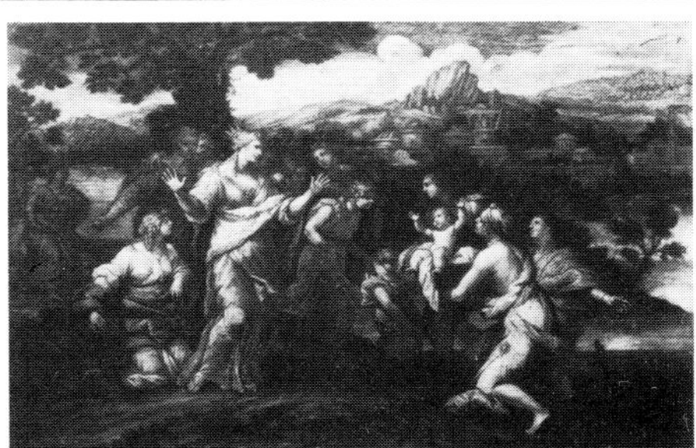

Abraham van Beyeren
1620/21–1690 Dutch

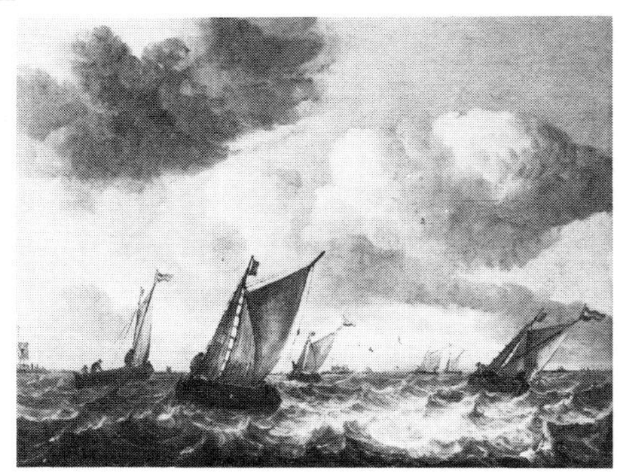

FISHING BOATS OFF THE COAST IN A CHOPPY SEA

Oil on panel
42·8 × 56·2 (16⅞ × 22⅛)
Unsigned
Assheton-Bennett bequest (1979.445)

Jules Bidlingmeyer
d. 1893 French

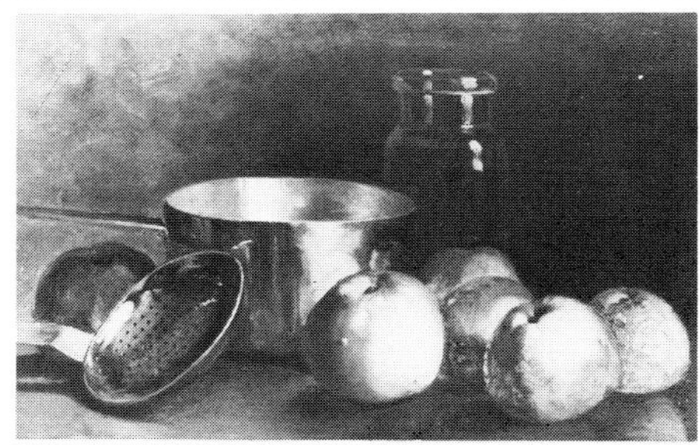

APPLES AND A PAN

Oil on canvas
38 × 45·7 (14$\frac{15}{16}$ × 18)
s(blc): *J Bidlingmeyer* (JB in mon)
Presented by George Thomas through the Royal Manchester Institution (1917.275)

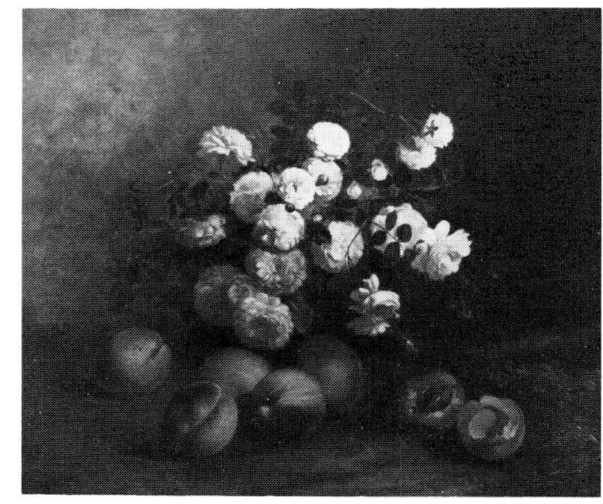

FLOWERS AND APRICOTS

Oil on canvas
36·8 × 45·1 (14½ × 17¾)
s(blc): *J Bidlingmeyer* (JB in mon)
Presented by George Thomas through the Royal Manchester Institution (1917.276)

Jacques-Émile Blanche
1861–1942 French

THE CORONATION OF GEORGE V
1911

Oil on canvas
92·5 × 73·1 ($36\frac{7}{16}$ × $28\frac{3}{4}$)
s(brc): *J. E. Blanche / 11*
Presented by the artist (1936.129)

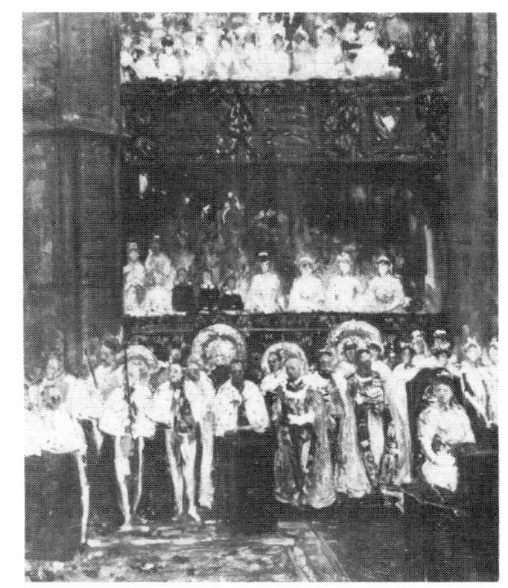

THOMAS HARDY (1840–1928)
1906

Oil on canvas
92 × 73·5 ($36\frac{3}{16}$ × $28\frac{15}{16}$)
s(brc): *J. E. Blanche / 1906*
Purchased (1936.134)

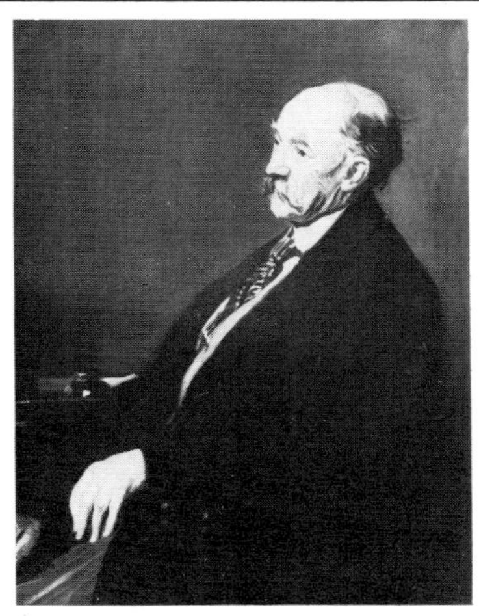

MISS WINNY MACEWAN

Oil on canvas
74 × 67·1 ($29\frac{1}{8}$ × $26\frac{3}{8}$)
s(trc): *J. E. Blanche*
Miss Helen J. MacEwan gift
(1936.366)

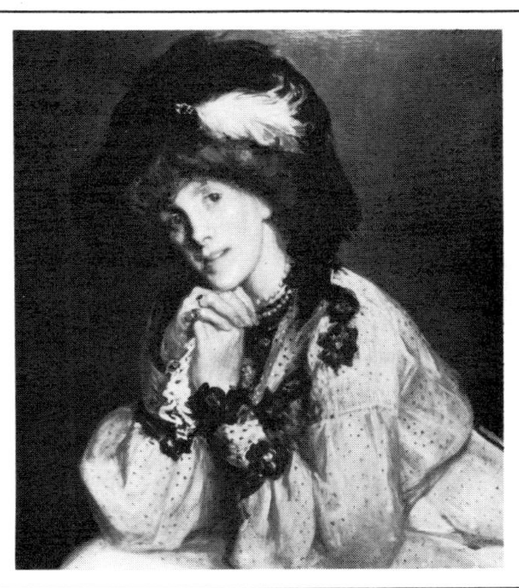

WALTER RICHARD SICKERT
(1860–1942)
Artist
1935

Oil on canvas
80·5 × 61·5 ($31\frac{11}{16} \times 24\frac{1}{4}$)
s(blc): *Sickert / 1935 . . .* (indecipherable) *friend / J. E. Blanche*
Purchased (1937.708)

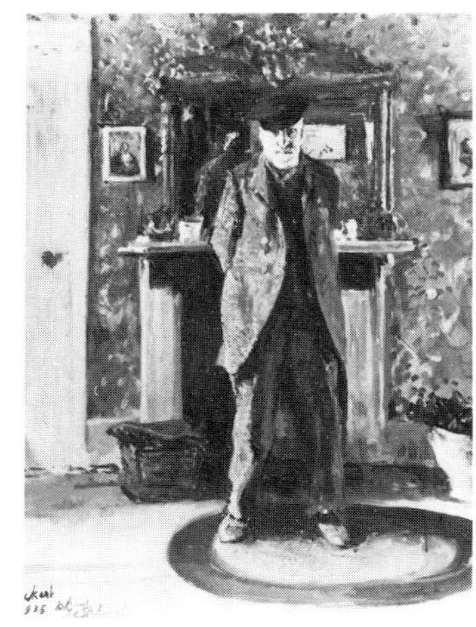

MRS. SICKERT (MOTHER OF W. R. S.)
1908

Oil on canvas
60·9 × 50 ($24 \times 19\frac{11}{16}$)
s(brc): *J E Blanche / Mrs Sickert / . . .* (?) */ Dieppe / 1908*
Purchased (1938.74)

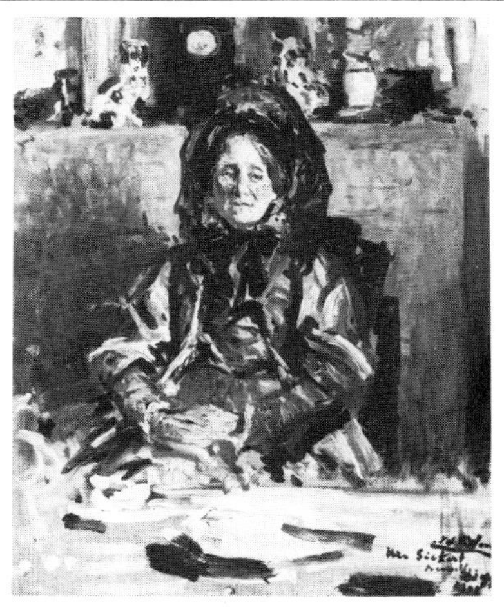

Abraham Bloemaert
1564–1651 Dutch

A PEDLAR WITH A DOG IN A LANDSCAPE

Oil on canvas
50·2 × 64·6 ($19\frac{3}{4} \times 25\frac{7}{16}$)
s(l): *A Bloemaert*
Purchased with the E. Assheton-Bennett Bequest Fund (1978.261)

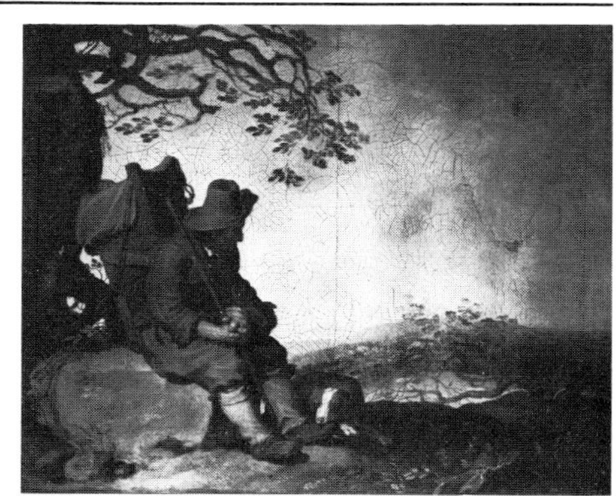

Boccaccio Boccaccino
c. 1467–1524/25 Italian

MADONNA AND CHILD

Oil on panel
56·5 × 45·6 ($22\frac{1}{4} \times 17\frac{15}{16}$)
Unsigned
G. Beatson Blair bequest, 1941
(1947.132)

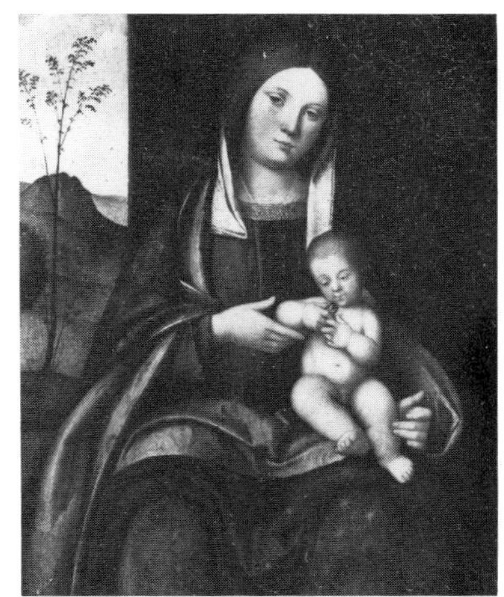

Max Bohm
1868–1923 American

FISHERMEN IN A STORMY SEA
1898

Oil on canvas
58·4 × 71·8 ($23 \times 28\frac{1}{4}$)
s(brc): *Max Bohm / 1898*
Henry Boddington gift (1912.71)

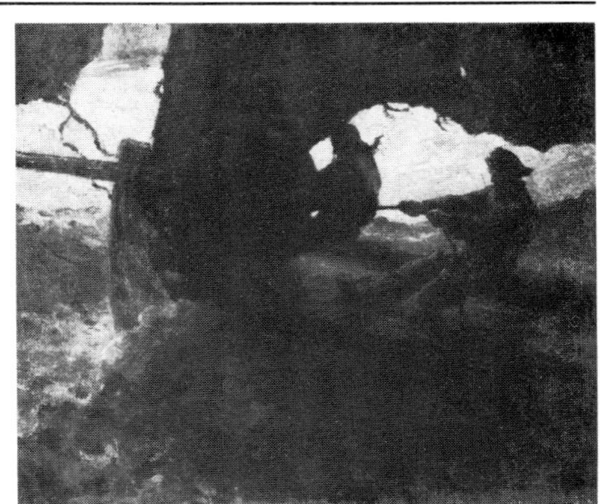

Marinus Boks
1849–1885 Dutch

LANDSCAPE WITH A FARMHOUSE

Oil on canvas laid down on board
13·4 × 29·7 ($5\frac{1}{4} \times 11\frac{11}{16}$)
Unsigned
Lady Mary Boyd Dawkins bequest
(1979.614)

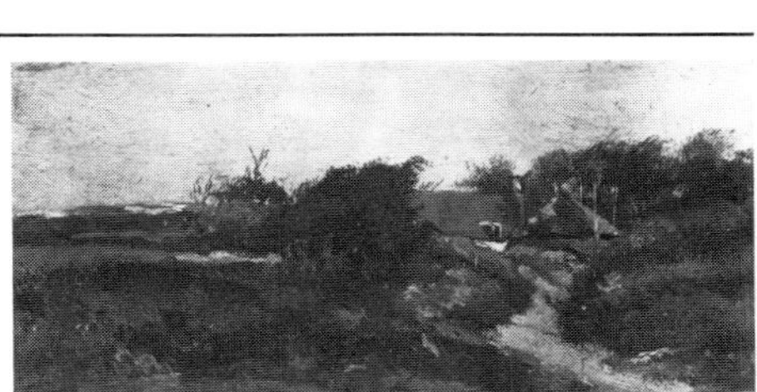

Matteo Bonechi
See Austrian or South German

Carlo Bononi
See School of Bernardo Strozzi

Pietro Paolo Bonzi
called il Gobbo dei Carracci
c. 1576–1636 Italian

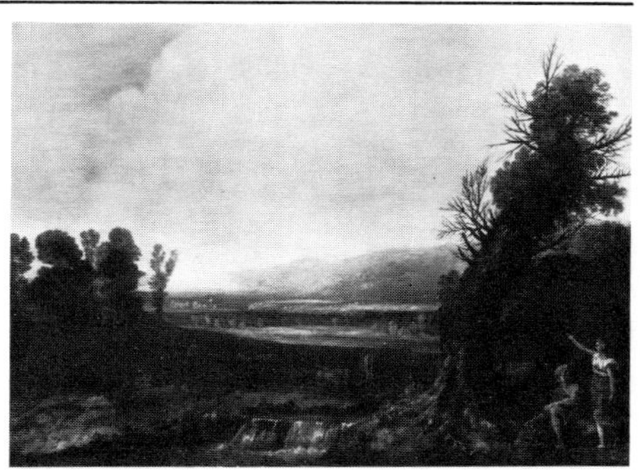

LANDSCAPE WITH ERMINIA AND THE SHEPHERDS

Oil on panel
37·4 × 53·4 ($14\frac{3}{4} \times 21$)
Unsigned
Purchased with the E. Assheton-Bennett Bequest Fund (1979.71)

Gerard Ter Borch
1617–1681 Dutch

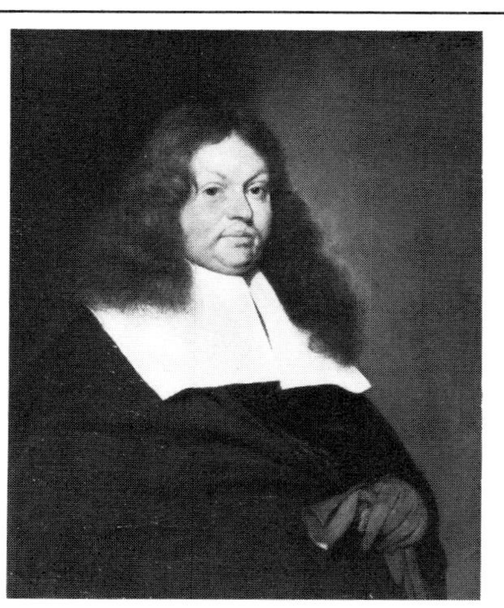

CORNELIS VOS, BURGOMASTER OF DEVENTER (1623–1684)

Oil on copper
22·7 × 19 ($8\frac{15}{16} \times 7\frac{1}{2}$)
Unsigned
Assheton-Bennett bequest (1979.446)

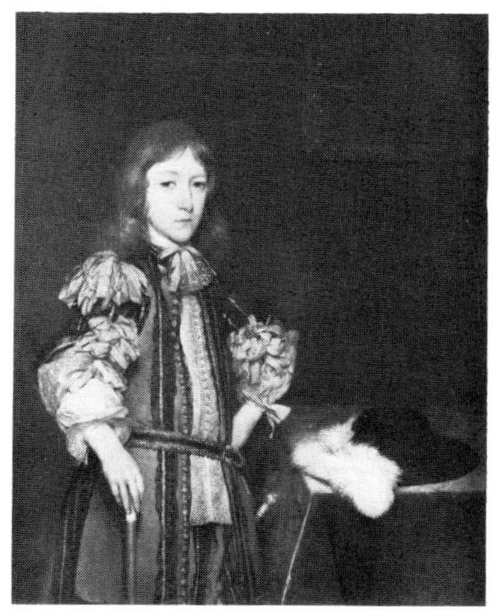

HENDRIK CASIMIR II, PRINCE OF NASSAU-DIETZ (1657–1696)
1670

Oil on canvas
33·4 × 27·8 ($13\frac{1}{8} \times 10\frac{15}{16}$)
s(r, below painting): *GTB* (mon), and inscr: *AETATIS 12 / 1670.*
Assheton-Bennett bequest (1979.447)

Attributed to Paris Bordon
1500–1571 Italian

THE HOLY FAMILY WITH ST. JOHN THE BAPTIST

Oil on canvas
94·3 × 135·9 ($37\frac{1}{8} \times 53\frac{1}{2}$)
Unsigned
Lt. Col. R. H. Antrobus gift
(1971.106)

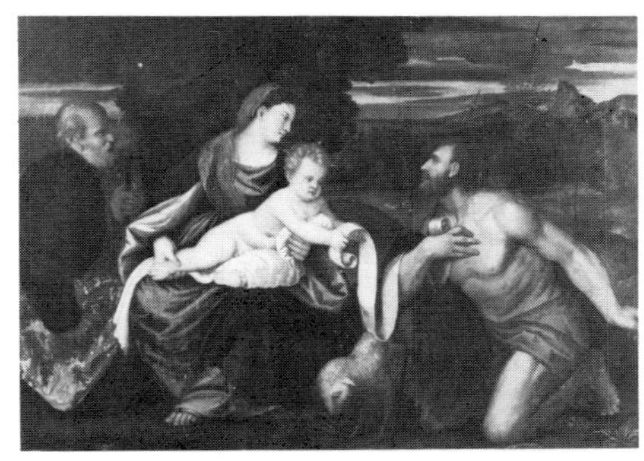

Johannes Bosboom
1817–1891 Dutch

ALMSHOUSES

Oil on panel
23·9 × 33·9 ($9\frac{7}{16} \times 13\frac{3}{8}$)
s(brc): *B.I*
Lady Mary Boyd Dawkins bequest
(1979.615)

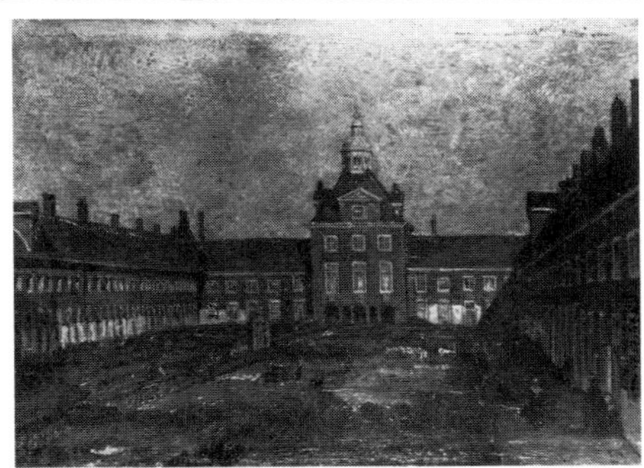

Eugène-Louis Boudin
1824–1898 French

ÉTAPLES
1889

Oil on panel
40·5 × 55·2 ($15\frac{15}{16} \times 21\frac{3}{4}$)
s(brc): *Etaples / E. Boudin 89*
Purchased (1908.2)

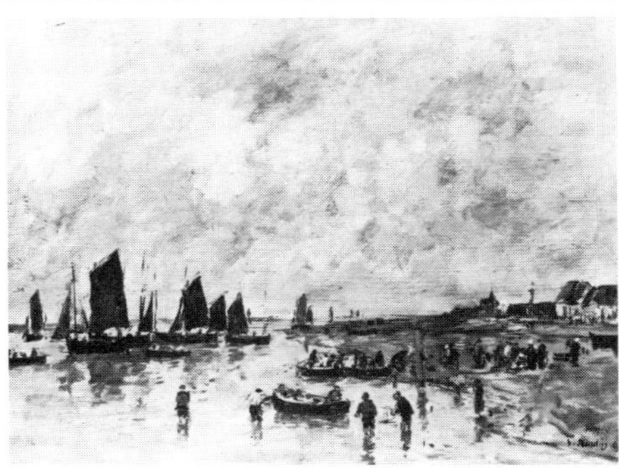

TROUVILLE HARBOUR

Oil on canvas
38·4 × 54·5 ($15\frac{1}{8} \times 21\frac{7}{16}$)
s(blc): *E. Boudin.*
G. Beatson Blair bequest, 1941
(1947.71)

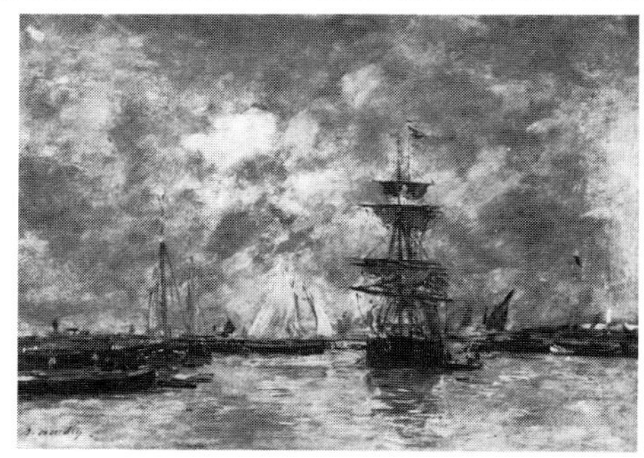

Manner of Eugène-Louis Boudin

A CALM

Oil on panel
23.4 × 33·2 ($9\frac{3}{16} \times 13\frac{1}{16}$)
inscr(blc): *E. Boudin* (?)
James Blair bequest (1917.225)

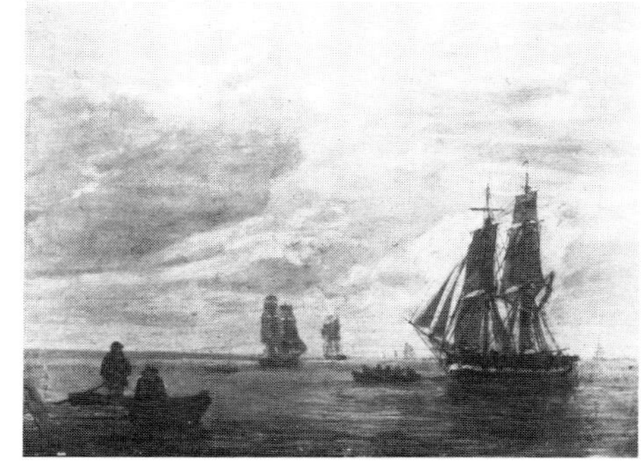

William-Adolphe Bouguereau
1825–1905 French

INNOCENCE
1898

Oil on canvas
95·3 × 58 ($37\frac{1}{2} \times 22\frac{7}{8}$)
s(br): *W-BOUGUEREAU – 1898*
James Blair bequest (1917.229)

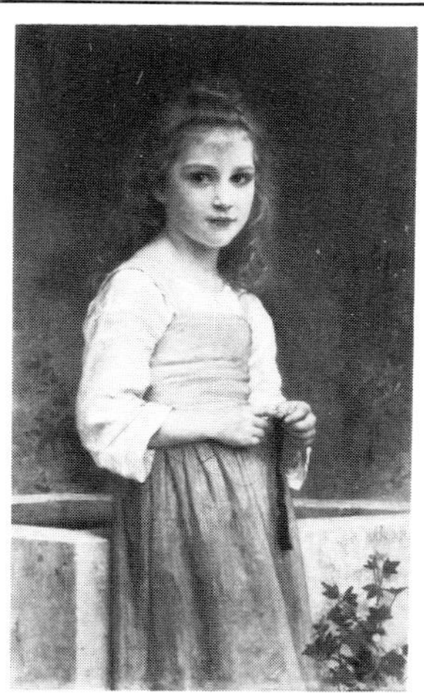

Quirin Gerritz. van Brekelenkam
c. 1620–1668 Dutch

A FAMILY SEATED ROUND A KITCHEN FIRE

Oil on canvas
41·4 × 55·7 ($16\frac{1}{4} \times 21\frac{15}{16}$)
s(br) : *Q.B.*
Assheton-Bennett bequest (1979.448)

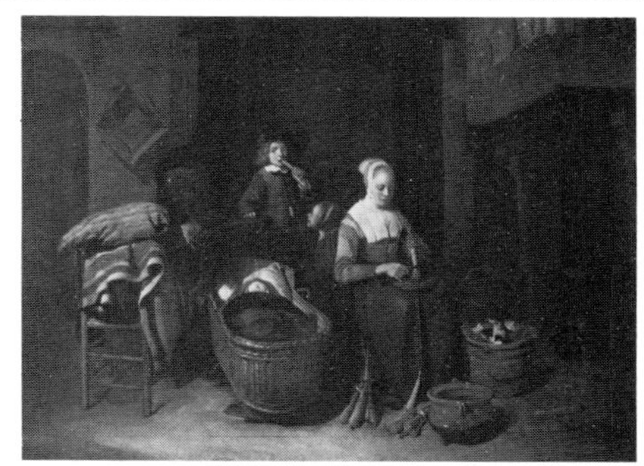

INTERIOR WITH A LADY CHOOSING FISH
1664

Oil on panel
49·8 × 39·4 ($19\frac{5}{8} \times 15\frac{1}{2}$)
s(br) : *Q.B. 1664.*
Assheton-Bennett bequest (1979.449)

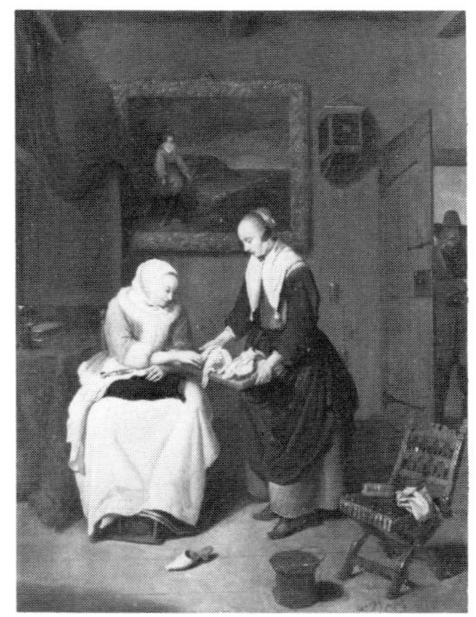

Follower of Adriaen Brouwer
1605/6–1638 Flemish

TAVERN SCENE WITH A LARGE CROWD OF PEASANTS DRINKING AND MERRYMAKING

Oil on panel
60·8 × 94·1 ($23\frac{7}{8} \times 37$)
inscr(br, on overturned bench) : *AB* (mon)
Assheton-Bennett bequest (1979.451)

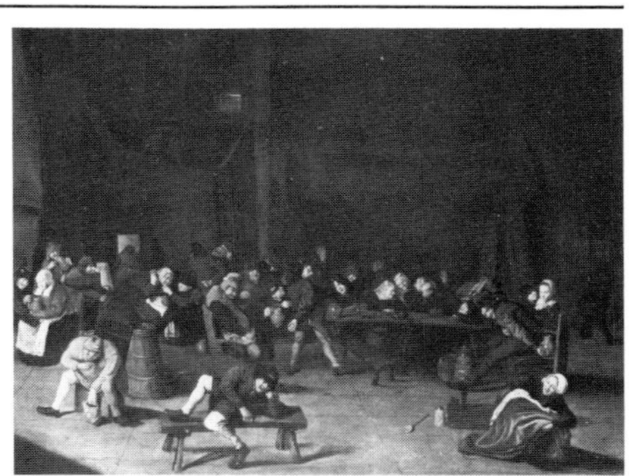

Manner of Adriaen Brouwer

PEASANTS EATING MUSSELS

Oil on panel
42·2 × 33·1 ($16\frac{5}{8} \times 13\frac{1}{16}$)
Unsigned
Assheton-Bennett bequest (1979.450)

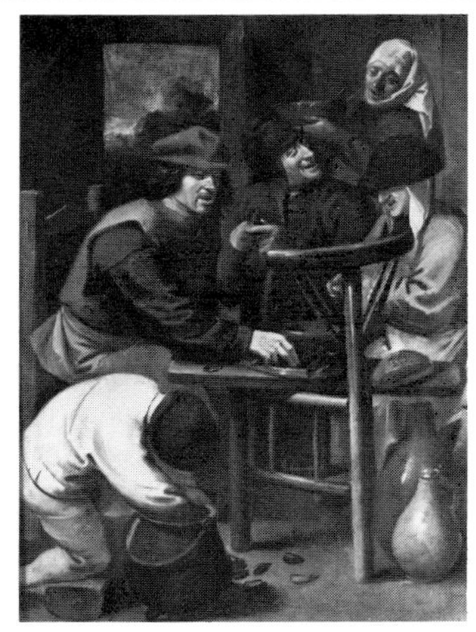

Henriette Browne (Mme. Jules de Saux; née Sophie de Bouteillier) 1829–1901 French

A BROTHER OF THE CHRISTIAN SCHOOLS

Oil on canvas
116·7 × 89·5 ($45\frac{15}{16} \times 35\frac{1}{4}$)
s(brc): *Henriette Browne.*
Presented by R. N. Philips to the Royal Manchester Institution, 1856, from which transferred (1884.10)

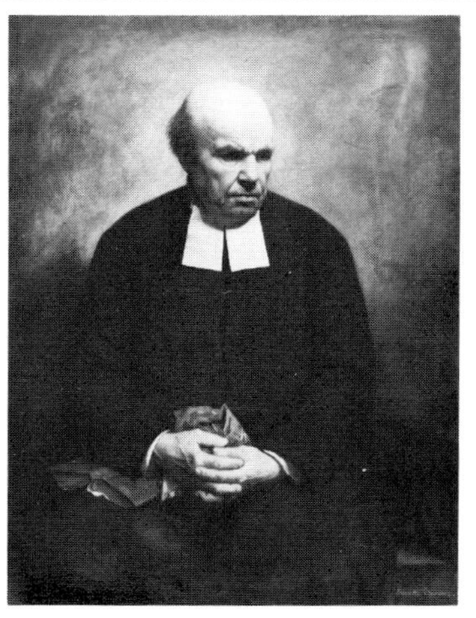

Follower of Jan Brueghel the Elder
1568–1625 Flemish

LANDSCAPE WITH WINDMILLS

Oil on copper
30 × 38 ($11\frac{13}{16} \times 14\frac{15}{16}$)
Unsigned
Mrs. R. Hatton gift (1908.34)

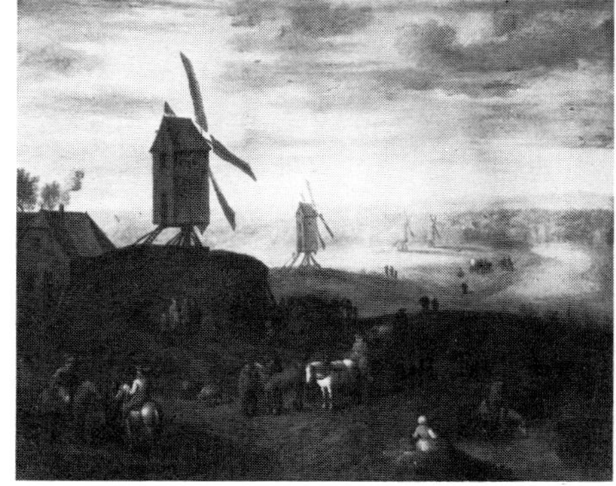

LANDSCAPE WITH FIGURES ON A PATH IN THE FOREGROUND, AND A CASTLE ON A RIVER

Oil on copper
17 × 22·9 ($6\frac{11}{16}$ × 9)
Unsigned
Assheton-Bennett bequest (1979.452)

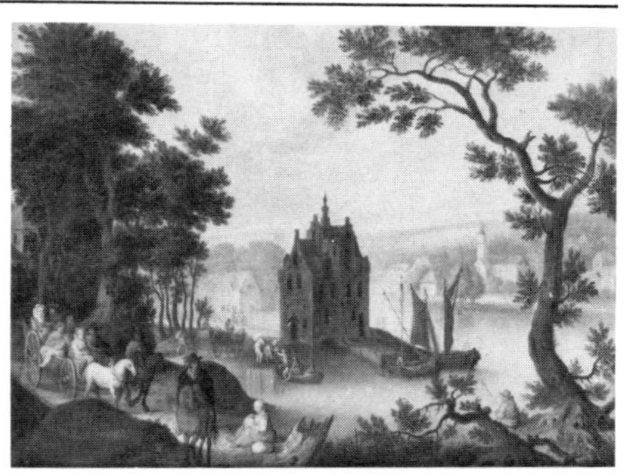

Léon-Émile Caille
1836–1907 French

CHIDING

Oil on panel
16·1 × 10·9 ($6\frac{3}{8}$ × $4\frac{5}{8}$)
s(brc): *Léon Caille* / . . . (date illegible)
Mothersill bequest to the Horsfall Museum, 1880, from which transferred (1918.422)

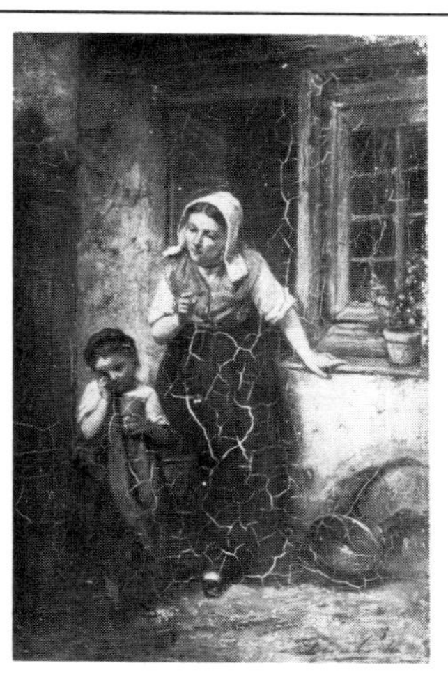

PRAYER
1872

Oil on panel
16·2 × 10·7 ($6\frac{3}{8}$ × $4\frac{3}{16}$)
s(brc): *Léon Caille, 1872*
Mothersill bequest, 1880, to the Horsfall Museum, from which transferred (1918.423)

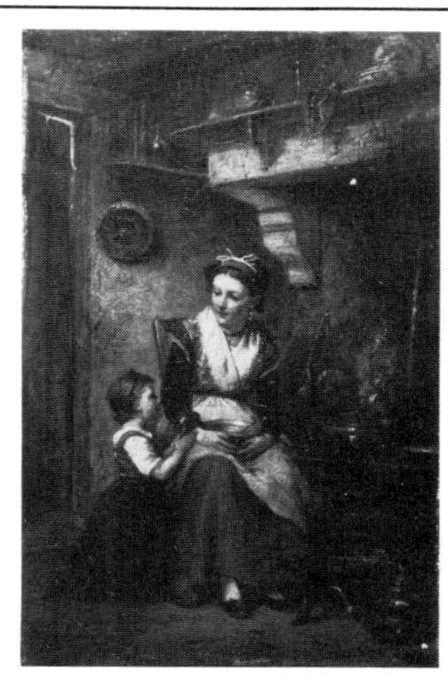

Juliette Cambier
1879–1963 Belgian

FLOWERS, HARMONY IN ROSE

Oil on canvas
46·3 × 38·5 ($18\frac{1}{4} \times 15\frac{3}{16}$)
s(brc): *Juliette Cambier / 1938* (?)
G. B. Alexander gift (1938. 513)

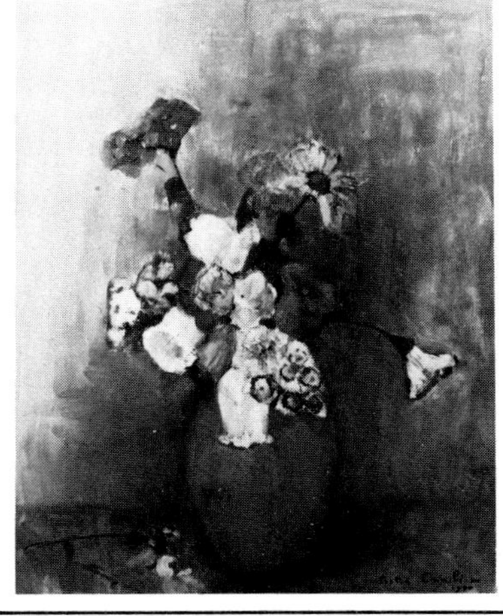

Jan van de Cappelle
c. 1623/5–1679 Dutch

SHIPPING ANCHORED IN A CALM SEA

Oil on panel
26·2 × 23·3 ($10\frac{5}{16} \times 9\frac{3}{16}$)
Unsigned
Assheton-Bennett bequest (1979.453)

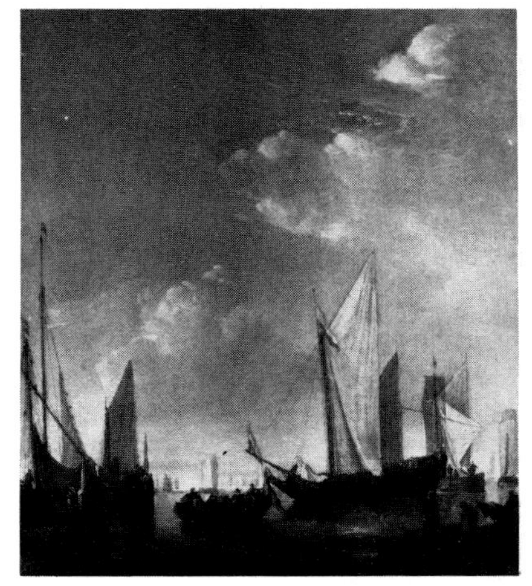

WINTER SCENE WITH THATCHED COTTAGES AND A FROZEN RIVER SPANNED BY A WOODEN BRIDGE

Oil on panel
33·4 × 42·3 ($13\frac{1}{8} \times 16\frac{5}{8}$)
s(bl): *IVC.*
Assheton-Bennett bequest (1979.455)

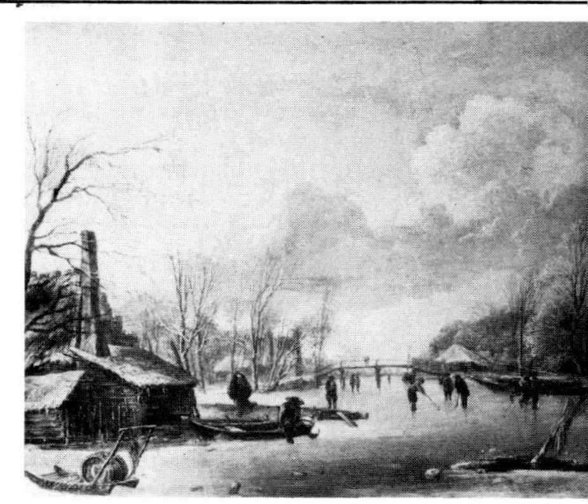

Follower of Jan van de Cappelle

SHIPPING AT ANCHOR OFF THE SHORE IN A CALM SEA; EVENING LIGHT

Oil on panel
53·4 × 65·9 (21$\frac{1}{16}$ × 25$\frac{15}{16}$)
inscr(bl): *IVC.*
Assheton-Bennett bequest (1979.454)

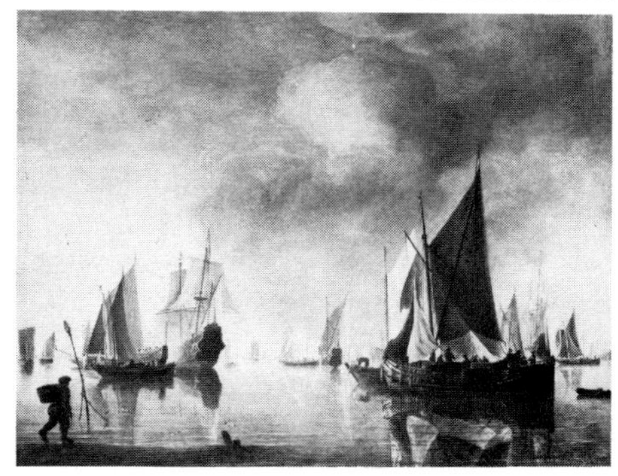

Jacques Carabain
1834–1933 Belgian

COAST SCENE

Oil on canvas
50·1 × 77·1 (19$\frac{3}{4}$ × 30$\frac{3}{8}$)
s(brc): *Jac. Carabain*
Transferred from the Horsfall Museum (1918.401)

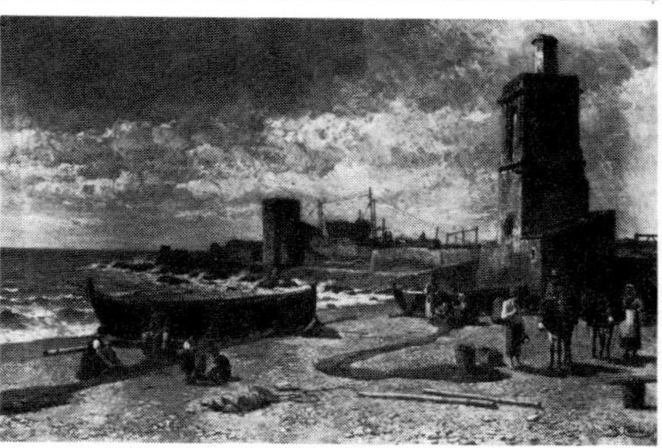

Attributed to Carlo Innocenzo Carlone
1686–1775 Italian

A SOLDIER ENTERING THE TENT OF A QUEEN

Oil on canvas
17·5 × 22 (6$\frac{7}{8}$ × 8$\frac{11}{16}$)
Unsigned
Purchased (1966.180)

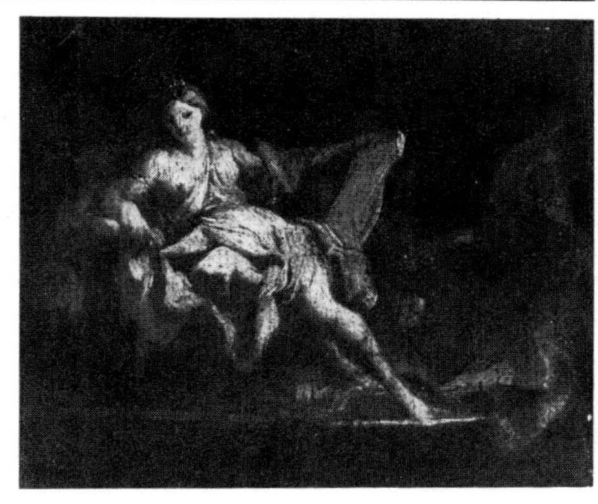

Angelo Caroselli
1585–1652 Italian

MADONNA AND CHILD WITH THE INFANT BAPTIST

Oil on panel
55·9 × 45·2 (22 × 17 13/16)
s(bl): *AC* (mon)
Presented by Mrs. E. F. Hickman in memory of her husband (1931.127)

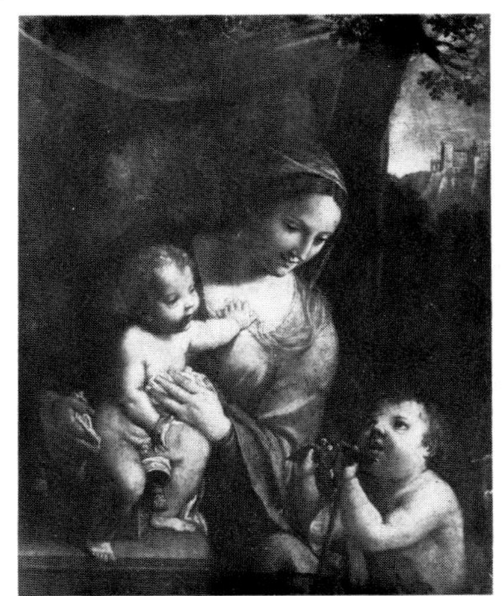

Jean-Jules-Louis Cavailles
1901–1977 French

INTERIOR, MUSIC ROOM

Oil on canvas
81·1 × 65 (31 15/16 × 25 5/8)
s(brc): *J. CAVAILLES*
Miss Dorothy Pilkington bequest (1974.91)

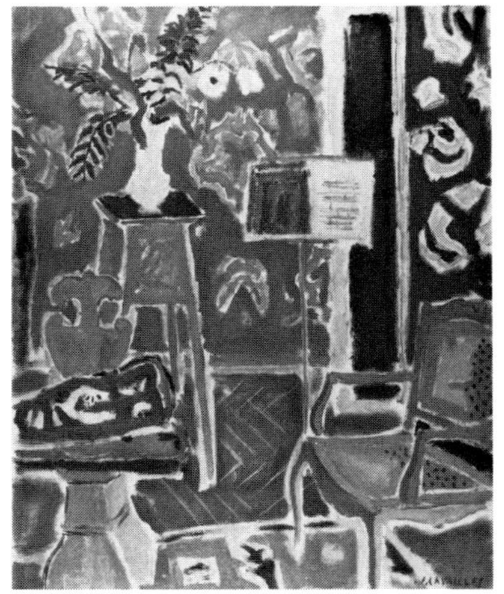

Jean Charles Cazin
1841–1901 French

THE BARLEYFIELD

Oil on canvas
45·8 × 55·4 (18 × 21 3/4)
s(brc): *J. C. CAZIN*
Purchased (1930.29)

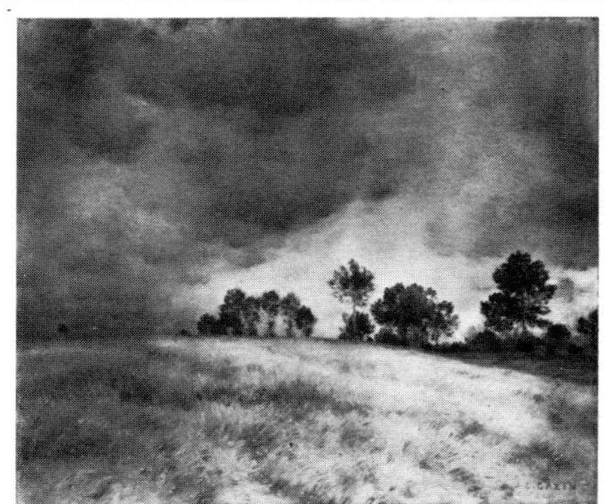

Jean-Ferdinand Chaigneau
1830–1906 French

SHEEP

Oil on panel
27·1 × 21·8 ($10\frac{11}{16} \times 8\frac{5}{8}$)
s(blc): *J Fd. Chaigneau* (JF in mon)
James Blair bequest (1917.226)

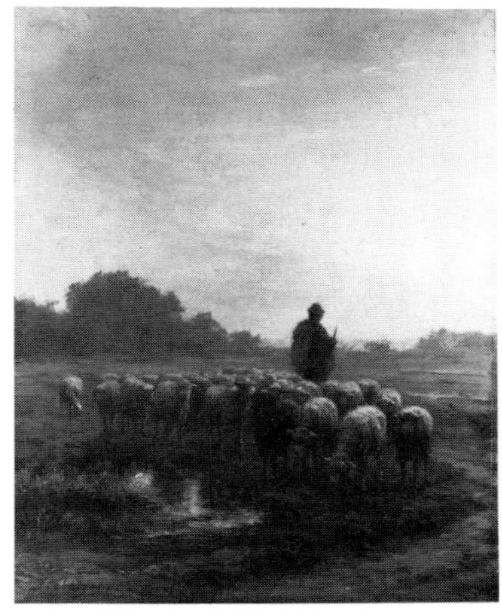

A FLOCK OF SHEEP

Oil on panel
23·9 × 33·1 ($9\frac{3}{8} \times 13\frac{1}{16}$)
s(blc): *J Fd. Chaigneau*
H. J. Sambrook bequest (1944.47)

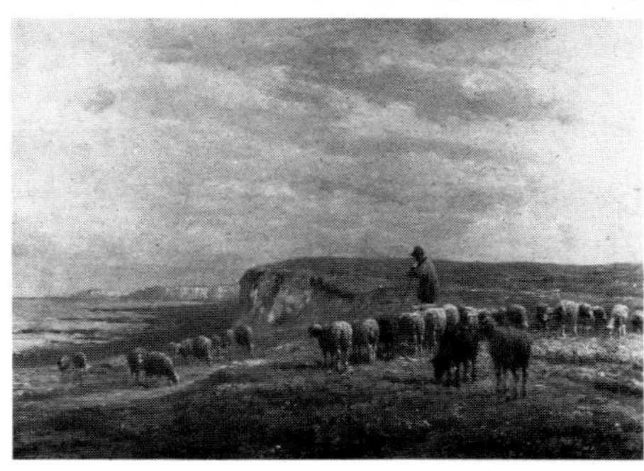

Jean-Laurent Challié
1880–1943 French

SNOW IN SUNSHINE

Oil on canvas
38·1 × 61·1 ($15 \times 24\frac{1}{16}$)
s(blc): *Challié*
Purchased (1928.122)

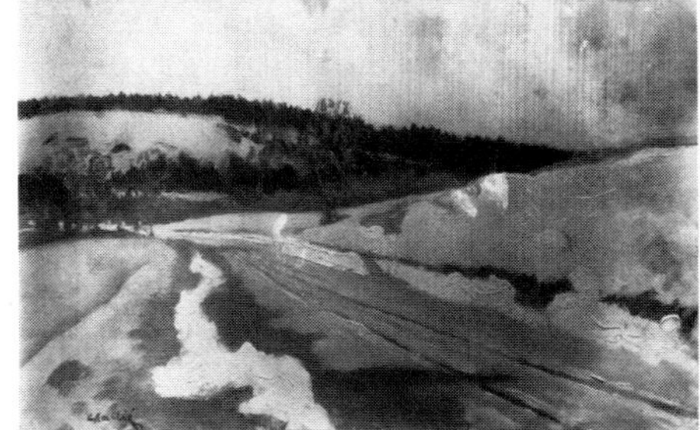

Louis Chéron
See Sir James Thornhill, British School Catalogue, Vol. I

Émile-François-Jacques Compard
b. 1900 French

PORTRAIT OF A WOMAN (L'ÉTUDIANTE) 1932

Oil on canvas
72·8 × 60 ($28\frac{5}{8} \times 23\frac{5}{8}$)
s(tlc): *Emile Compard*
Sir Thomas Barlow gift (1936.278)

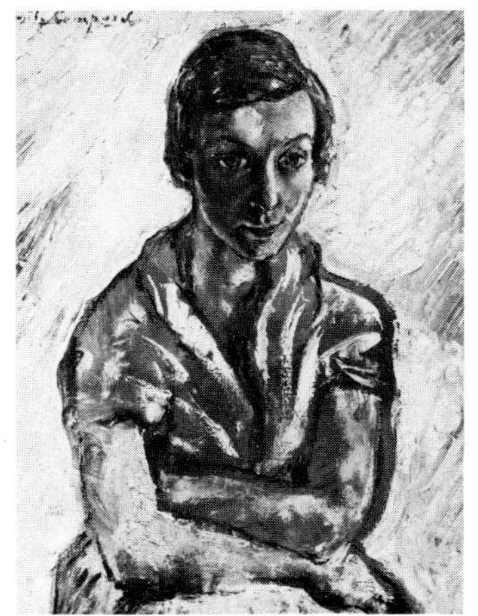

Sebastiano Conca
1680–1764 Italian

THE GOVERNMENT OF POPE BENEDICT XIV

Oil on canvas
44·5 × 91 ($17\frac{1}{2} \times 35\frac{13}{16}$)
Unsigned
Purchased (1966.296)

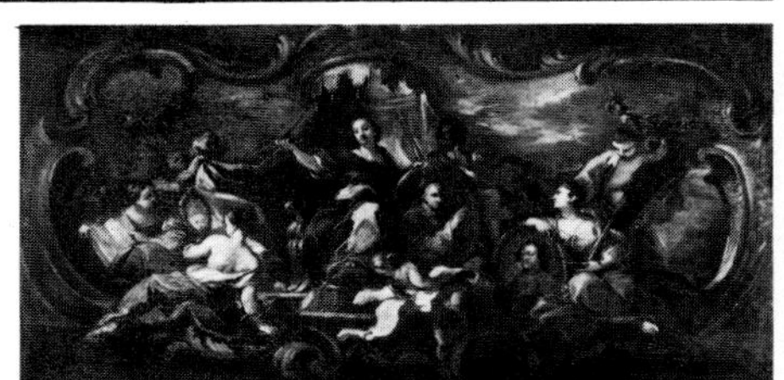

THE BLESSINGS OF GOOD GOVERNMENT

Oil on canvas
44·6 × 91·1 ($17\frac{9}{16} \times 35\frac{7}{8}$)
Unsigned
Purchased (1966.297)

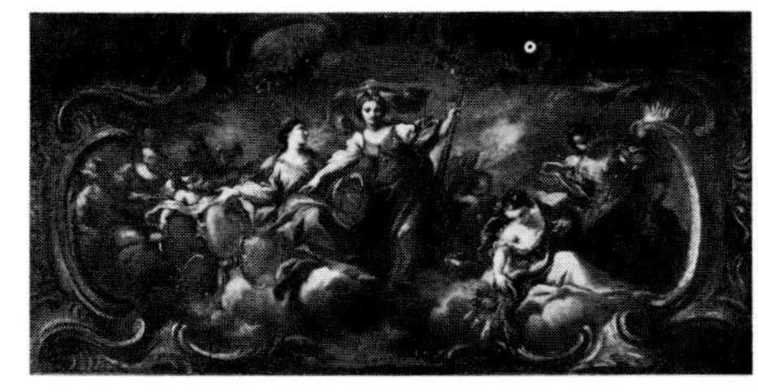

Jean-Baptiste-Camille Corot
1796–1875 French

SUNSET : FIGURES UNDER TREES

Oil on canvas
33·8 × 43·8 (13$\frac{15}{16}$ × 17$\frac{1}{4}$)
s(brc) : *COROT*
Purchased (1908.7)

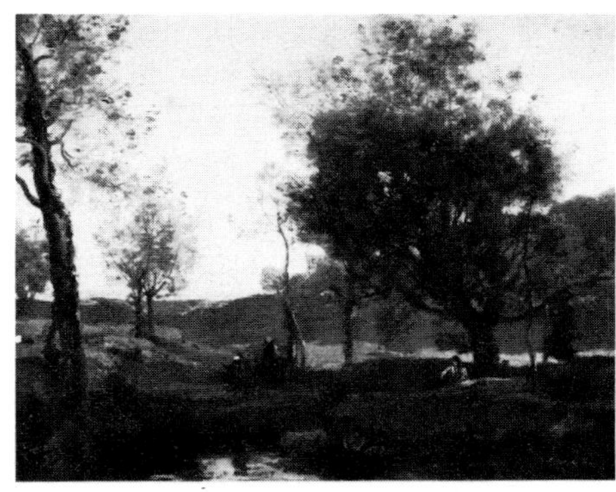

RIDER IN THE WATER

Oil on canvas
60 × 81·9 (23$\frac{5}{8}$ × 32$\frac{1}{4}$)
Unsigned
Stamped(blc) : *VENTE / COROT*
G. Beatson Blair bequest, 1941
(1947.140)

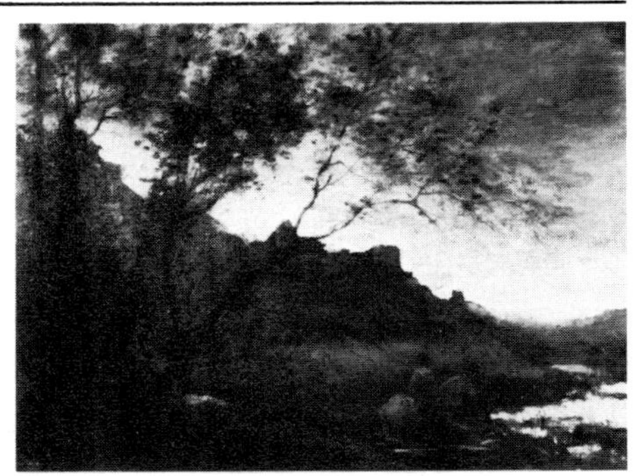

Niccolò di Corsi
active 20th century Italian

MORNING MISTS IN VENICE

Oil on canvas laid down on board
45·4 × 51·1 (17$\frac{7}{8}$ × 20$\frac{1}{8}$)
Unsigned
Alderman E. F. M. Sutton gift
(1930.79)

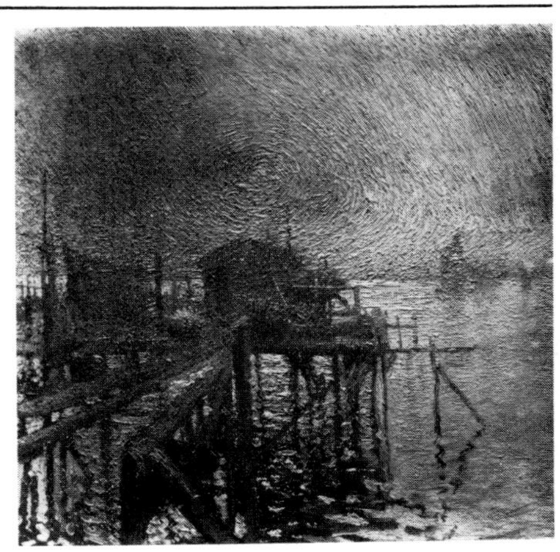

Pietro da Cortona
See Berrettini

Gustave Courbet
1819–1877 French

LE RUISSEAU DU PUITS NOIR

Oil on panel
55·5 × 46 (21⅞ × 18⅛)
s(blc): *G. Courbet*
Purchased (1955.104)

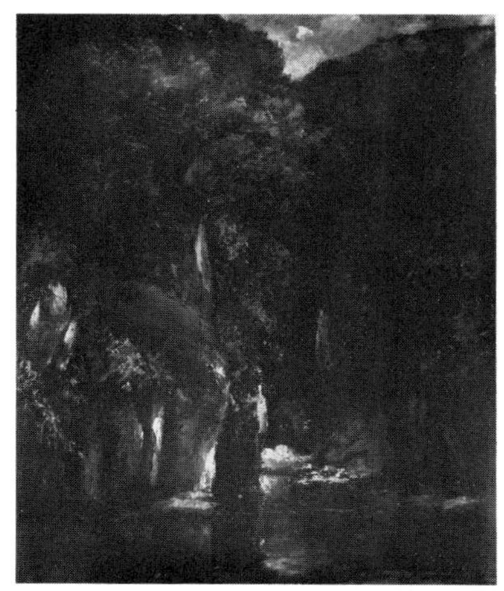

Giuseppe Maria Crespi
1665–1747 Italian

A SINGER WITH A DONKEY

Oil on canvas
57·7 × 45 (22¾ × 17¾)
Unsigned
Purchased (1963.147)

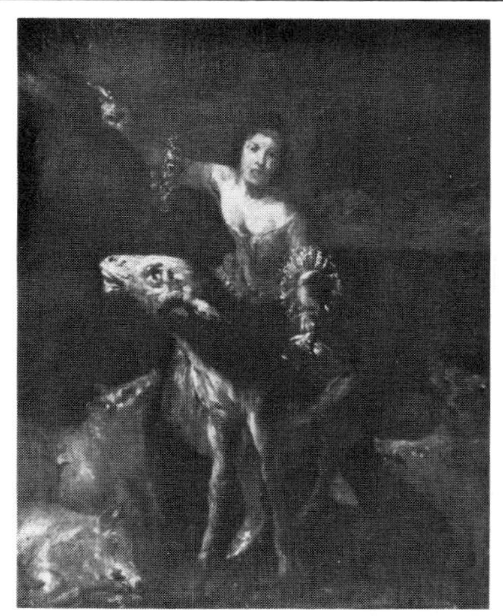

Aelbert Cuyp
1620–1691 Dutch

POULTRY WITH A DISTANT VIEW OF DORDRECHT

Oil on canvas
64·7 × 77·8 (25½ × 30⅝)
s(blc): *A. cŭÿp fecit*
Mrs. E. Wood bequest (1908.23)

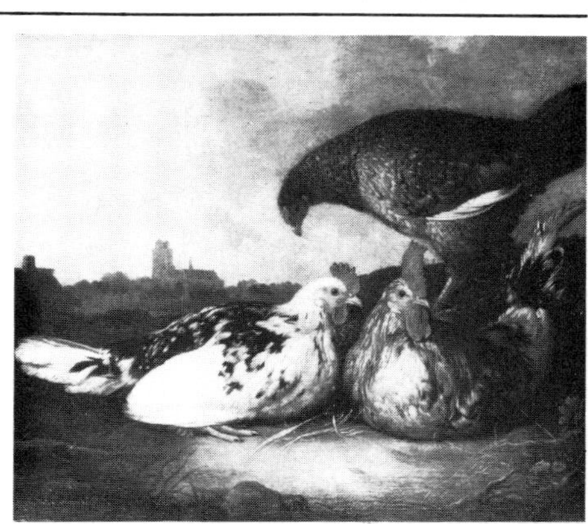

RIVER SCENE WITH A VIEW OF DORDRECHT AND A WINDMILL: ANGLERS, RIGHT

Oil on panel
19 × 32·2 ($7\frac{1}{2} \times 12\frac{11}{16}$)
s(b, centre): *A cuÿp*
Assheton-Bennett bequest (1979.456)

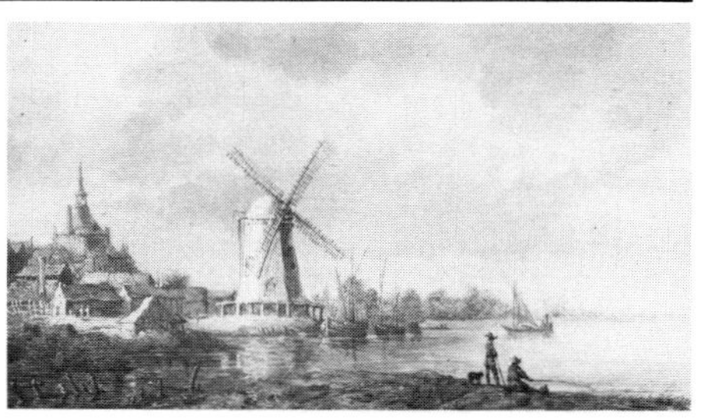

Manner of Bernardo Daddi
c. 1290–1348 Italian

VIRGIN AND CHILD WITH THE GOLDFINCH

Tempera on panel
62 × 32·2 ($24\frac{3}{8} \times 12\frac{11}{16}$) arched top
Unsigned. Inscr(b):
AVE·MARIA·GRAÇIA·PL
Purchased with the aid of a grant from the Victoria and Albert Museum (1959.29)

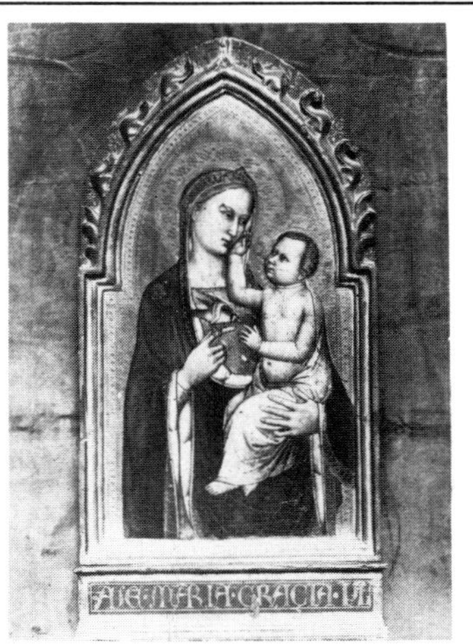

Manner of Hilaire-Germain-Edgar Degas
(English School?)
1834–1917 French

WOMAN IN A CAFÉ

Oil on canvas
49·7 × 35 ($19\frac{5}{8} \times 13\frac{3}{4}$)
Inscr(trc): *Degas*
G. Beatson Blair bequest, 1941 (1947.163)

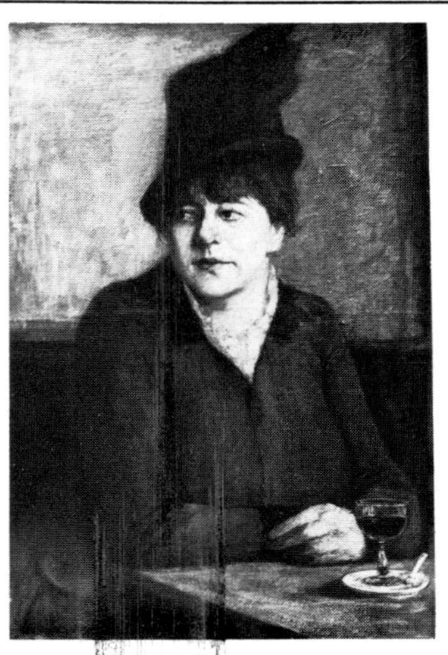

André Derain
1880–1954 French

HEAD OF A GIRL

Oil on canvas
46 × 38 ($18\frac{1}{8}$ × 15)
s(brc): *Derain*
Purchased (1947.189)

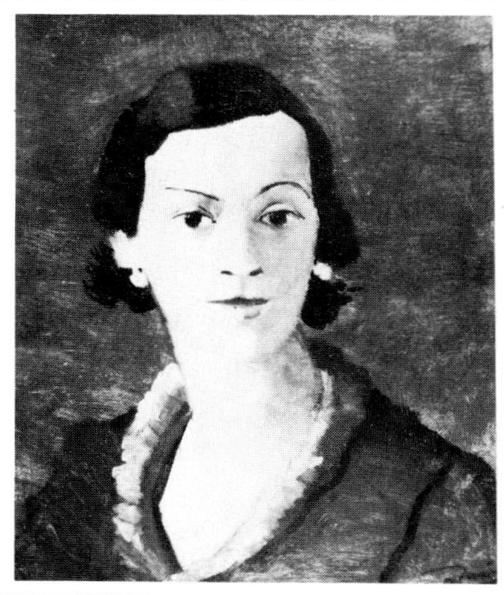

Johannes Joseph Destrée
1827–1888 Belgian

HAARLEM FROM THE DUNES
1851

Oil on canvas
88·5 × 113 ($34\frac{13}{16}$ × $44\frac{1}{2}$)
s(blc): *J. J. Destree pt. 1851*
H. B. Wood gift (1935.212)

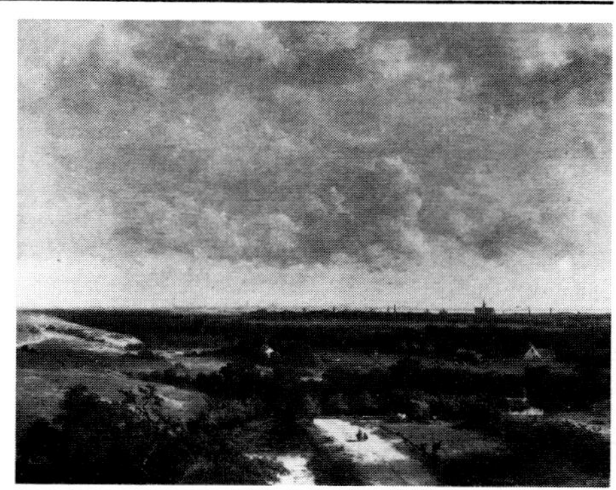

Gerard Dou
1613–1675 Dutch

PORTRAIT OF A GIRL

Oil on panel
21·2 × 17·6 ($8\frac{9}{16}$ × $6\frac{15}{16}$), oval
s(centre to r): *G DOV* (GD in mon)
Assheton-Bennett bequest (1979.457)

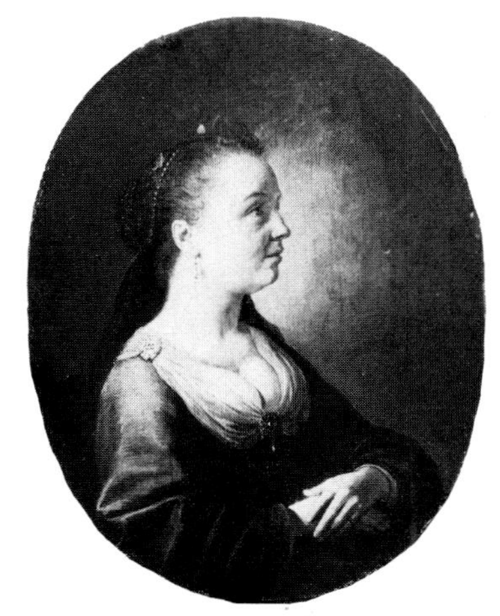

Claude Marie Dubufe
1790–1864 French

MRS. HERVEY FRANCIS DE MONTMORENCY AND HER DAUGHTER FRANCES
1835

Oil on canvas
145·8 × 113·3 ($57\frac{3}{8} \times 44\frac{5}{8}$)
s(brc): *Dubufe*
Presented by the National Art-Collections Fund from the collection of the late Mr. E. E. Cook (1955.123)

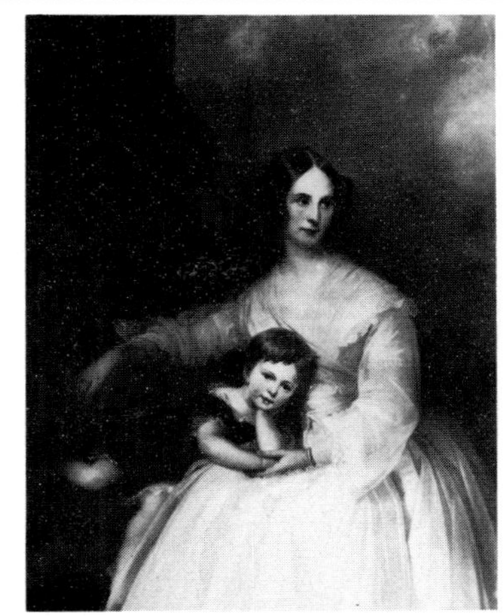

Jacob Duck
See Netherlandish School, 17th century

Raoul Dufy
1877–1953 French

EQUESTRIAN STATUE OF HENRI IV, PARIS
1921

Oil on canvas
54·2 × 65 ($21\frac{3}{8} \times 25\frac{5}{8}$)
s(brc): *Raoul Dufy 1921*
Miss Dorothy Pilkington bequest (1974.90)

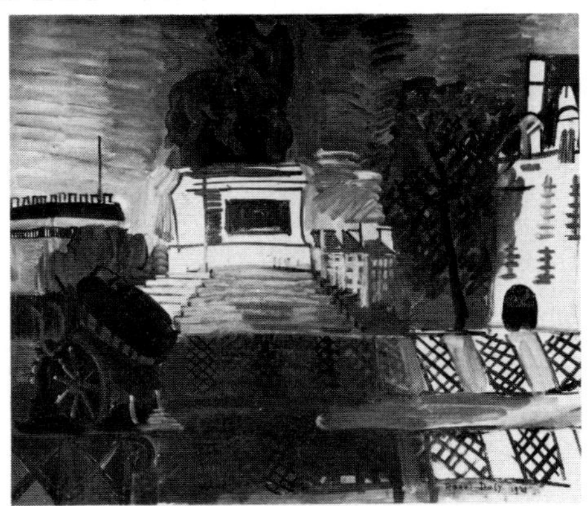

Gaspard Dughet (or **Gaspard Poussin**)
1615–1675 French

LANDSCAPE WITH SHEPHERDS

Oil on canvas
46·5 × 36·2 ($18\frac{5}{16} \times 14\frac{1}{4}$)
Unsigned
Purchased (1950.63)

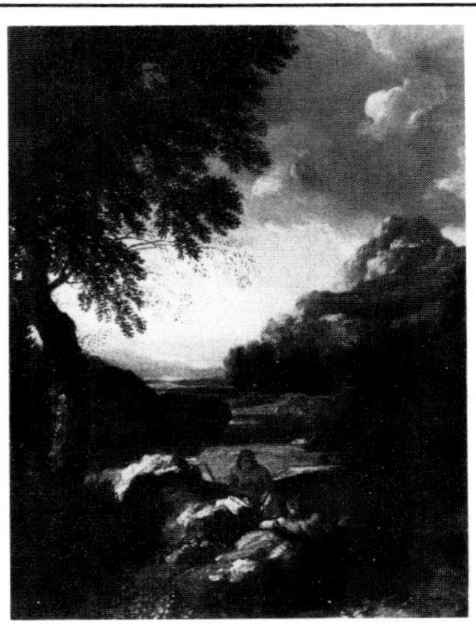

Attributed to Sir Anthony van Dyck

1599–1641 Flemish

THE HOLY FAMILY

Oil on canvas
122 × 97·9 ($48\frac{1}{16}$ × $38\frac{1}{2}$)
Unsigned
G. Beatson Blair bequest, 1941
(1947.137)

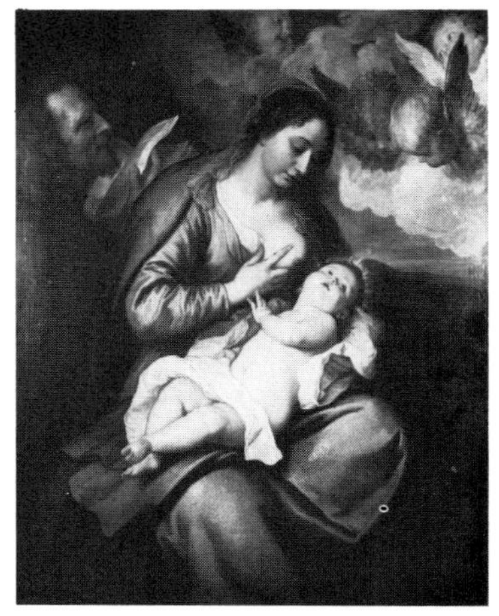

Studio of Sir Anthony van Dyck

ST. SEBASTIAN

Oil on canvas
195·6 × 135·4 (77 × $53\frac{5}{16}$)
Unsigned
Presented by Richard Holt to the Royal Manchester Institution, 1845, from which transferred (1882.43)

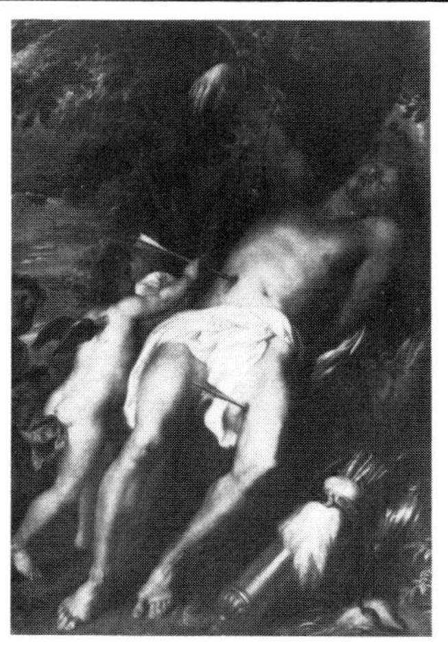

After Sir Anthony van Dyck

EQUESTRIAN PORTRAIT OF CHARLES I

Oil on canvas
157·9 × 128·2 ($62\frac{3}{16}$ × $50\frac{1}{2}$)
Unsigned
W. Bently Capper gift (1902.1)

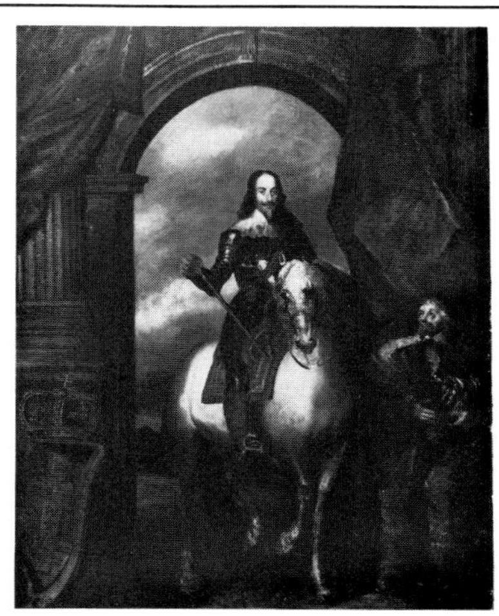

Egyptian, Alexandrian, 2nd or 3rd century A.D.

HEAD OF A YOUNG WOMAN

Tempera on linen
24·4 × 25·7 ($9\frac{9}{16}$ × $10\frac{1}{8}$) irregular
Unsigned
G. Beatson Blair bequest, 1941
(1947.147)

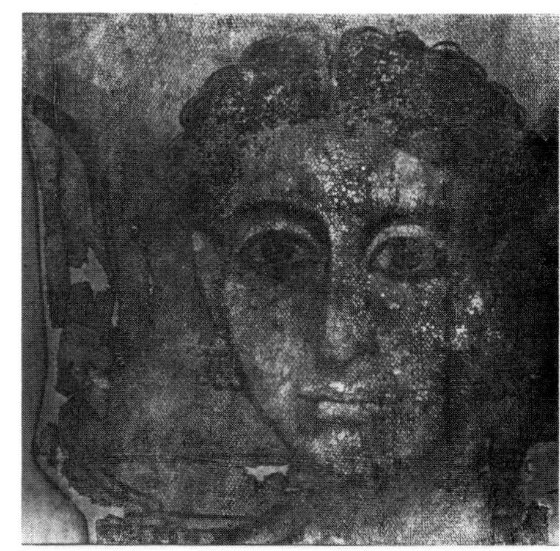

Egyptian, Fayoum, 2nd or 3rd century A.D.

PORTRAIT OF A WOMAN

Encaustic on panel
30·5 × 22·4 (12 × $8\frac{13}{16}$) irregular
Unsigned
J. Haworth bequest (1937.128)

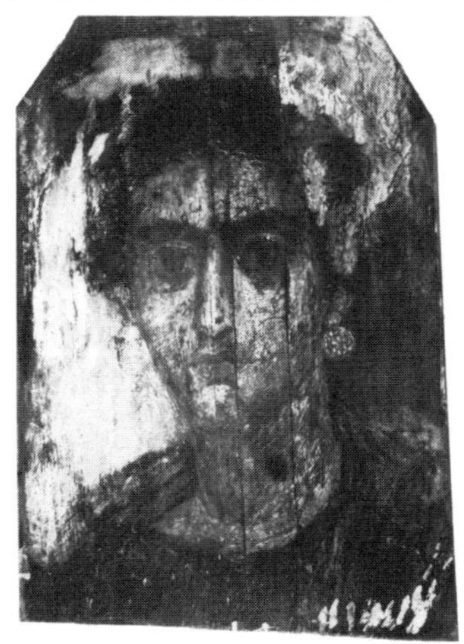

Wilhelm Heinrich Ernst Eitner
b. 1867 German

MONTE CRISSILANO

Oil on canvas
80·7 × 100 ($31\frac{3}{4}$ × $39\frac{3}{8}$)
s(blc): *E. Eitner*
Mrs. O. Samson gift (1944.27)

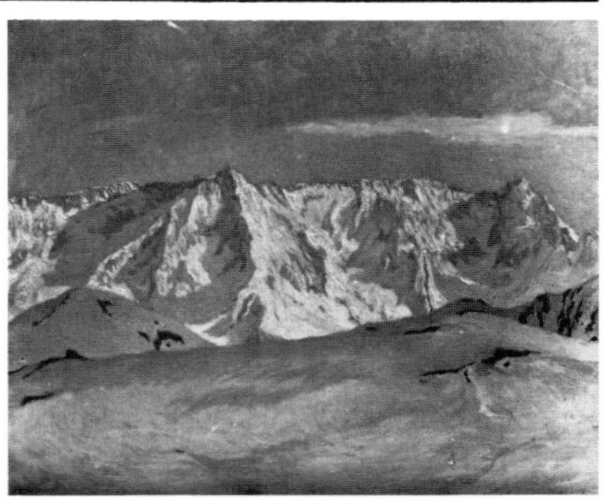

Jan Ekels the Younger
1759–1793 Dutch

INTERIOR WITH MAN READING
1784

Oil on canvas
57·4 × 46·6 ($22\frac{5}{8} \times 18\frac{5}{16}$)
s(blc): *I EKELS / A 1784* (?)
J. Porter gift (1935.286)

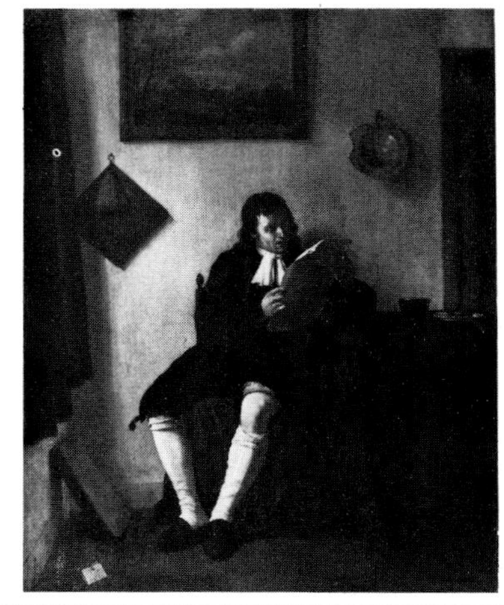

Hans Erni
b. 1909 Swiss

COMPOSITION NO. 36
1935

Oil on canvas
61 × 50 ($24 \times 19\frac{11}{16}$)
Unsigned
A. C. Sewter gift (1956.406)

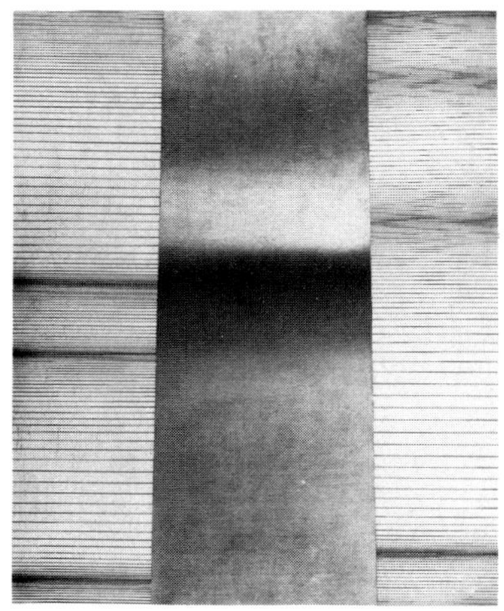

Max Ernst
1891–1976 French

LA VILLE PETRIFIÉE
1933

Oil on paper stuck down on board
50·5 × 60·9 ($19\frac{7}{8} \times 23\frac{15}{16}$)
s(brc): *max ernst*
Purchased (1955.112)

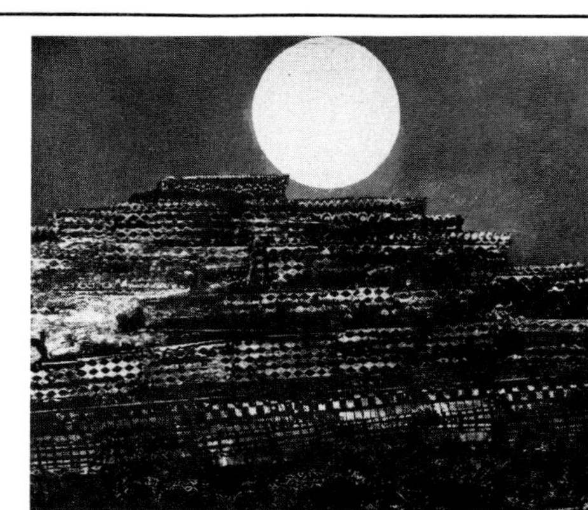

Georges d'Espagnat
1870–1950 French

WOMAN READING

Oil on canvas
50·1 × 60·9 ($19\frac{11}{16} \times 23\frac{15}{16}$)
s(tlc): *G d E*
Purchased (1908.4)

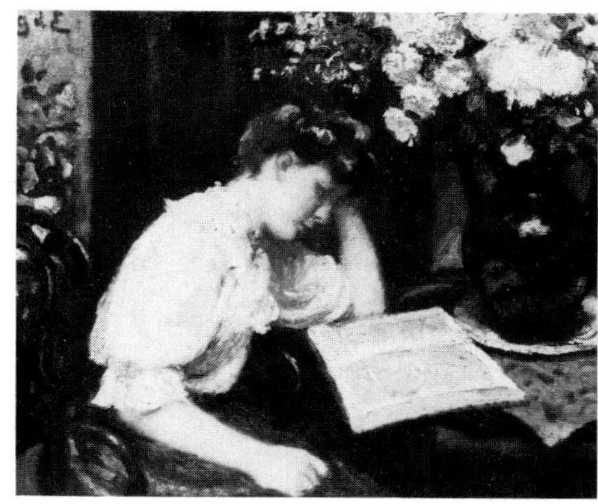

Ignace-Henri-Jean-Théodore Fantin-Latour
1836–1904 French

FLOWERS
1872

Oil on canvas
40·2 × 50·6 ($15\frac{13}{16} \times 19\frac{15}{16}$)
s(trc): *Fantin. Sept. 1872.*
Godfrey Gottschalk bequest (1882.11)

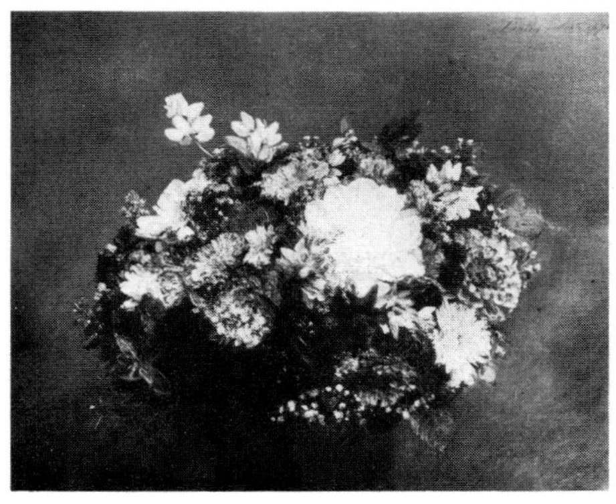

SELF-PORTRAIT
1867

Oil on canvas
64 × 55·2 ($25\frac{3}{16} \times 21\frac{3}{4}$)
s(trc): *Fantin*
Purchased (1919.8)

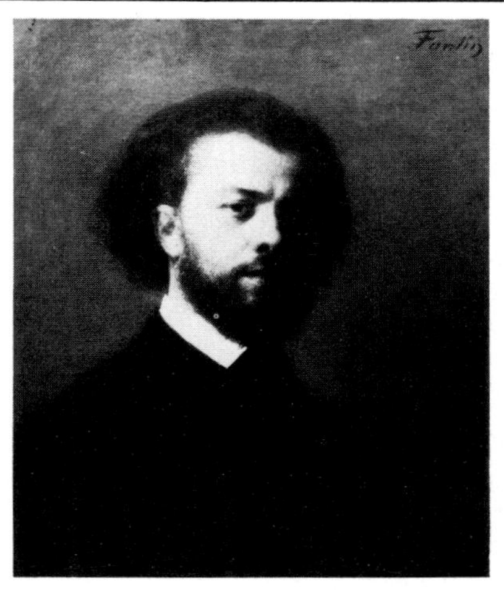

LA SOURCE
1871

Oil on canvas
22·8 × 14·2 (9 × 5⅝)
Unsigned
Lloyd Roberts bequest (1920.538)

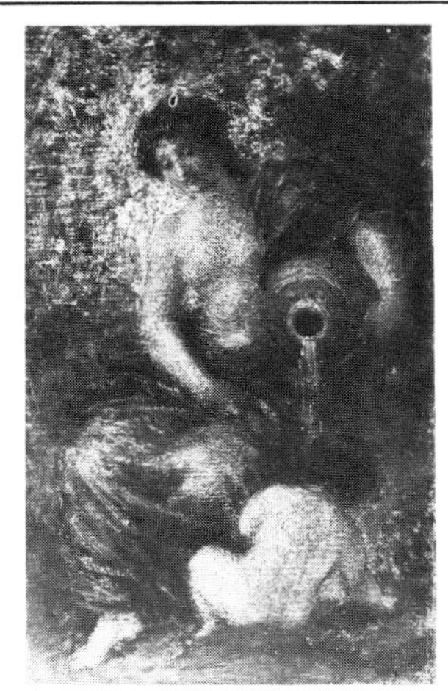

PEACHES AND GRAPES
1874

Oil on canvas
26·1 × 36 (10¼ × 14⅛)
s(blc): *Fantin . 74*
Lloyd Roberts bequest (1920.539)

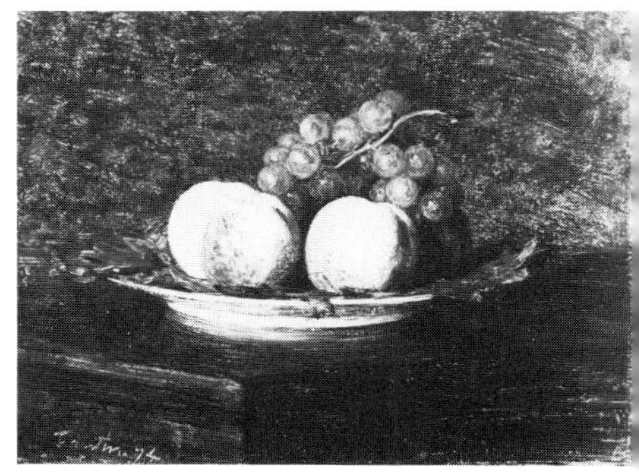

CUPID AND VENUS
c. 1871–74

Oil on canvas
24·6 × 18·9 (9¾ × 7 7/16)
s(blc): *Fantin*
Lloyd Roberts bequest (1920.540)

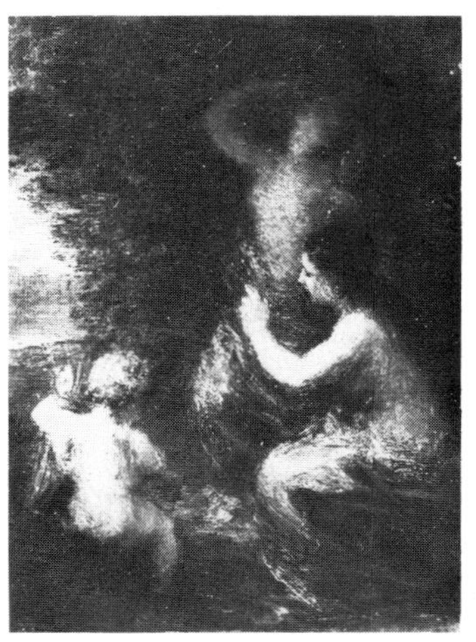

GRAPES AND AN APPLE
1870

Oil on canvas
16·7 × 22·5 ($6\frac{9}{16} \times 8\frac{7}{8}$)
s(tlc): *Fantin 70*
Lloyd Roberts bequest (1920.549)

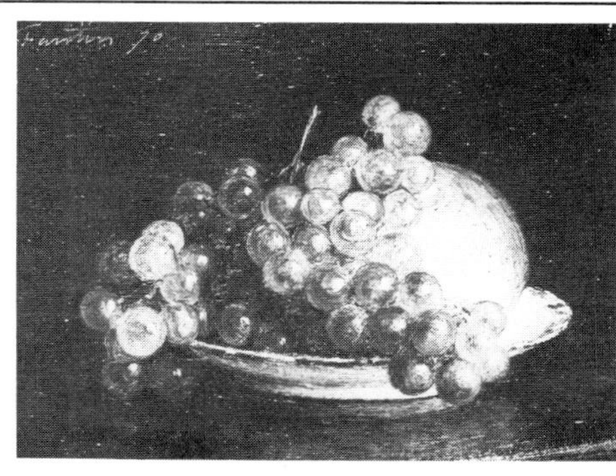

A WOODLAND GLADE
c. 1872

Oil on canvas
20·6 × 25·7 ($8\frac{1}{8} \times 10\frac{1}{8}$)
s(blc): *Fantin*
Lloyd Roberts bequest (1920.557)

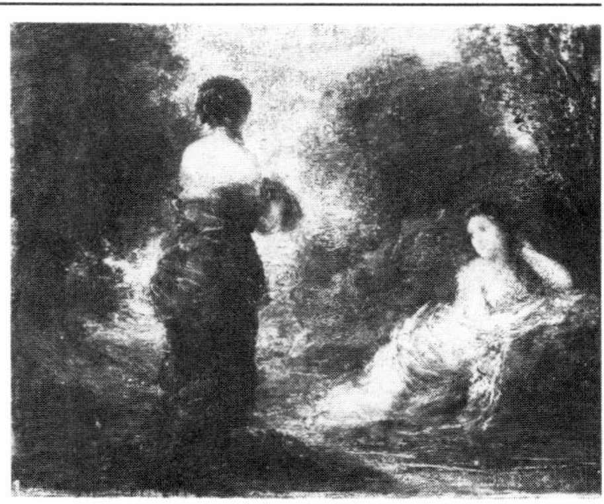

FLOWERS IN A VASE
1873

Oil on canvas
40·2 × 32·2 ($15\frac{13}{16} \times 12\frac{11}{16}$)
s(br): *Fantin. 73.*
Lloyd Roberts bequest (1920.559)

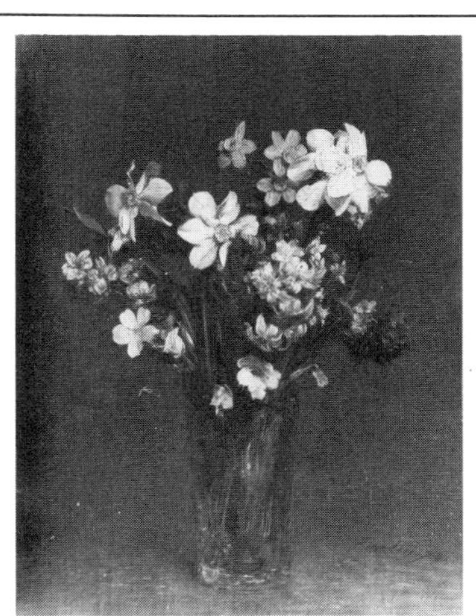

THE BATHERS

Oil on canvas
$23 \times 27{\cdot}4$ ($9\frac{1}{16} \times 10\frac{13}{16}$)
Unsigned
Lloyd Roberts bequest (1920.560)

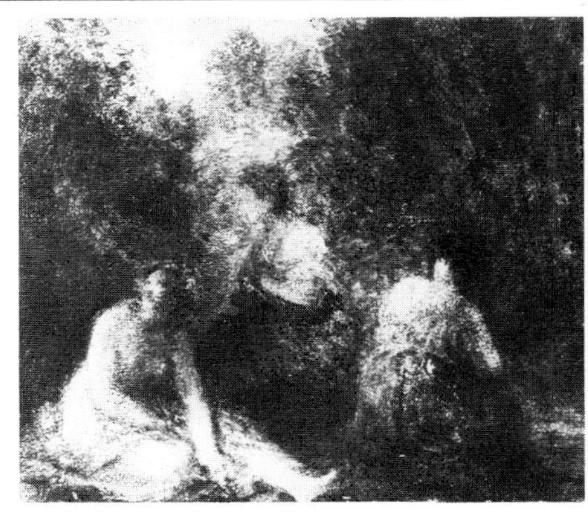

L'AMOUR VAINQUEUR

Oil on canvas
81×60 ($31\frac{7}{8} \times 23\frac{5}{8}$)
s(blc): *Fantin*
Purchased (1934.527)

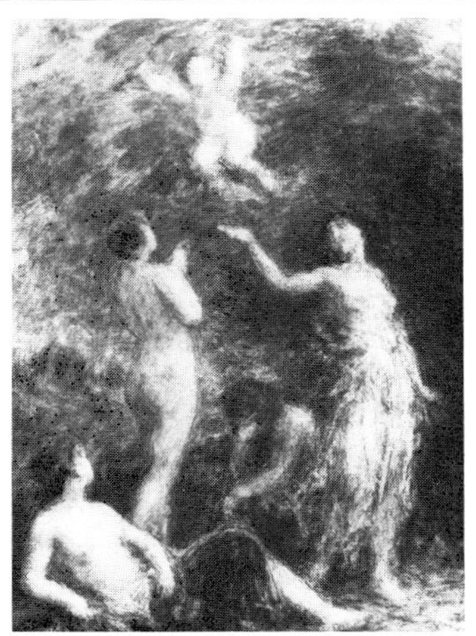

STILL LIFE: ROSES IN A GLASS VASE
1879

Oil on canvas
$43{\cdot}9 \times 38$ ($17\frac{5}{16} \times 15$)
s(tlc): *Fantin 79.*
Assheton-Bennett bequest (1979.532)

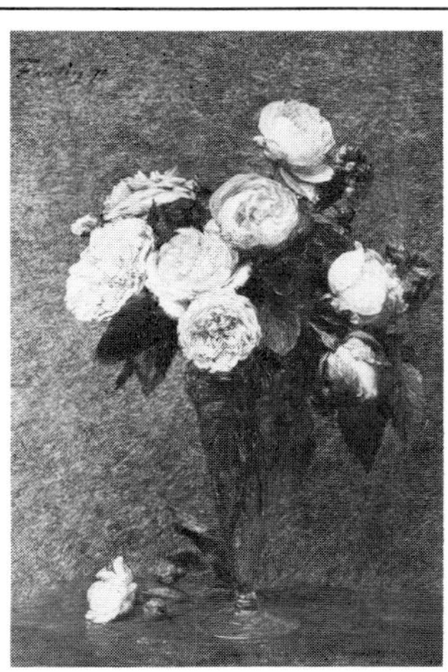

Lucy Citti Ferreira
active 20th century, Brazilian

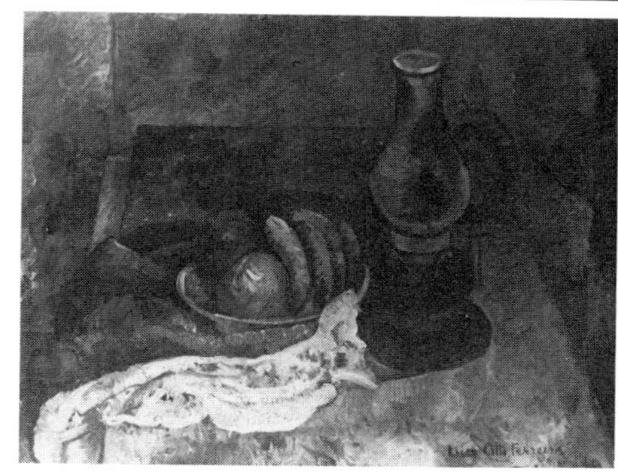

STILL LIFE WITH LAMP

Oil on canvas
$51{\cdot}8 \times 68{\cdot}2$ ($20\frac{3}{8} \times 26\frac{7}{8}$)
s(brc): *Lucy Citti Ferreira*
Presented by the artist (1949.257)

Domenico Fetti
See Jean-Honoré Fragonard

Jacques-Eugène Feyen
1815–1908 French

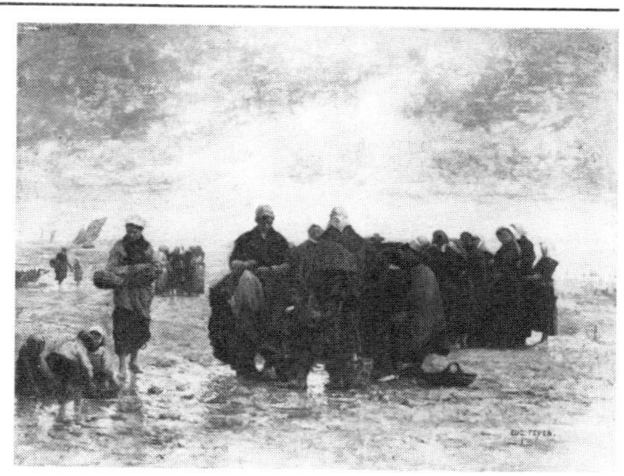

ON THE SHORE

Oil on panel
$16 \times 22{\cdot}1$ ($6\frac{5}{16} \times 8\frac{11}{16}$)
s(brc): *EUG. FEYEN*
James Blair bequest (1917.221)

Jacques-Louis Forain
1852–1931 French

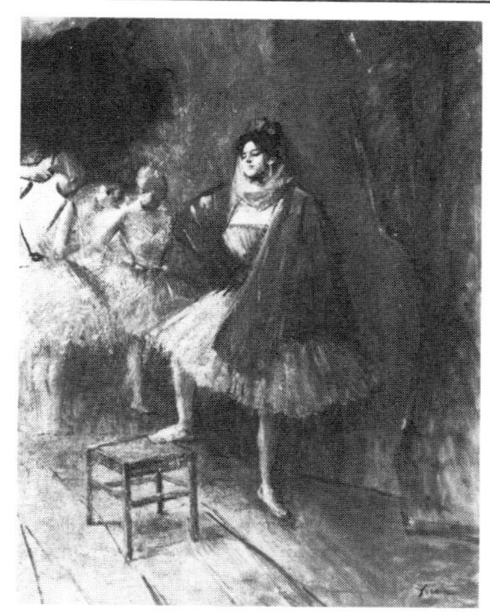

DANCERS IN THE WINGS

Oil on canvas
$70 \times 55{\cdot}4$ ($27\frac{9}{16} \times 21\frac{13}{16}$)
s(brc): *forain*
Purchased (1938.366)

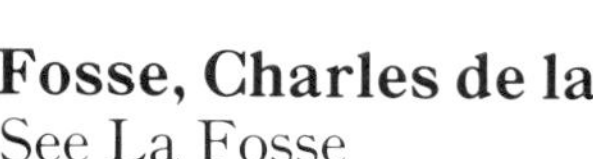

Fosse, Charles de la
See La Fosse

Attributed to
Jean-Honoré Fragonard
1732–1806 French
after Domenico Fetti (formerly attributed to Domenico Fetti)

PORTRAIT OF THE ACTOR TRISTANO MARTINELLI(?)
(formerly called CLAUDIO MONTEVERDI)

Oil on canvas
45·3 × 37·5 ($17\frac{7}{8} \times 14\frac{3}{4}$) Unsigned
Presented by Ernest Innes through the National Art-Collections Fund
(1930.171)

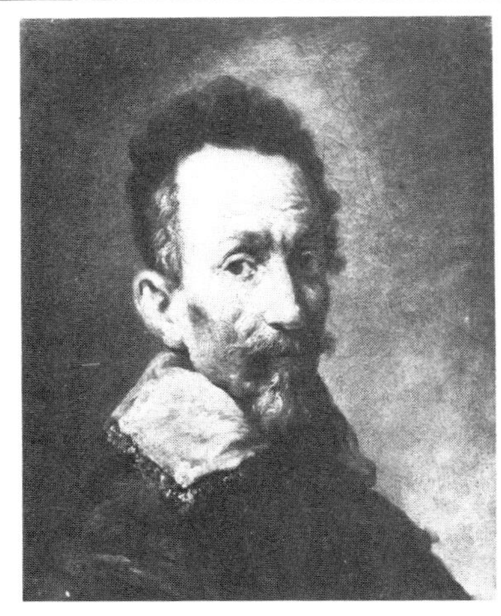

Ambrosius Francken I
See Cornelis de Baellieur the Elder

Frans Francken the Younger
1581–1642 Flemish

THE SEVEN WORKS OF MERCY

Oil on panel
50·2 × 89 ($19\frac{3}{4} \times 35\frac{1}{16}$)
s(brc): *D.J.F.F.IN.* (F.F. in mon)
Purchased (1912.51)

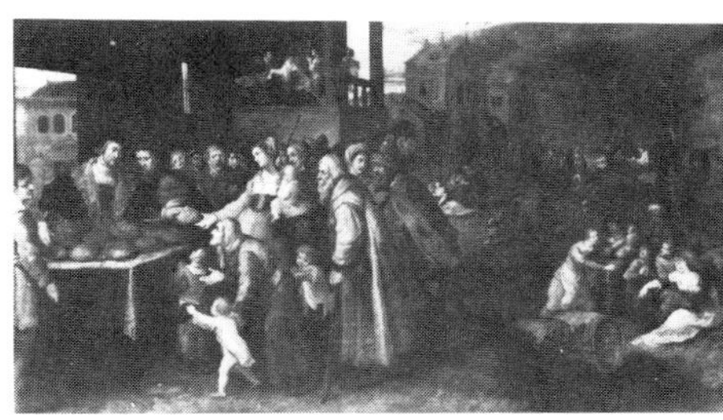

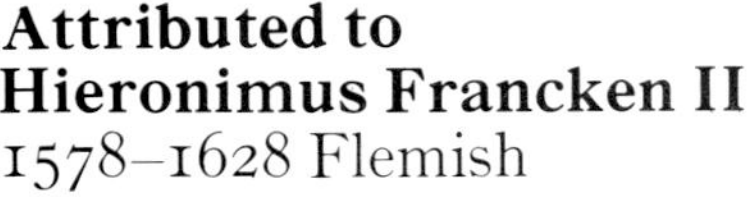

Attributed to
Hieronimus Francken II
1578–1628 Flemish

THE ADORATION OF THE SHEPHERDS

Oil on copper
36·1 × 28·1 ($14\frac{1}{4} \times 11\frac{1}{4}$)
Unsigned
E. Neild gift (1912.52)

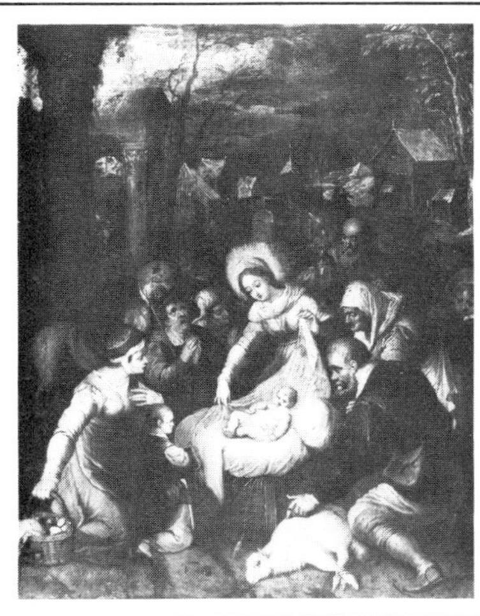

André Fraye
1888–1963 French

OLD HARBOUR AND CATHEDRAL, MARSEILLES
1920

Oil on canvas
65 × 81·2 (25⅝ × 31 15/16)
s(blc): *Andre Fraye*
Presented by the Contemporary Art Society (1935.179)

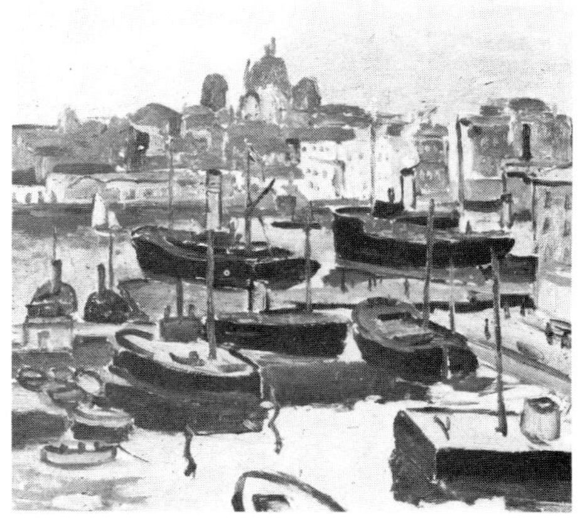

Pierre Edouard Frère
1819–1886 French

ROASTING CHESTNUTS

Oil on panel
26·9 × 21·3 (10⅝ × 8⅜)
Unsigned
Lloyd Roberts bequest (1920.546)

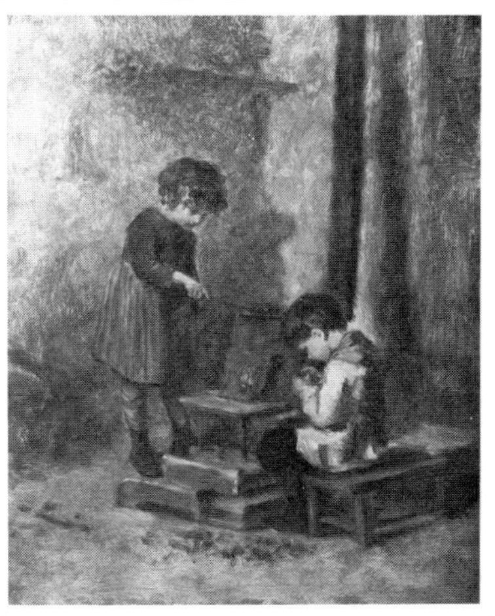

Albert Freyse
d. 1652 German

ALLEGORY OF VIRTUE
Oil on panel
53·1 × 44·6 (20⅞ × 17 9/16)
s(br): *A. Freÿse. 164* . . . (last figure illegible)
inscr: *WERTUGEND LIEBT HAT EHR ZU LOHN/IN GOTT/BEHARDT DIE HIMMELS KRON/ERKEN DICH SELBST/REGIER DICH SELBST/BESSER/DIE BEGIERDEN/ZERBROCHEN/ALS HERNACH DIE/SUBSTANZ MIT/GROSEM SCHMERZN* [sic]
Presented by Dr. and Mrs. Langley (1953.113)

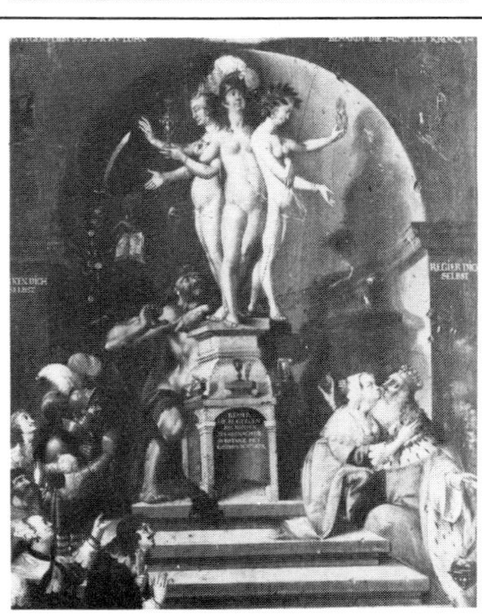

Théophile Gardini
active 20th century Italian

SPRING AT NAYLAND, SUFFOLK
1938

Oil on panel
40·7 × 51·1 ($16\frac{1}{16} \times 20\frac{1}{8}$)
s(brc): *T Gardini*
Dr. Jane Walker bequest (1939.36)

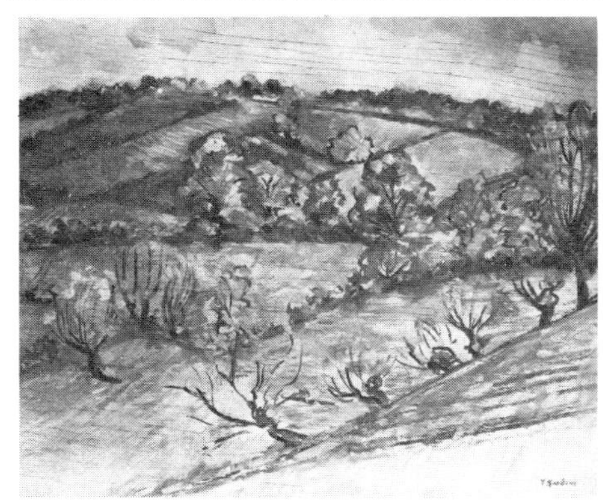

Louis Gauffier
1761–1801 French

PYGMALION AND GALATEA
1797

Oil on canvas
67·5 × 51·2 ($29\frac{9}{16} \times 20\frac{3}{16}$)
s(brc): *L. Gauffier. Flor.ce 1797.*
Purchased with the aid of a grant from the National Art-Collections Fund (1979.546)

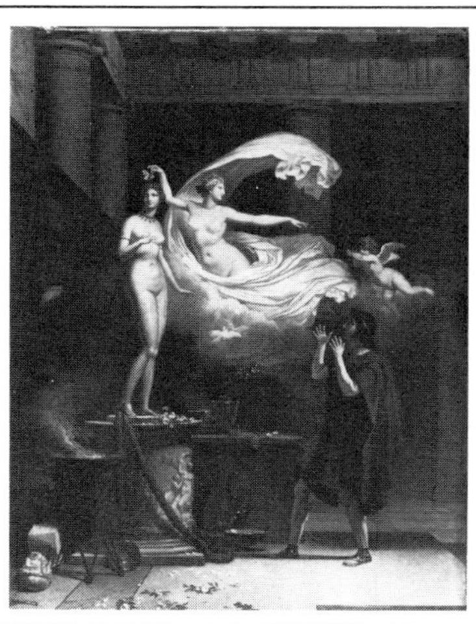

Paul Gauguin
1848–1903 French

HARBOUR SCENE, DIEPPE

Oil on canvas
60·2 × 72·3 ($23\frac{11}{16} \times 28\frac{7}{16}$)
s(brc): *P Gauguin*
Mrs. P. Duxbury gift (1944.46)

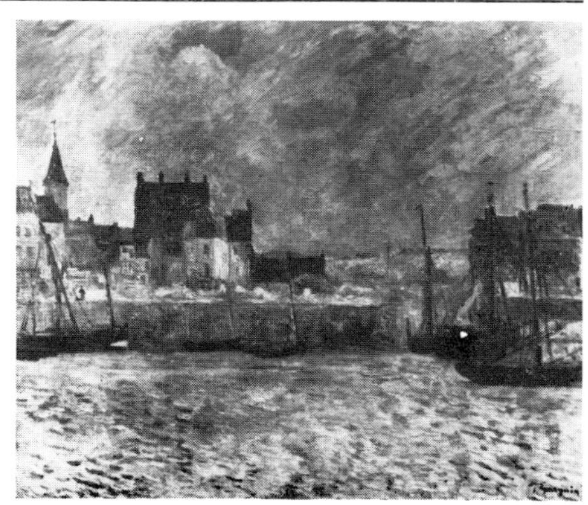

Giovanni Battista Gaulli, called il Baciccio
1639–1709 Italian

ST. JOHN THE BAPTIST

Oil on canvas
183·5 × 118·5 ($72\frac{1}{4} \times 46\frac{11}{16}$)
Unsigned
Purchased with the aid of a grant from the Victoria and Albert Museum (1968.104)

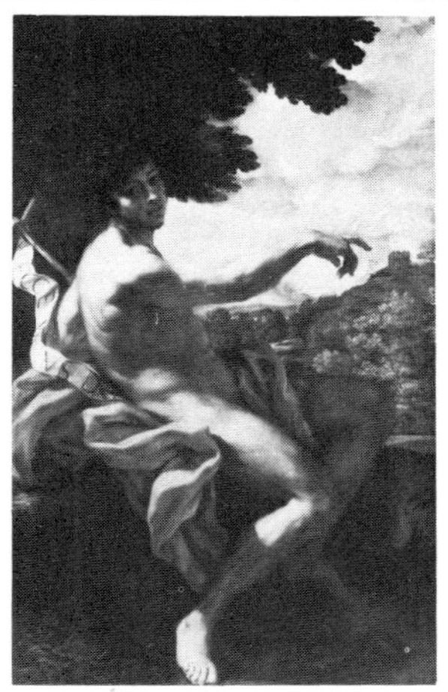

?German, 18th century
(formerly attributed to Cornelis van Poelenburgh)

THE BATH OF DIANA

Oil on copper
23 × 28 ($9\frac{1}{16} \times 11\frac{1}{16}$)
Unsigned
James Blair bequest (1917.154)

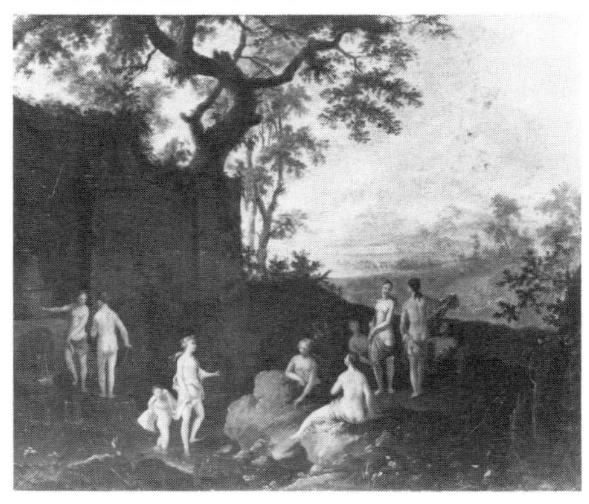

Jacob de Gheyn the Younger
1565–1629 Dutch

MASTER AND PUPIL
1620

Oil on panel
58 × 69·5 ($22\frac{7}{8} \times 27\frac{3}{8}$)
Inscr. (on cartouche):
EPANNONEAPELLIΣ/
EDEINEEYNNIAEYEIA
s(on base of background frame):
[G] *HEYN FE AN° 1620*
Purchased (1949.224)

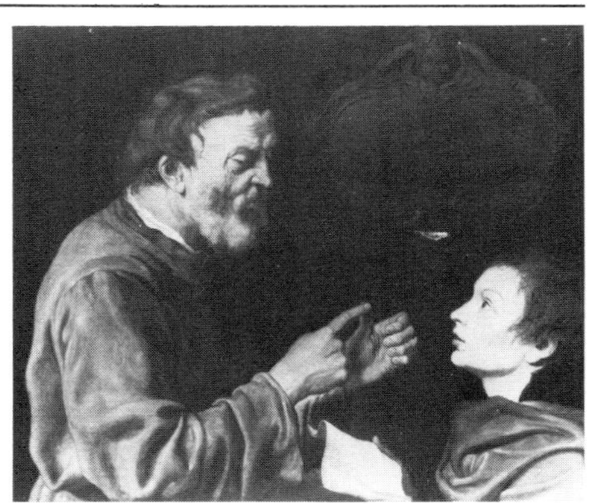

Attributed to Ridolfo Ghirlandaio
1483–1561 Italian
(formerly attributed to Piero di Cosimo)

THE ADORATION OF THE SHEPHERDS

Oil on panel
114 ($44\frac{7}{8}$) diameter
Unsigned
Purchased with the aid of the Sir John S. Randles Bequest Fund (1947.188)

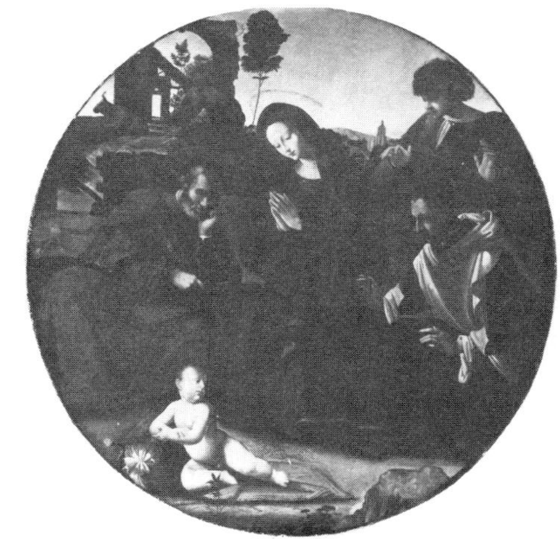

Alberto Giacometti
1901–1966 Swiss

THE ARTIST'S MOTHER
1949

Oil on canvas
74·3 × 38·8 ($29\frac{1}{4} \times 15\frac{5}{16}$)
s(brc): *Alberto Giacometti 1949*
Presented by the Contemporary Art Society (1952.277)

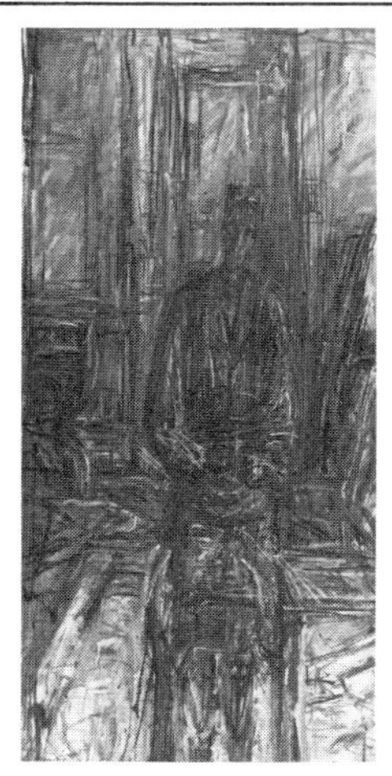

Luca Giordano
1632–1705 Italian

THE CAVE OF ETERNITY

Oil on canvas
69 × 84·5 ($27\frac{3}{16} \times 33\frac{1}{4}$)
Unsigned
Purchased (1964.284)

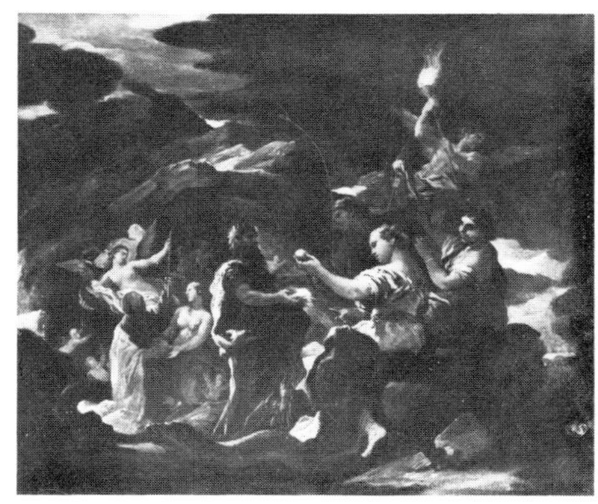

ɜrigory Gluckmann

ɔ. 1898 Russian

ʼEMALE NUDE

Ɔil on panel
ɜ0·7 × 16·5 ($8\frac{1}{8} \times 6\frac{1}{2}$)
ɜ(brc): *Grigory / Gluckmann / Paris*
Eric C. Gregory gift (1946.35)

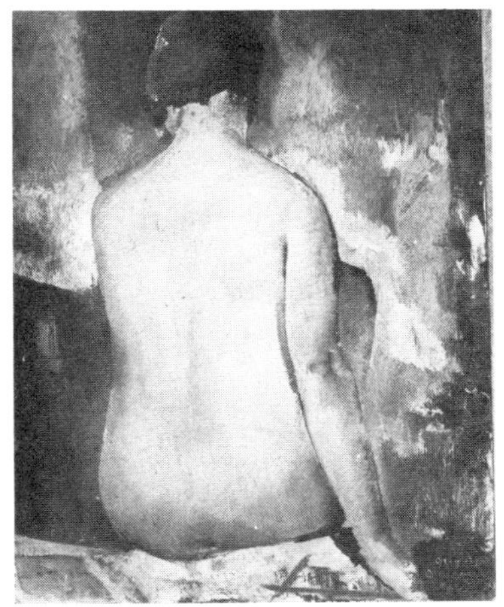

Attributed to Laureys Goubau

ɪctive 1651–1669 Dutch
(formerly attributed to Willem van Mieris)

A GIRL AT A KITCHEN WINDOW SLICING A LEMON

Oil on panel
37·6 × 30·7 ($14\frac{13}{16} \times 12\frac{1}{16}$)
Unsigned
Assheton-Bennett bequest (1979.477)

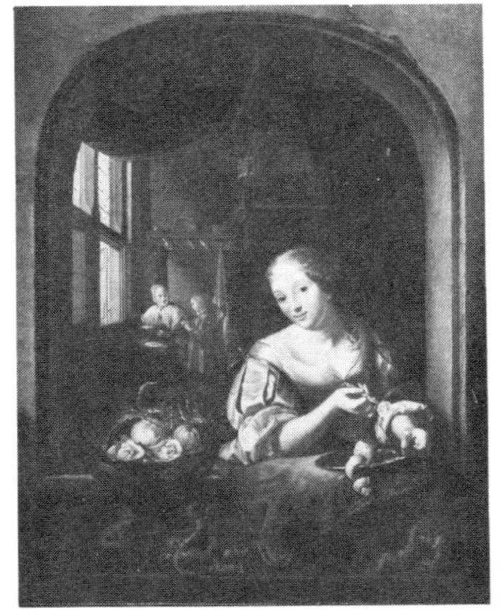

Jan van Goyen

1596–1656 Dutch

LANDSCAPE WITH A COTTAGE AND A BARN
1632

Oil on panel
24·7 × 34·6 ($9\frac{1}{4} \times 13\frac{5}{8}$)
s(br, on fence): *VG 1632*
Assheton-Bennett bequest (1979.458)

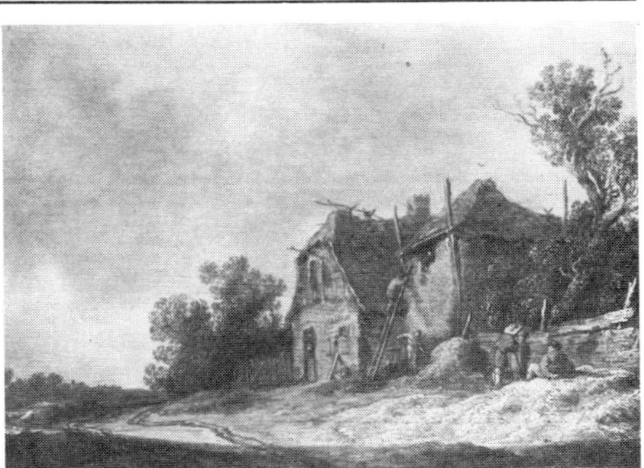

WINTER SCENE WITH A SLEDGE IN THE FOREGROUND AND FIGURES GATHERING ROUND A TENT ON THE ICE
1653

Oil on panel
27·9 × 43·1 (11 × 17)
s(b, centre): *VG 1653.*
Assheton-Bennett bequest (1979.459)

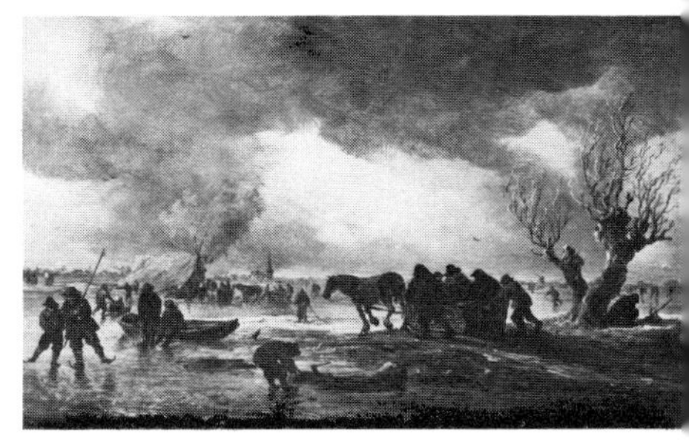

Pieter Franz de Grebber
*c.*1600–*c.*1652 Dutch

THE NATIVITY
1634(?)

Oil on canvas
141·5 × 177·2 (55 11/16 × 69 3/4)
s(br): *P.DG* (mon) *1634* (?)
Presented by the children of John Albert and Edith Eckersley Bright (1926.34)

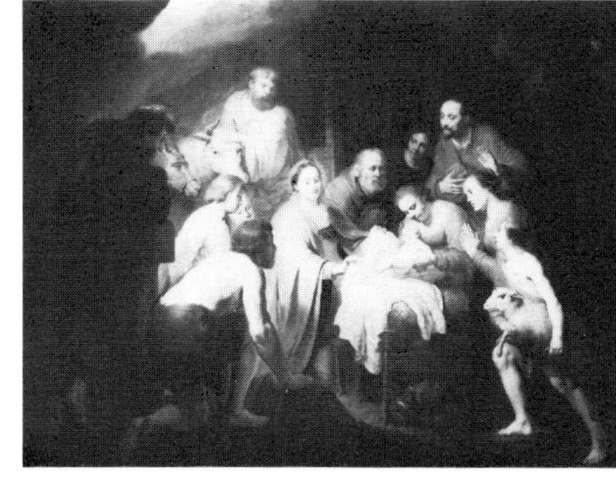

Attributed to Francesco Guardi
1712–1793 Italian

PIAZZA SAN MARCO, VENICE

Oil on panel
18·2 × 32·1 (7 3/16 × 12 5/8)
Unsigned
Assheton-Bennett bequest (1979.518)

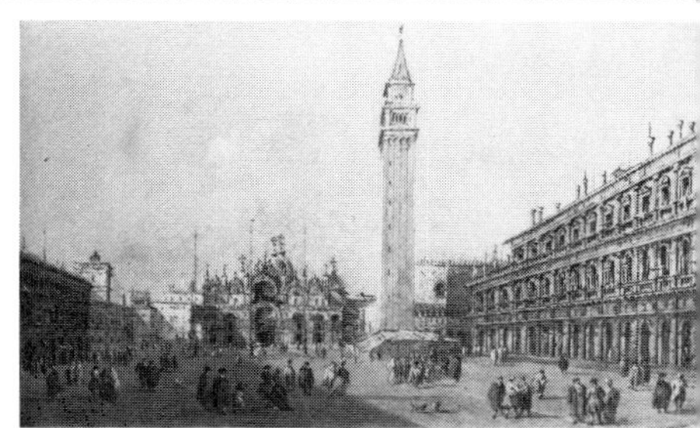

THE PIAZZETTA, VENICE

Oil on panel
18·1 × 31·8 ($7\frac{1}{8} \times 12\frac{7}{16}$)
Unsigned
Assheton-Bennett bequest (1979.519)

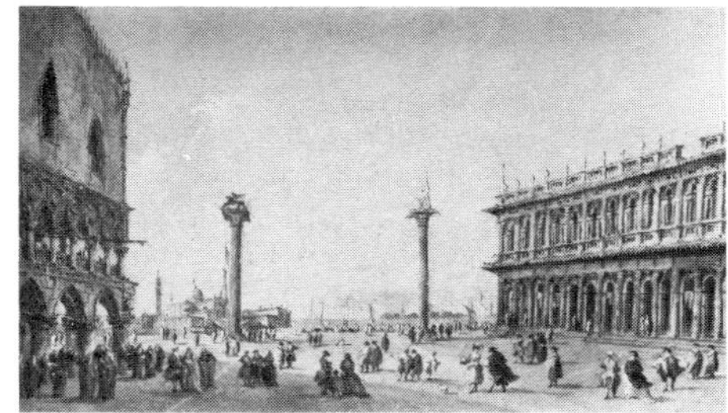

THE BRIDGE OVER THE BRENTA AT DOLO

Oil on panel
20 × 24·7 ($7\frac{7}{8} \times 9\frac{3}{4}$)
Unsigned
Assheton-Bennett bequest (1979.520)

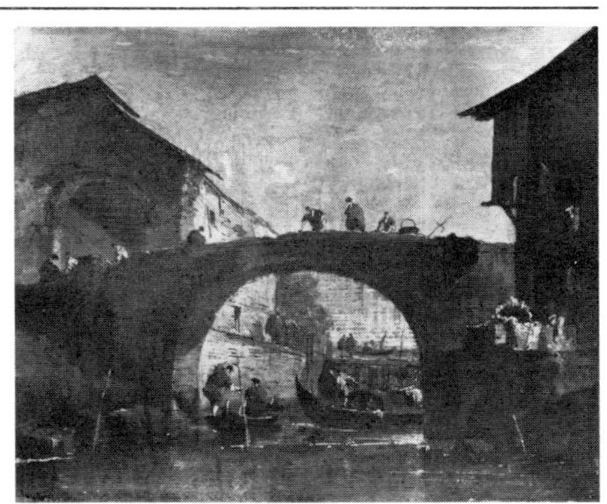

STORM AT SEA

Oil on panel
12 × 18·6 ($4\frac{11}{16} \times 7\frac{5}{16}$)
Unsigned
Assheton-Bennett bequest (1979.521)

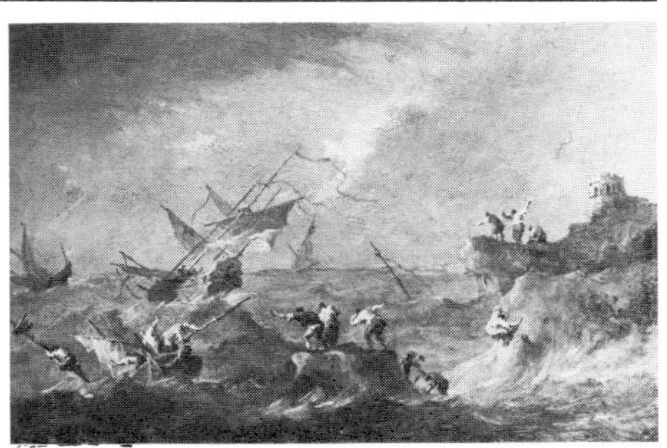

AN ISLAND IN THE LAGOON

Oil on panel
$11{\cdot}9 \times 18{\cdot}6$ ($4\frac{11}{16} \times 7\frac{3}{8}$)
Unsigned
Assheton-Bennett bequest (1979.522)

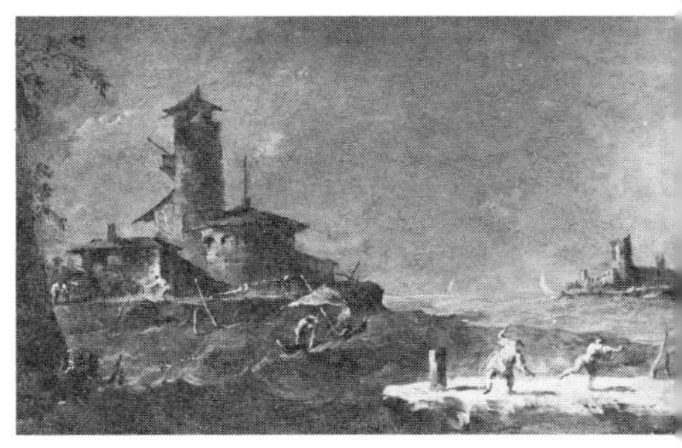

LAGOON CAPRICCIO WITH A RUINED ARCH

Oil on panel
$6{\cdot}8 \times 14{\cdot}3$ ($2\frac{11}{16} \times 5\frac{5}{8}$)
Unsigned
Assheton-Bennett bequest (1979.523)

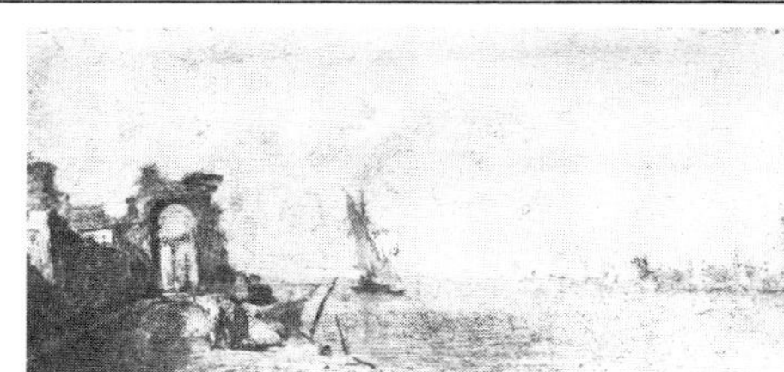

LAGOON CAPRICCIO WITH A CHURCH AND A BRIDGE

Oil on panel
$6{\cdot}8 \times 14{\cdot}3$ ($2\frac{11}{16} \times 5\frac{5}{8}$)
Unsigned
Assheton-Bennett bequest (1979.524)

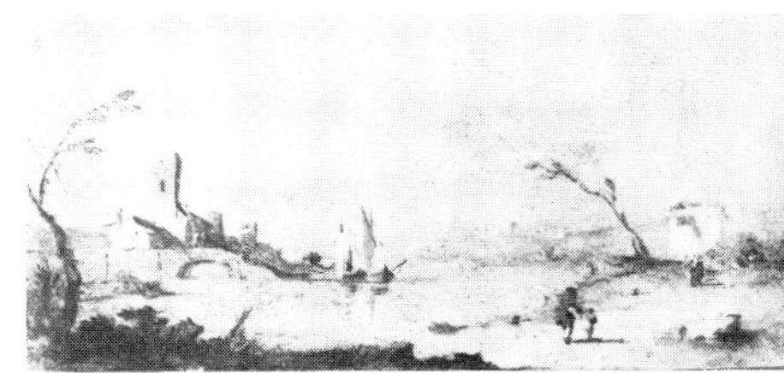

LAGOON CAPRICCIO WITH A CHURCH

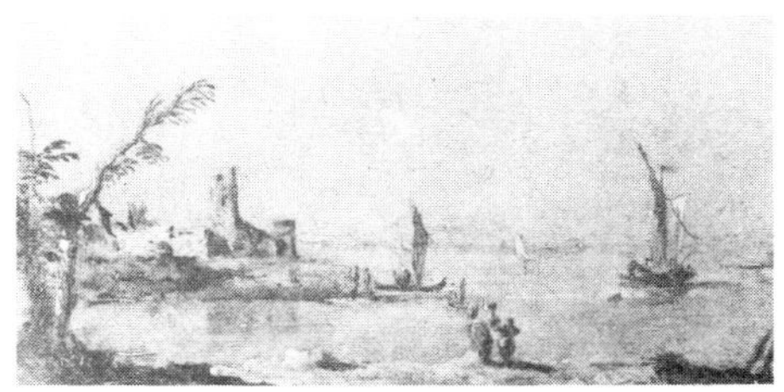

Oil on panel
6·8 × 14·3 ($2\frac{11}{16} \times 5\frac{5}{8}$)
Unsigned
Assheton-Bennett bequest (1979.525)

LAGOON CAPRICCIO WITH A PEASANT AND CATTLE

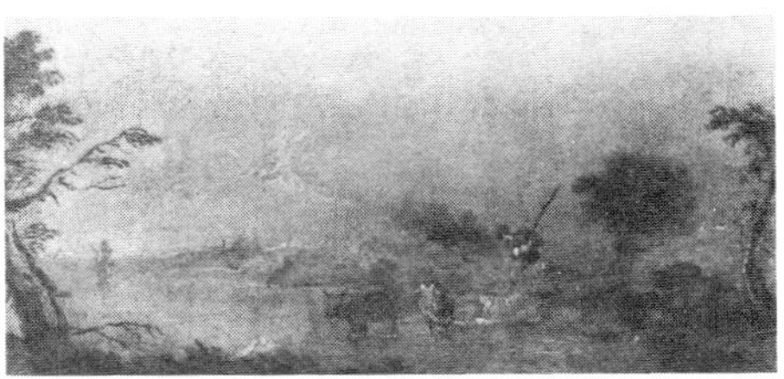

Oil on panel
6·7 × 14·3 ($2\frac{5}{8} \times 5\frac{5}{8}$)
Unsigned
Assheton-Bennett bequest (1979.526)

CAPRICCIO WITH A CHURCH SEEN THROUGH A PORTICO

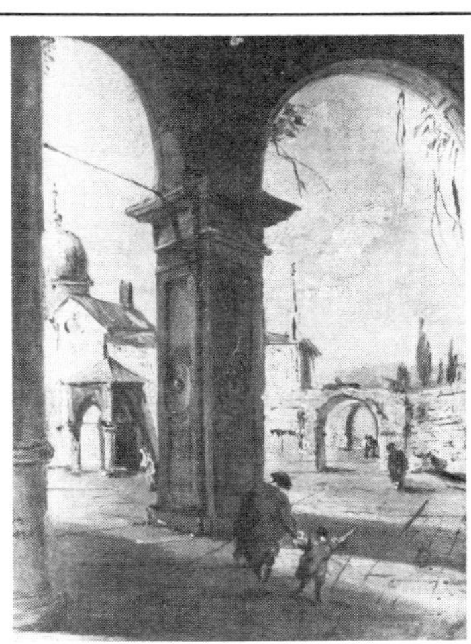

Oil on panel
13·9 × 10·2 ($5\frac{1}{2} \times 4$)
Unsigned
Assheton-Bennett bequest (1979.527)

Attributed to
Giovanni Francesco Guerrieri
1589–1655/59 Italian
(formerly attributed to Gerrit van Honthorst)

LOT AND HIS DAUGHTERS

Oil on canvas
136·3 × 99·3 (53⅝ × 39⅛)
Unsigned
James Bradock gift to the Royal Manchester Institution, 1832, from which transferred (1882.45)

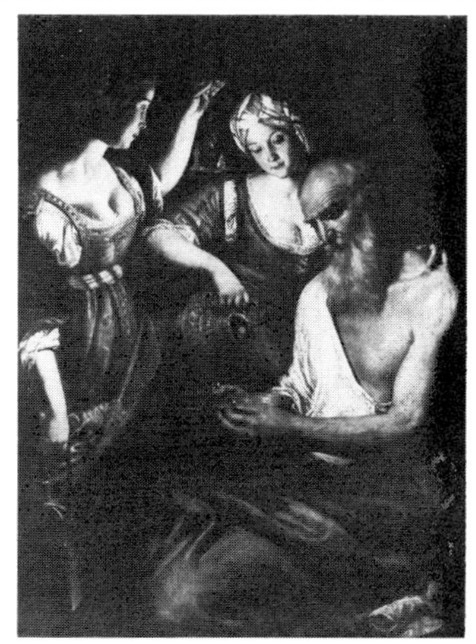

Alvaro Guevara
1894–1951 Chilean

THE HUNTER

Oil on canvas
88·8 × 65 (34 15/16 × 25⅝)
s(brc): *A. Guevara*
Dr. Jane Walker bequest (1939.14)

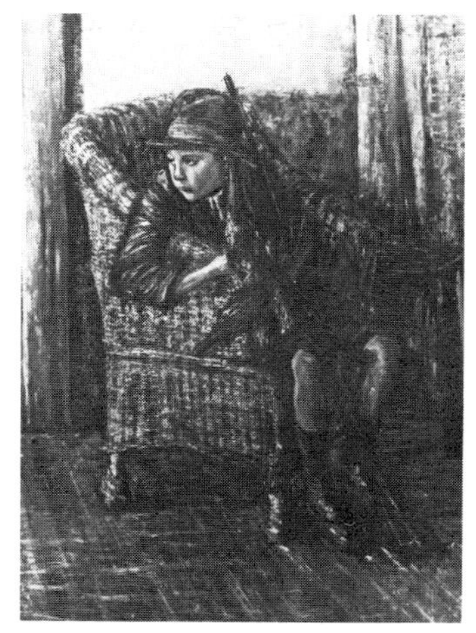

Follower of Frans Hals
*c.*1580?–1666 Dutch

A FISHER BOY

Oil on panel
28·6 × 21·9 (11¼ × 8⅝)
inscr(trc): *FH* (mon)
Assheton-Bennett bequest (1979.460)

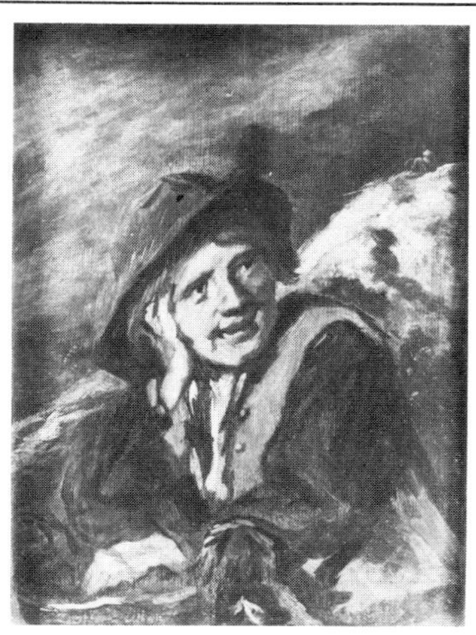

Henri Harpignies
1819–1916 French

THE WINDING RIVER
1882

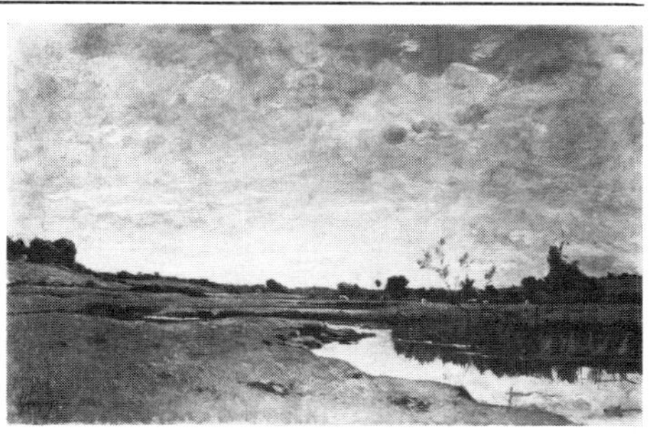

Oil on canvas
32·4 × 51·5 ($12\frac{3}{4} \times 20\frac{1}{4}$)
s(blc): *H Harpignies. 1882.*
Purchased (1920.132)

THE CASTLE OF CLISSON
1895

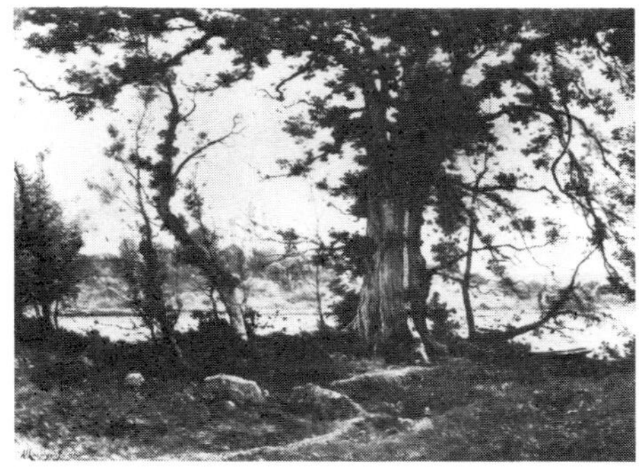

Oil on canvas
117·5 × 160·7 ($46\frac{1}{2} \times 63\frac{1}{4}$)
s(blc): *H. Harpignies · 95*
Purchased (1930.82)

Jan Davidsz. de Heem
1605/6–1684 Dutch

STILL LIFE: FRUIT AND OYSTERS ON A TABLE

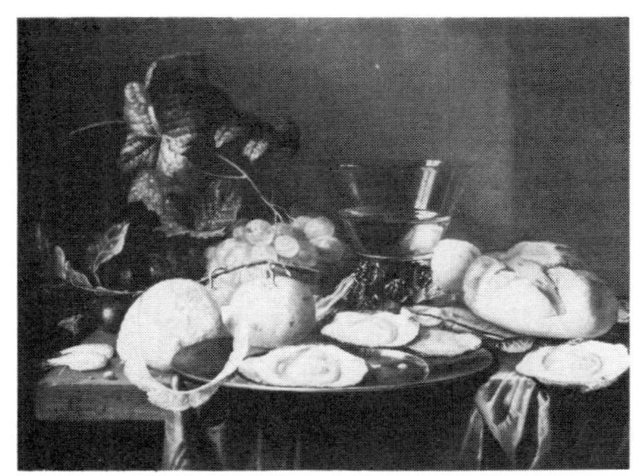

Oil on panel
33·6 × 49·8 ($13\frac{1}{4} \times 19\frac{9}{16}$)
s(bl): *J D D Heem.f* (JDDH in mon)
Assheton-Bennett bequest (1979.461)

Maerten van Heemskerk
1498–1574 Dutch

PORTRAIT OF MARGARETHA BANKEN (?MARGUERITE DE BINCHEM)
Wife of Aert van der Goes

Oil on panel
89·5 × 72·3 ($35\frac{1}{4} \times 28\frac{7}{16}$)
inscr(trc): *AN°AETATIS / 65*
Purchased (1958.55)

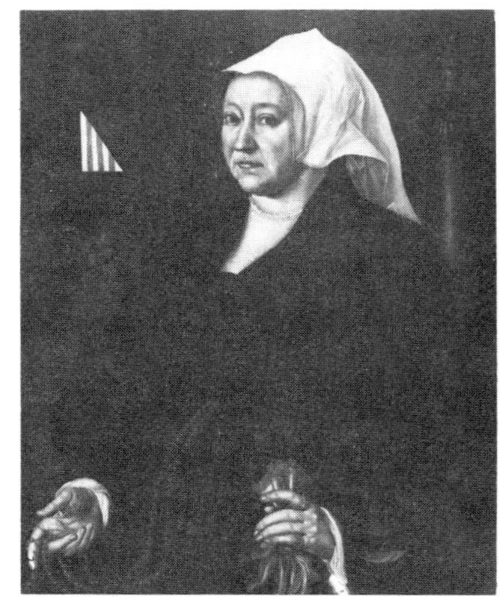

Thomas Heeremans
c. 1640–1697 Dutch

RIVER SCENE WITH A RUINED TOWER ON THE BANK AND FIGURES IN ROWING BOATS

Oil on panel
20·5 × 26·7 ($8\frac{1}{16} \times 10\frac{3}{8}$)
Unsigned
Assheton-Bennett bequest (1979.462)

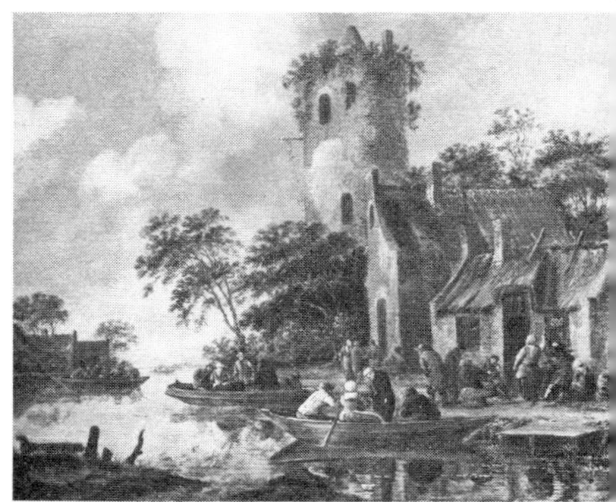

Louis-Adolphe Hervier
1818–1879 French

A FARMYARD
1874

Oil on canvas
47·1 × 39·4 ($18\frac{5}{8} \times 15\frac{1}{2}$)
s(br): *HERVIER / 74*
Purchased (1919.5)

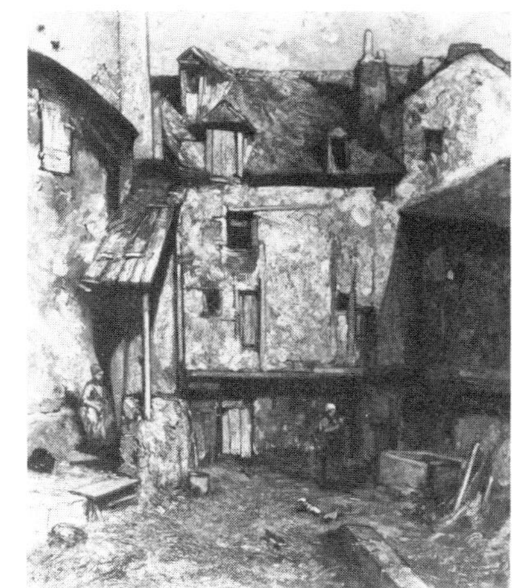

Jan van der Heyden
1637–1712 Dutch

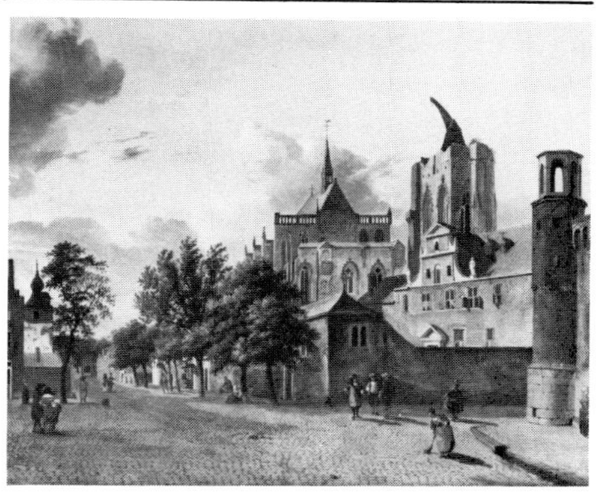

A STREET IN COLOGNE WITH THE UNFINISHED CATHEDRAL IN THE CENTRE
1694

Oil on panel
31·7 × 40·5 ($12\frac{1}{4}$ × 16)
s(br, on base of gate tower): *I V Heyden f. 1694.*
Assheton-Bennett bequest (1979.463)

Manner of Meindert Hobbema
1638–1709 Dutch

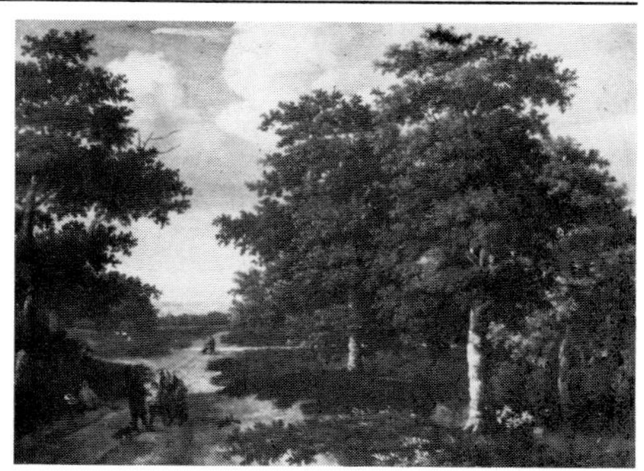

FIGURES HALTED AT THE OUTSKIRTS OF A WOOD, A POOL AT THE RIGHT

Oil on panel
46·8 × 63·1 ($18\frac{7}{16}$ × $24\frac{3}{4}$)
inscr(blc): *M. Hobbema f.*
Assheton-Bennett bequest (1979.464)

Manner of Melchior de Hondecoeter
1636–1695 Dutch

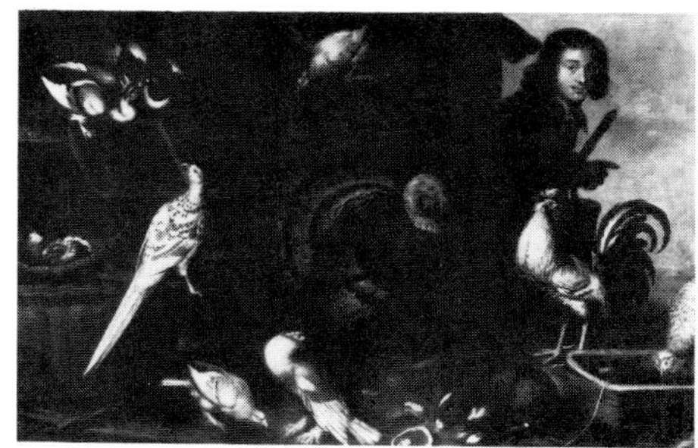

DOMESTIC FOWLS AND A MAN

Oil on canvas
120 × 188·5 ($47\frac{1}{4}$ × $74\frac{3}{16}$)
inscr(brc): *Melchior d Hondecoeter*
G. Spiegelberg gift (1910.41)

Gerrit van Honthorst
See Giovanni Francesco Guerrieri

Pieter de Hoogh
1629–after 1684 Dutch

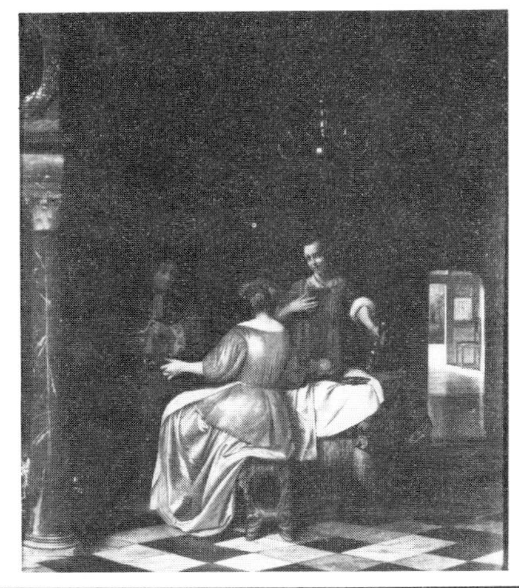

INTERIOR WITH A GENTLEMAN AND TWO LADIES CONVERSING; AN OPEN DOORWAY LEADING TO A COURTYARD, RIGHT

Oil on canvas
70 × 61·8 ($27\frac{1}{2} \times 24\frac{5}{16}$)
s(blc, on base of column): *P d hooch.*
Assheton-Bennett bequest (1979.465)

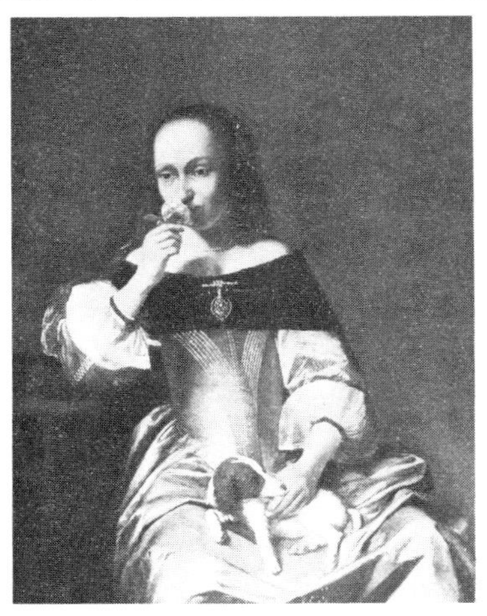

INTERIOR WITH A LADY SEATED, A DOG ON HER LAP

Oil on canvas
35·5 × 28·3 ($14 \times 11\frac{1}{8}$)
s(trc): *P D HOOCH.*
Assheton-Bennett bequest (1979.466)

Samuel van Hoogstraten
1627–1678 Dutch
(formerly attributed to Rembrandt and to Nicholas Maes)

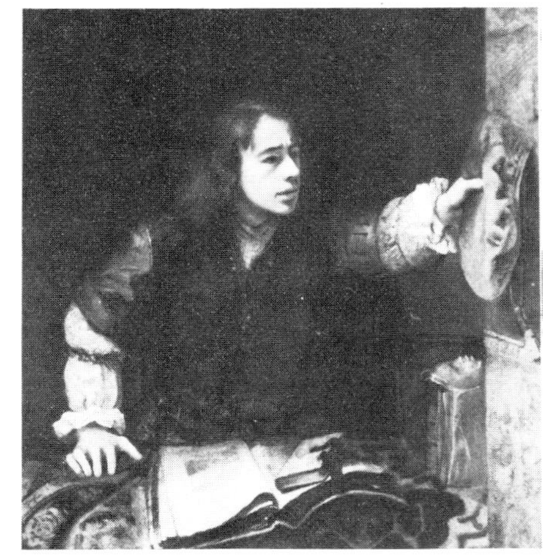

A YOUNG MAN REACHING FOR HIS CAP

Oil on canvas
114·1 × 108·2 ($44\frac{15}{16} \times 42\frac{5}{8}$)
Unsigned
Purchased with the aid of a grant from the Victoria and Albert Museum (1973.290)

Arnold Houbraken
1660–1719 Dutch

SUSANNAH AND THE ELDERS

Oil on copper
36·5 × 27·3 (14⅜ × 10¾)
Unsigned
Presented by Mrs. E. F. Hickman in memory of her husband (1931.128)

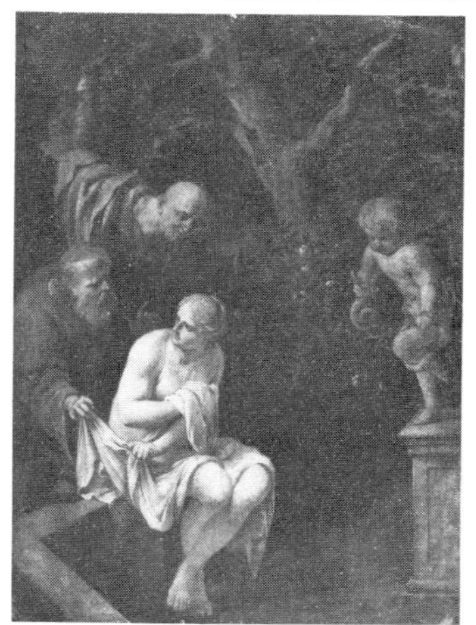

Jan van Huysum
1682–1749 Dutch

STILL LIFE: FLOWERS AND FRUIT

Oil on panel
88·9 × 67·5 (35 × 26⅝)
s(bl, on table, each side of fallen carnation): *Jan van Huysum f.*
Assheton-Bennett bequest (1979.467)

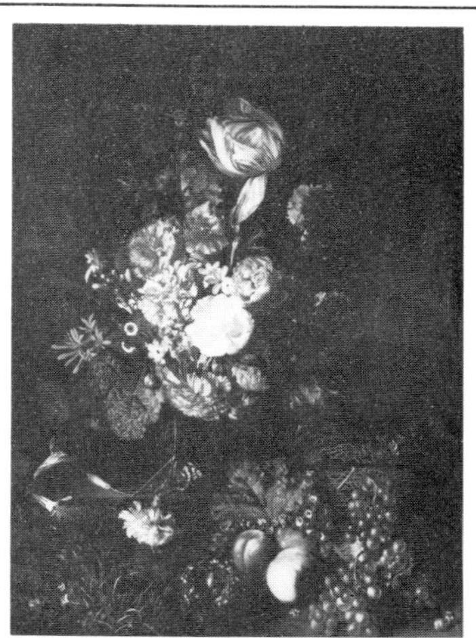

Eugène Isabey
1804–1886 French

THE SMITHY

Oil on panel
32·9 × 21·8 ($12\frac{15}{16} \times 8\frac{9}{16}$)
s(blc): *E. Isabey*
Purchased (1913.15)

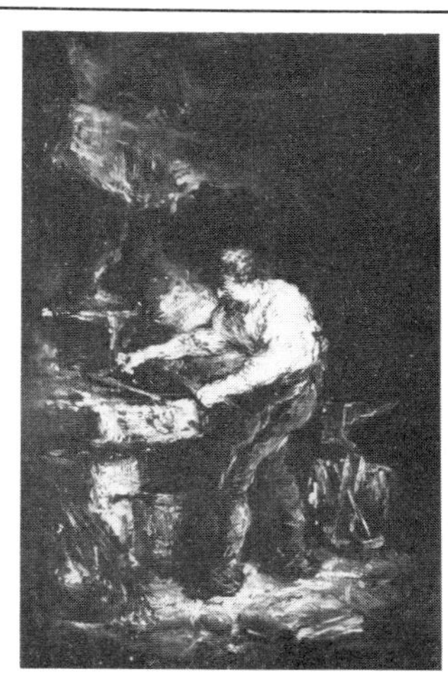

Italian, *c.* 1700
(formerly called School of Salvator Rosa)

LANDSCAPE WITH ABRAHAM AND ISAAC

Oil on canvas
58·6 × 86·6 ($23\frac{1}{8} \times 34\frac{1}{8}$)
Unsigned
P. King gift in memory of his grandfather, Capt. J. D. King, through the National Art-Collections Fund (1931.64)

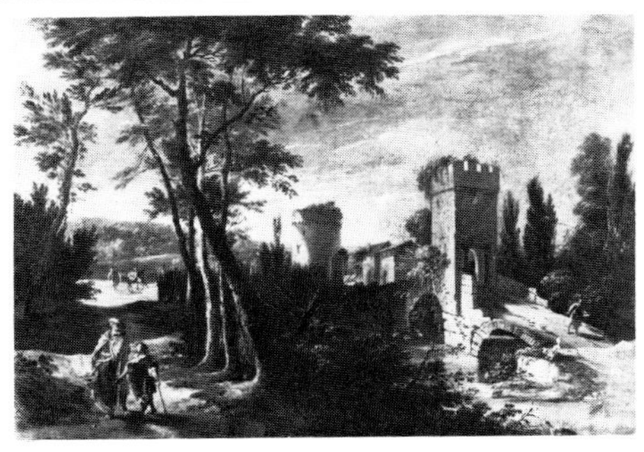

Italian or Dutch, late 17th century

CLASSICAL LANDSCAPE WITH A RIVER

Oil on canvas
50 × 66·8 ($19\frac{11}{16} \times 26\frac{5}{16}$)
Unsigned
Lt. Col. R. H. Antrobus gift (1971.108)

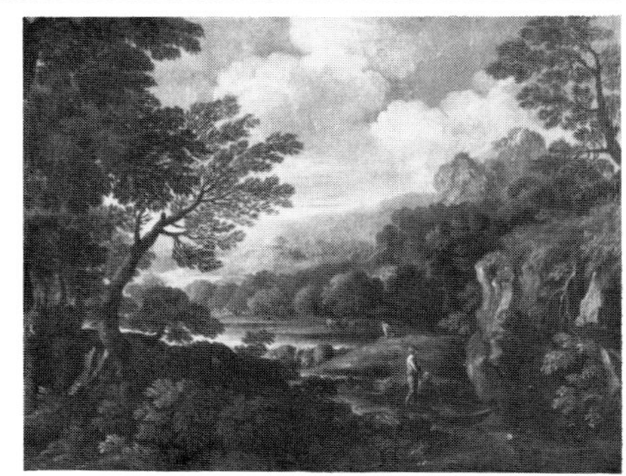

Gustave Jean Jacquet
1846–1909 French

MEDITATION

Oil on canvas
32·6 × 24·8 ($12\frac{13}{16} \times 9\frac{3}{4}$)
s(tlc): *G Jacquet*
James Blair bequest (1917.224)

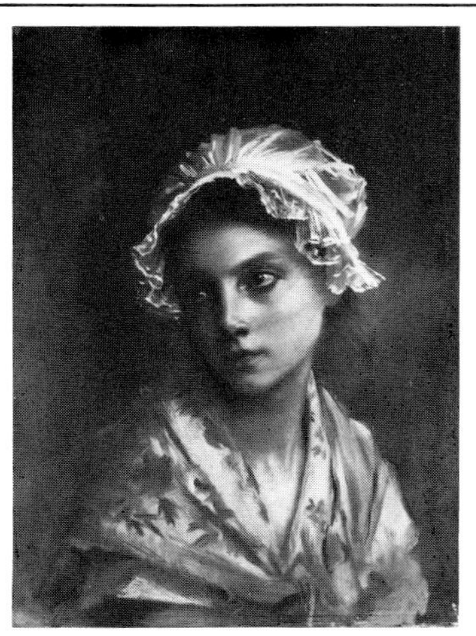

HEAD OF A GIRL

Oil on panel
33 × 23·7 (13 × 9 5/16)
s(l): *G J Jacquet* (GJ in mon)
John E. Yates bequest (1934.406)

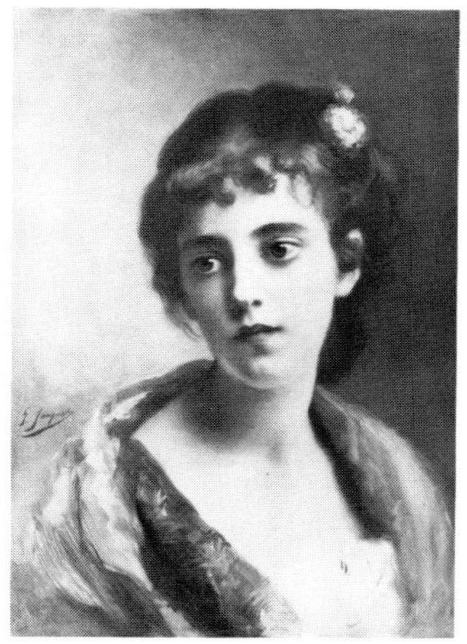

Willem Kalf
1619–1693 Dutch

STILL LIFE: FRUIT, GOBLET AND SALVER

Oil on canvas
58·9 × 50·7 (23 1/8 × 20 1/16)
s(bl): *W. KALF.*
Assheton-Bennett bequest (1979.468)

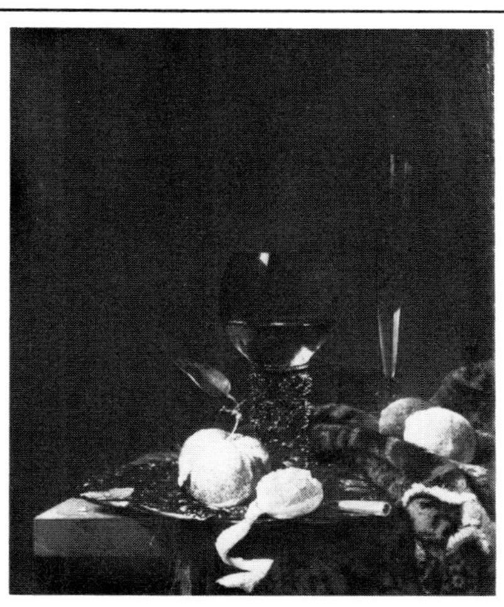

Stanislawa de Karlowska (Mrs. Robert Bevan)
1876–1952 Polish

AT WOODNESBOROUGH, KENT

Oil on canvas
45·9 × 37·8 (18 1/16 × 14 7/8)
s(brc): *S de Karlowska*
C. W. Baty gift (1936.262)

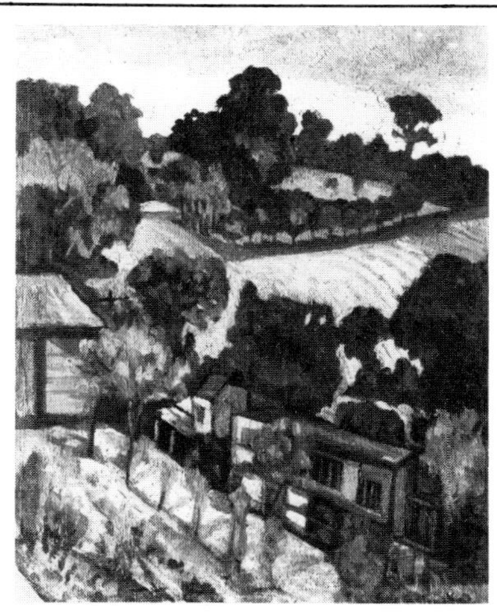

ADAMSON ROAD, N.W.3

Oil on canvas
55·7 × 48·3 ($21\frac{15}{16}$ × 19)
s(blc): *S de Karlowska*
Presented by Mrs. C. W. Baty and Mr. R. A. Bevan, daughter and son of the artist (1968.91)

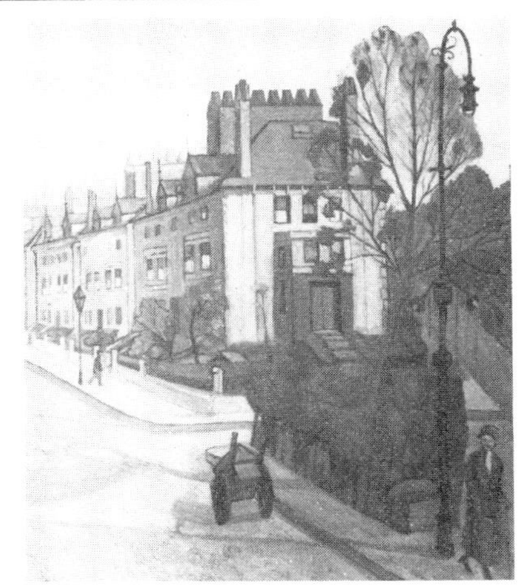

Herman Frederik Carel ten Kate
1822–1891 Dutch

INTERIOR OF A DUTCH INN
1851

Oil on canvas
28·4 × 33·6 ($11\frac{1}{8}$ × $13\frac{1}{4}$)
s(brc): *Herman ten Kate f. '51*
Purchased (1931.51)

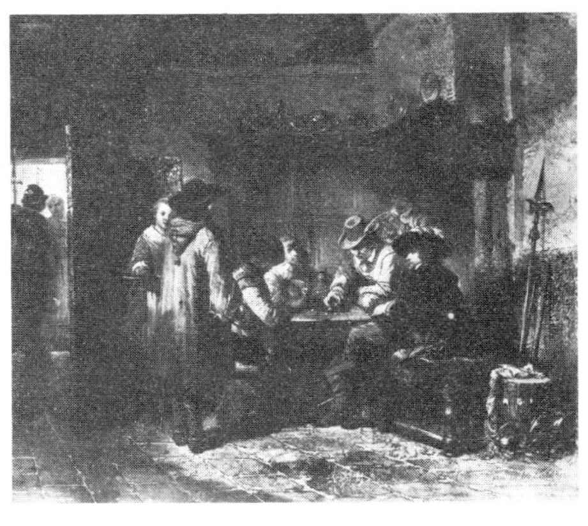

Angelica Kauffman
See English School Catalogue, Vol. I

Adriaen Thomas Key
See Frans Pourbus the Elder

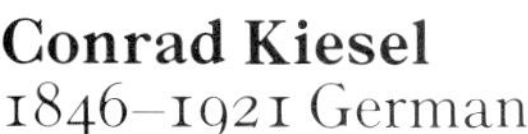

Conrad Kiesel
1846–1921 German

MARGUERITES

Oil on canvas
119·7 × 78·4 ($47\frac{1}{8}$ × $30\frac{7}{8}$)
s(brc): *Conrad Kiesel pxt.*
James Blair bequest (1917.242)

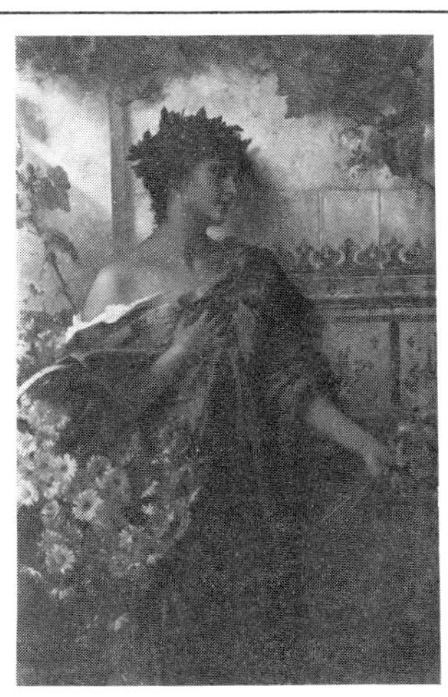

Elias Kohn
active 20th century Israeli

ISRAELI LANDSCAPE

Oil on canvas
81·3 × 100·5 (32 × 39 9/16)
s(blc): *Elias Kohn*
Presented by the Leonard Cohen Fund (1968.154)

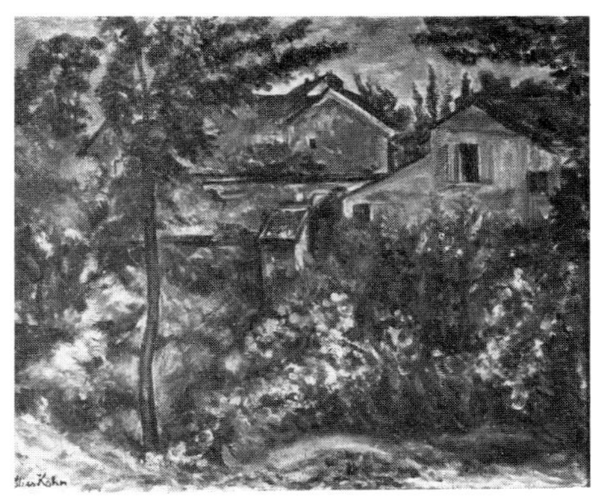

FRENCH LANDSCAPE

Oil on hardboard
32·3 × 47·2 (12 11/16 × 18 9/16)
s(blc): *Elias Kohn*
Presented by the Leonard Cohen Fund (1968.155)

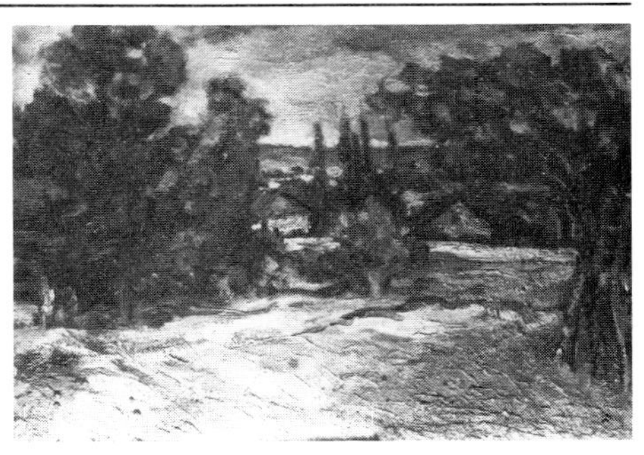

Philips Koninck
1619–1688 Dutch

FLAT LANDSCAPE WITH A VIEW TO DISTANT HILLS
1648

Oil on panel
29·8 × 40·8 (11 3/4 × 16 1/16)
s(b, centre to l): *P koninck 1648.*
Assheton-Bennett bequest (1979.469)

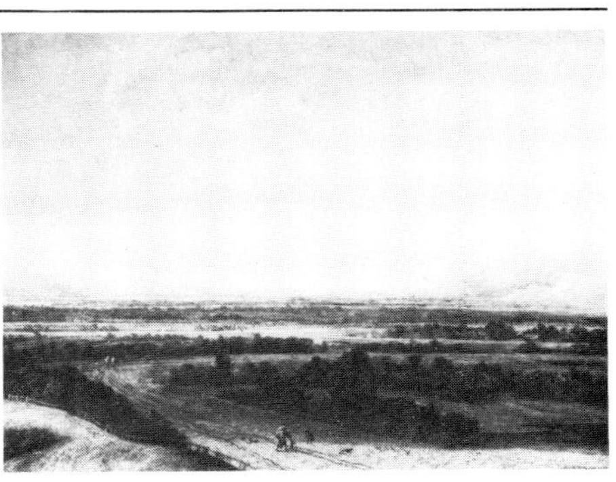

A WOMAN WITH A GLASS OF WINE, AND A MAN LOOKING IN AT HER
1649

Oil on panel
33 × 24·8 (13 × 9¾)
s(brc): *P. Koninck 1649*
Assheton-Bennett bequest (1979.470)

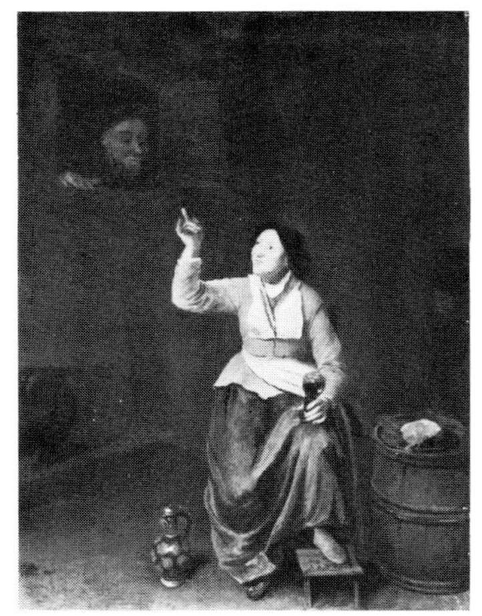

Charles de La Fosse
1636–1716 French

APOLLO AND PHAETON WITH THE SEASONS
c. 1689

Oil on canvas
123·5 × 91 (48⅝ × 35 13/16)
Unsigned
Purchased (1964.40)

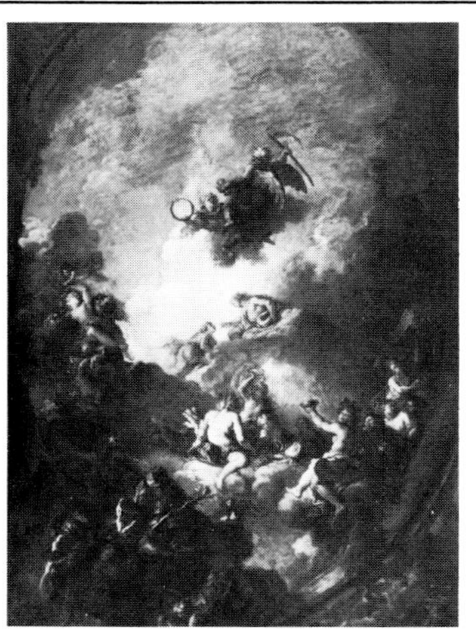

Elie Lascaux
1888–1968 French

LES VIGNES SOUS LA NEIGE
1929

Oil on canvas
54·1 × 65·1 (21 5/16 × 25⅝)
s(brc): *LASCAUX*
Miss Dorothy Pilkington bequest (1974.92)

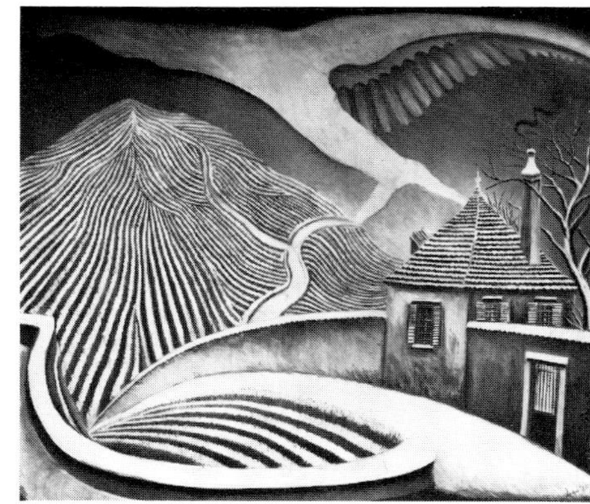

Fernand Léger
1881–1955 French

PAINTING 1926

Oil on canvas
65·1 × 46 ($25\frac{5}{8}$ × $18\frac{1}{8}$)
s(brc): *F. LÉGER . 26*
Purchased (1949.102)

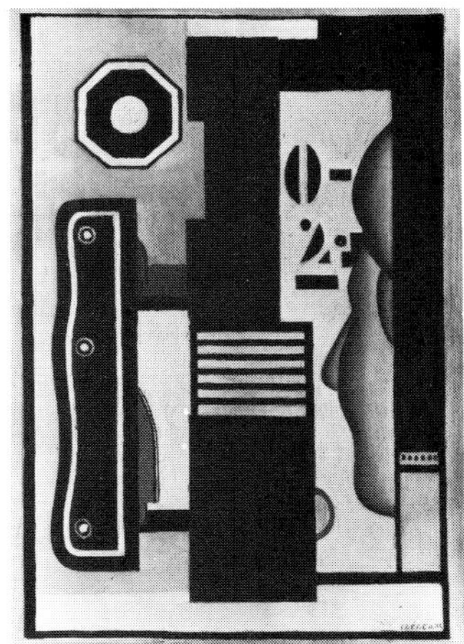

Alphonse Legros
1837–1911 French

STUDY OF A HEAD
C. NAPIER HEMY (1841–1917)
Artist
1879

Oil on canvas
51 × 40·8 ($20\frac{1}{16}$ × $16\frac{1}{16}$)
Unsigned
Presented by the artist to the Royal Manchester Institution, 1879, from which transferred (1882.8)

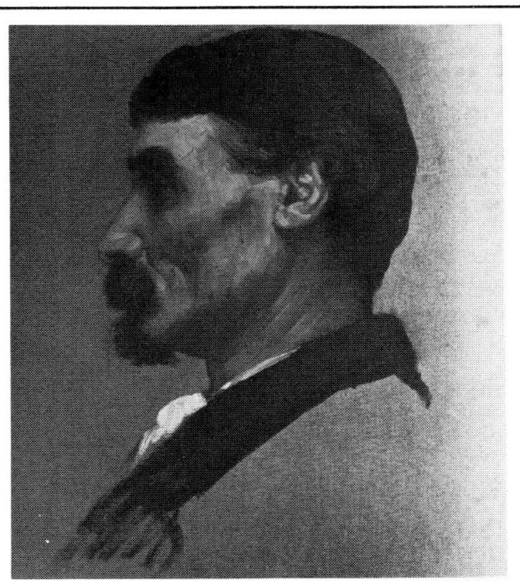

STUDY OF A HEAD

Oil on canvas laid down on panel
58·3 × 45·2 ($22\frac{15}{16}$ × $17\frac{13}{16}$)
s(tr): *A.L*
Presented by the artist to the Royal Manchester Institution, 1879, from which transferred (1882.9)

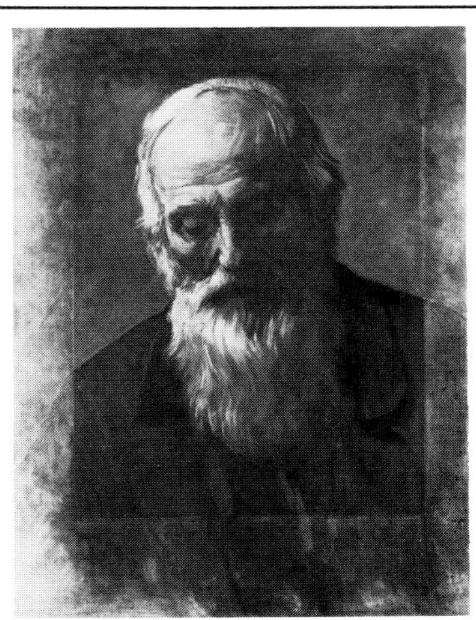

ST. JEROME
1881

Oil on canvas
176·4 × 107·6 ($69\frac{7}{16} \times 42\frac{3}{8}$)
s(brc): *A. Legros. 1881*
Presented by the artist to the Royal Manchester Institution, 1881, from which transferred (1882.10)

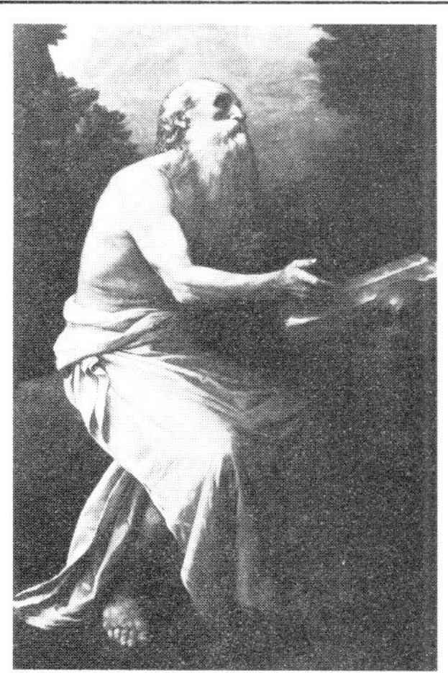

STUDY OF A HEAD

Oil on canvas
61·1 × 51 ($24\frac{1}{16} \times 20\frac{1}{16}$)
s(trc): *A. Legros*
Presented by the artist (1884.2)

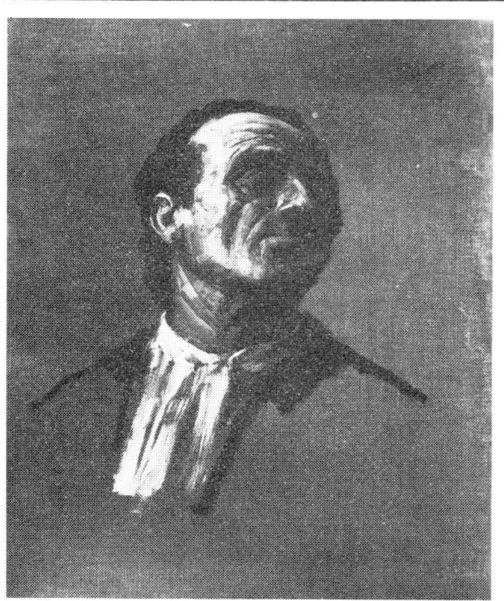

HEAD OF AN OLD MAN

Oil on canvas
61·3 × 50·7 ($24\frac{1}{8} \times 19\frac{15}{16}$)
s(trc): *A. Legros / 1881.*
Guy Knowles gift (1933.68)

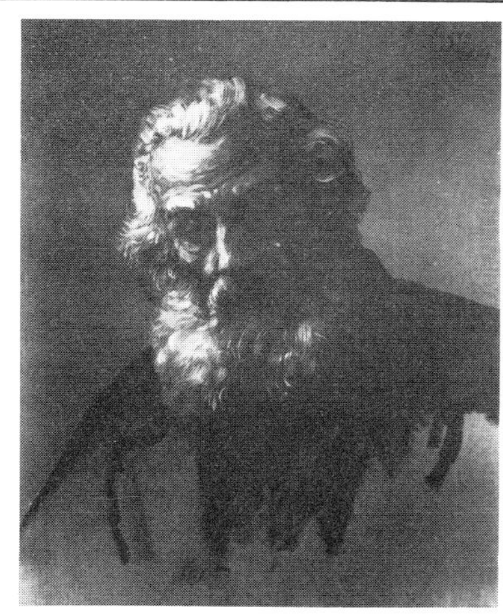

Henri-Eugène-Augustin Le Sidaner
1862–1939 French

COURTYARD FROM A WINDOW

Oil on canvas
80·7 × 99·9 ($31\frac{3}{4} \times 39\frac{5}{16}$)
s(brc): *Le SIDANER*
Purchased (1929.27)

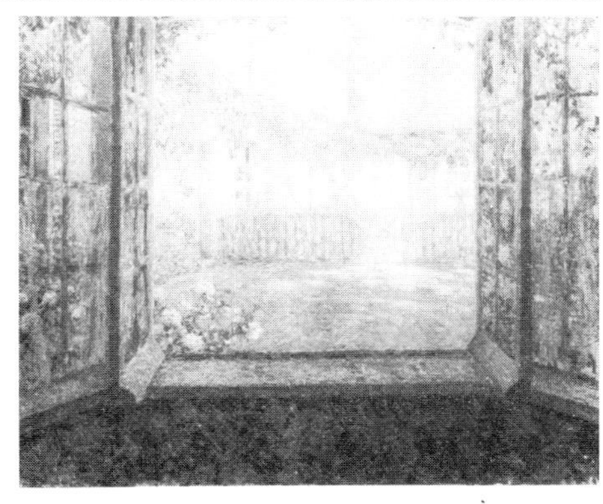

Léon-Augustin Lhermitte
1844–1925 French

A FLOOD
1876

Oil on canvas
42·8 × 64·8 ($16\frac{7}{8} \times 25\frac{1}{2}$)
s(blc): *L. Lhermitte – 76*
G. Beatson Blair bequest, 1941
(1947.92)

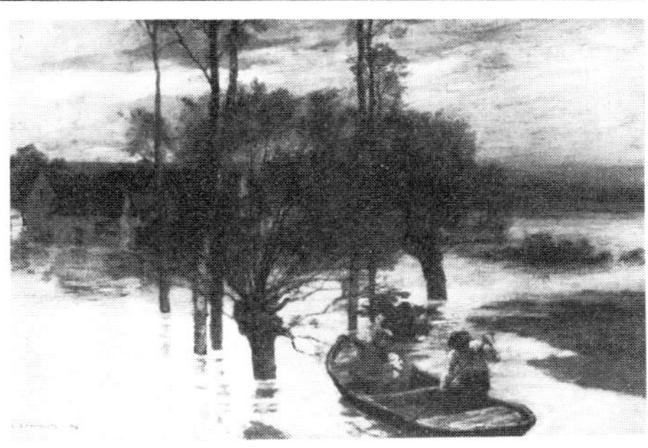

Johannes Lingelbach
1622–1674 Dutch

A PARTY OF FALCONERS OUTSIDE THE GATES OF A CHÂTEAU

Oil on canvas
35·1 × 42·2 ($13\frac{7}{8} \times 16\frac{5}{8}$)
s(brc): *J Lingelbach.*
Assheton-Bennett bequest (1979.471)

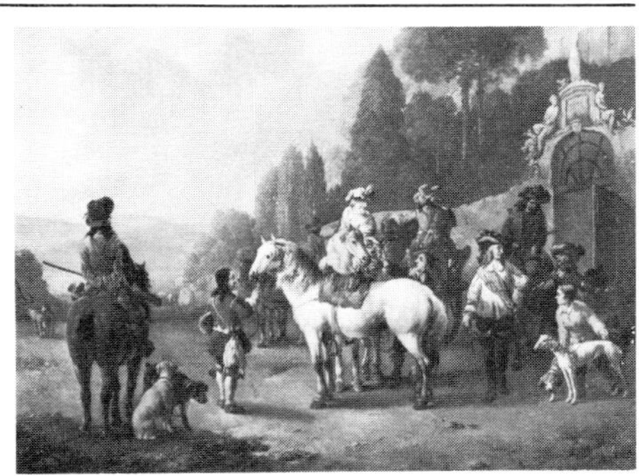

Gustave Loiseau
1865–1935 French

THE SEINE NEAR PORT MARLY
1903

Oil on canvas
50·2 × 61 ($19\frac{3}{4}$ × 24)
s(brc): *G. Loiseau. 03*
Purchased (1908.3)

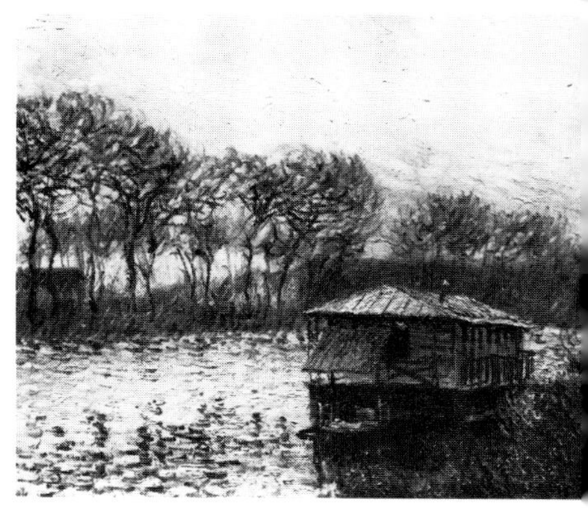

Jadwiga Luyten-Behnisch
active 1915–1928 Polish?

PLUMS

Oil on canvas
40·7 × 51 ($15\frac{15}{16}$ × $20\frac{1}{8}$)
s(blc): *Luyten Behnisch*
Purchased (1928.103)

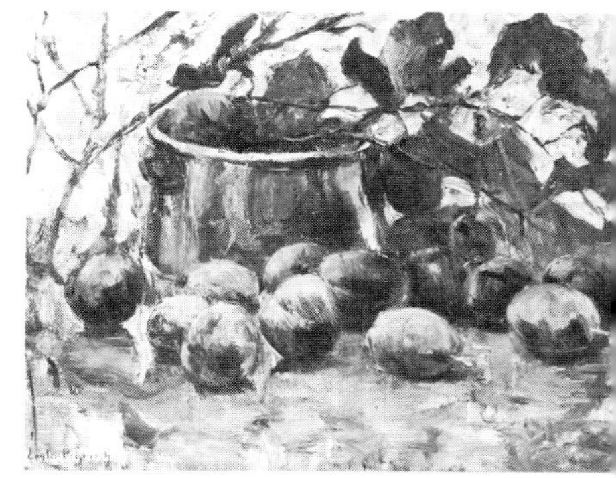

Nicholas Maes
See Samuel van Hoogstraten

Jean Hippolyte Marchand
1883–1940 French

OLIVE TREES, VENCE

Oil on canvas
65·1 × 92·1 ($25\frac{5}{8}$ × $36\frac{1}{4}$)
s(brc): *J. Marchand*
Charles L. Rutherston gift (1925.317)

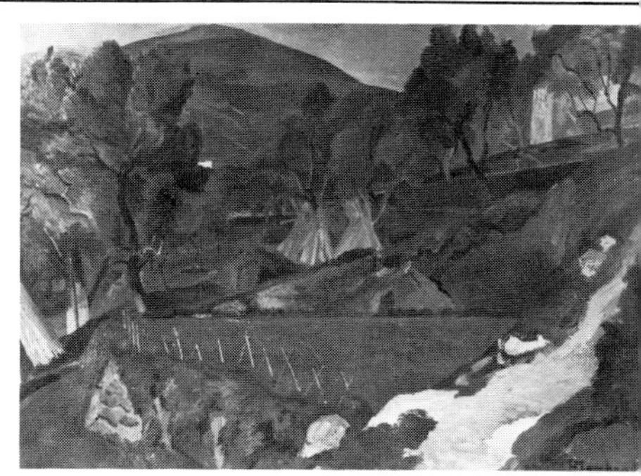

THE LADY IN BROWN

Oil on canvas
65·3 × 54·7 ($25\frac{11}{16} \times 21\frac{9}{16}$)
s(brc) : *J. Marchand*
Charles L. Rutherston gift (1925.583)

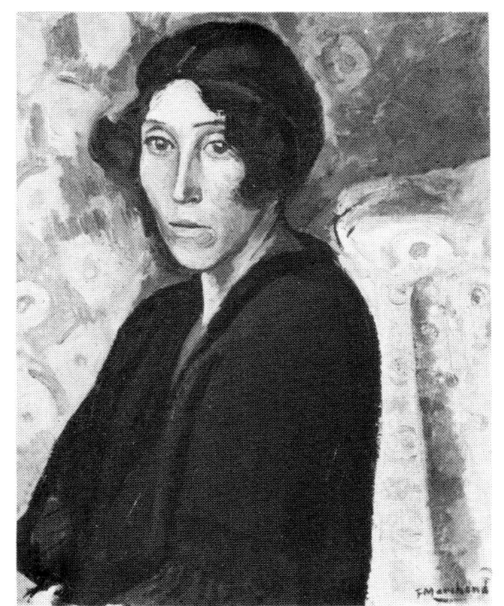

PORTRAIT OF A LADY

Oil on canvas
65·4 × 53·3 ($25\frac{3}{4} \times 21$)
s(tlc) : *J Marchand*
Mrs. Archibald gift (1937.676)

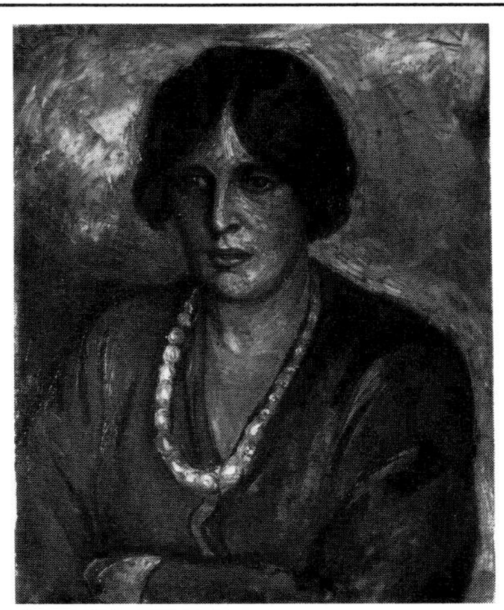

FRENCH VILLAGE

Oil on canvas
60·6 × 73·5 ($23\frac{7}{8} \times 28\frac{15}{16}$)
s(blc) : *J Marchand*
F. Hindley Smith bequest (1940.4)

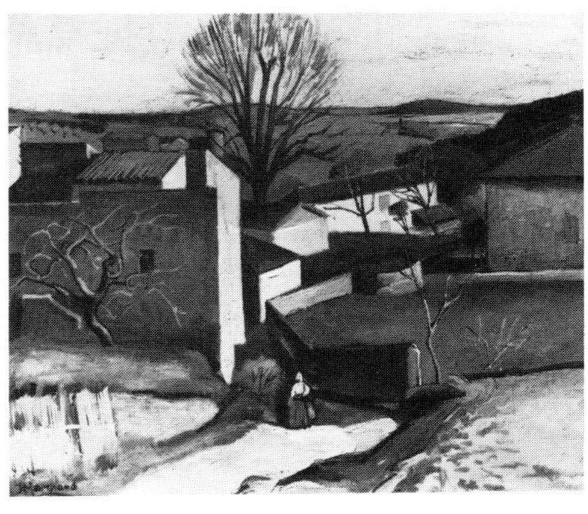

Louis Marcoussis (Ludwig Casimir Ladislas Markous)
1883–1941 French

STILL LIFE 1927

Oil on canvas
80·9 × 100·2 ($31\frac{13}{16}$ × $39\frac{7}{16}$)
s(bl): *Marcoussis / Bormes / 27*
Purchased (1951.59)

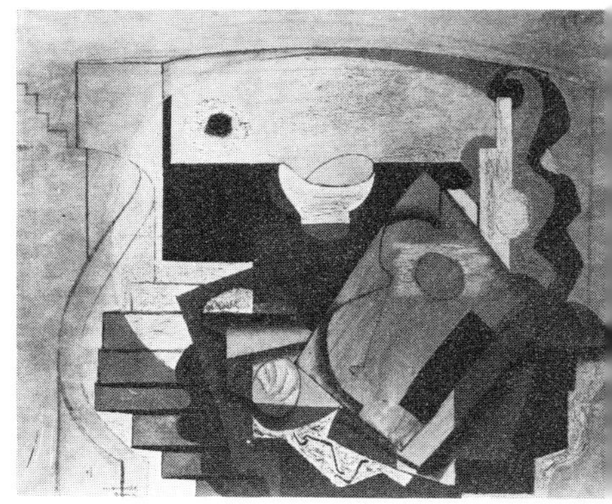

Jacob Hendricus Maris
1837–1899 Dutch

IN THE GARDEN

Oil on panel
29 × 19·6 ($11\frac{7}{16}$ × $7\frac{3}{4}$)
s(brc): *J Maris*
Purchased (1911.77)

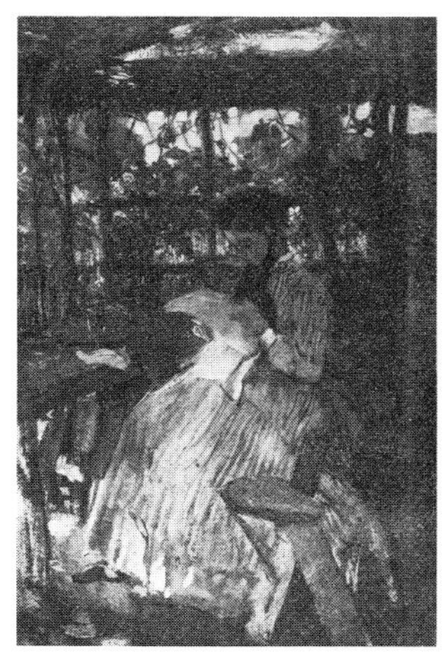

THE GATHERING STORM

Oil on canvas
48·1 × 90·5 ($18\frac{15}{16}$ × $35\frac{5}{8}$)
Unsigned
Presented by the family of R. E. Haslam, through the National Art-Collections Fund (1927.39)

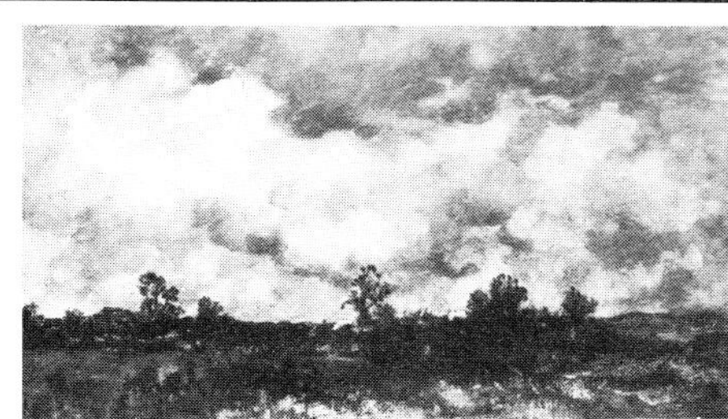

Willem Maris
1884–1910 Dutch

COWS AT PASTURE

Oil on canvas
25 × 42·5 ($9\frac{7}{8}$ × $16\frac{3}{4}$)
s(l): *Willem Maris f*
G. Beatson Blair bequest, 1941
(1947.93)

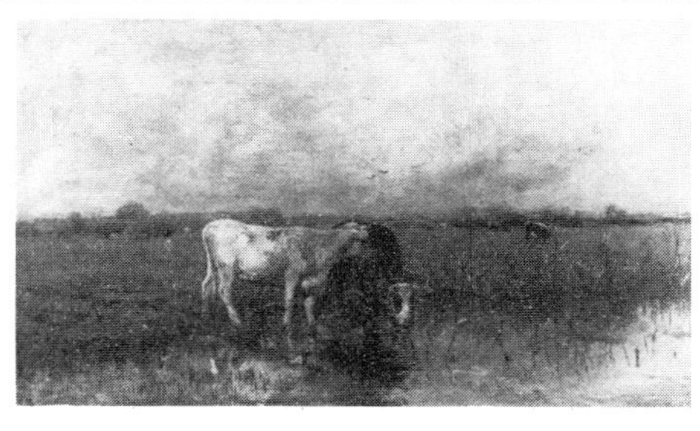

Benito Quinquella Martin
See Quinquella Martin

Master of Frankfurt
c. 1460–1515 Flemish
ST. CATHERINE AND ST. BARBARA WITH DONORS
(wings of a triptych)
Oil on panel
89·9 × 26 ($35\frac{3}{8}$ × $10\frac{1}{4}$) each
Inscr (*verso*): *VOS QVI TRANSITIS NOSTRE MEMORES ROGO SITIS QVOD SVMVS HOC/ ERITIS FVIMVS QUA[N]DOQVE QVOD ESTIS/COGITA/MORI*
Purchased with the aid of a grant from the National Art-Collections Fund (1957.510)

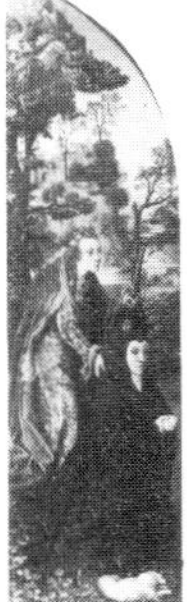
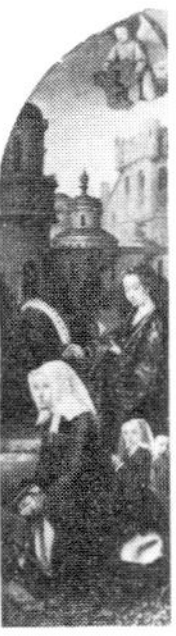
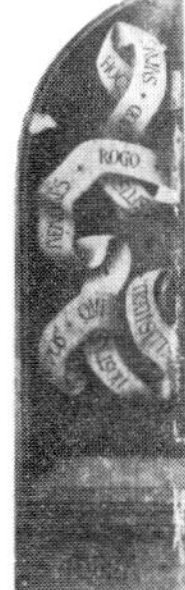
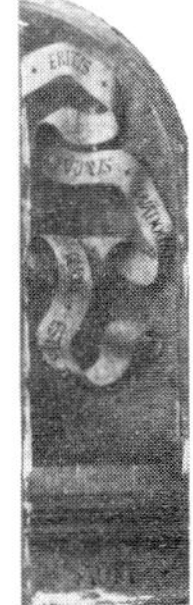

Master of the Magdalen Legend
active late 15th century Flemish

VIRGIN AND CHILD

Oil on panel
25·2 × 15·4 ($9\frac{15}{16}$ × $6\frac{1}{8}$)
Unsigned
Henry Boddington gift (1911.27)

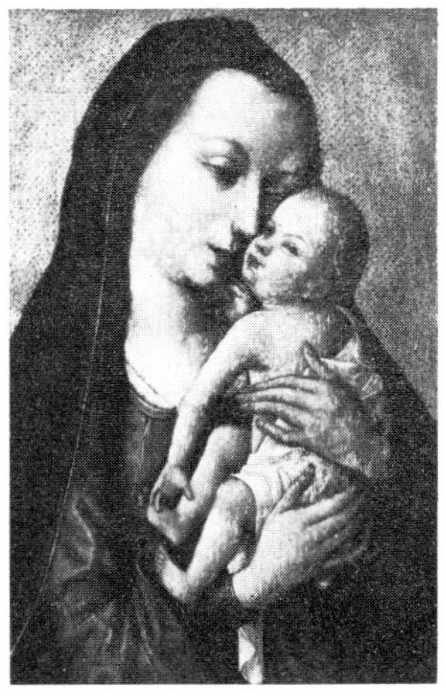

School of Matteo di Giovanni
active 1452, d. 1495 Italian

THE CRUCIFIXION

Tempera on panel
31·4 × 71·1 (12$\frac{3}{8}$ × 28)
Unsigned
Purchased (1951.2)

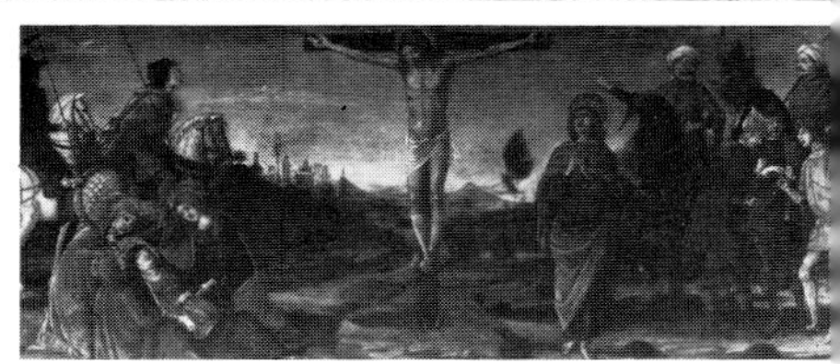

Maxime-Émile-Louis Maufra
1861–1918 French

SPRINGTIME AT LAVARDIN (TOURAINE)
1907

Oil on canvas
65 × 80·6 (25$\frac{9}{16}$ × 31$\frac{3}{4}$)
s(brc): *Maufra 1907*
Presented by Messrs. Durand-Ruel and Sons, Paris (1908.6)

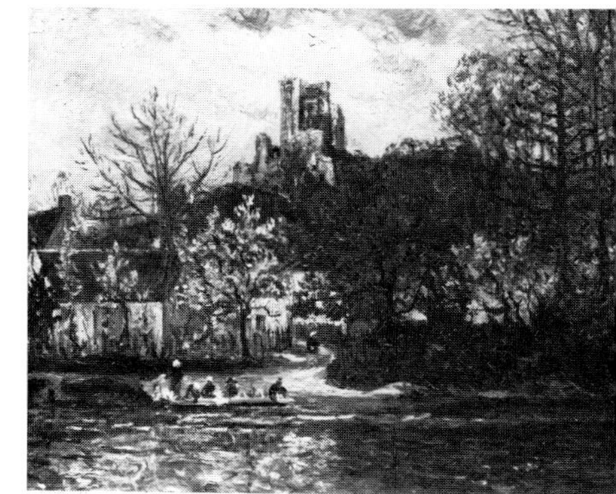

Paul Maze
b. 1887 French

VILLEFRANCHE

Oil on canvas
45·9 × 38·2 (18$\frac{1}{16}$ × 15)
s(brc): *Maze*
Dr. Jane Walker bequest (1939.27)

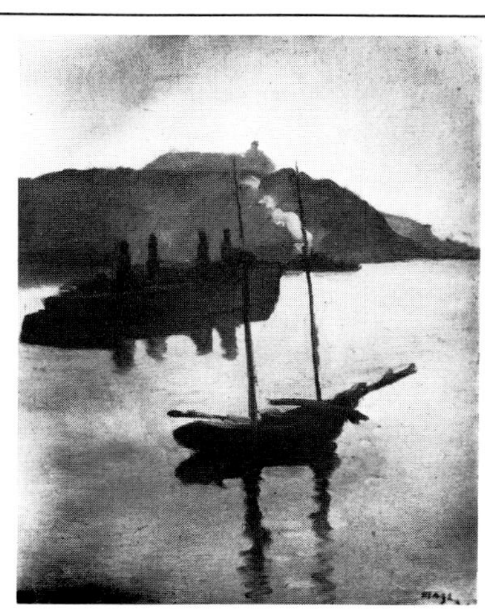

Jean-Louis-Ernest Meissonnier
1815–1891 French

A GENERAL OFFICER

Oil on panel
12·9 × 9·4 ($5\frac{1}{8} \times 3\frac{11}{16}$)
s(brc): *EM* (mon)
Assheton-Bennett bequest (1979.533)

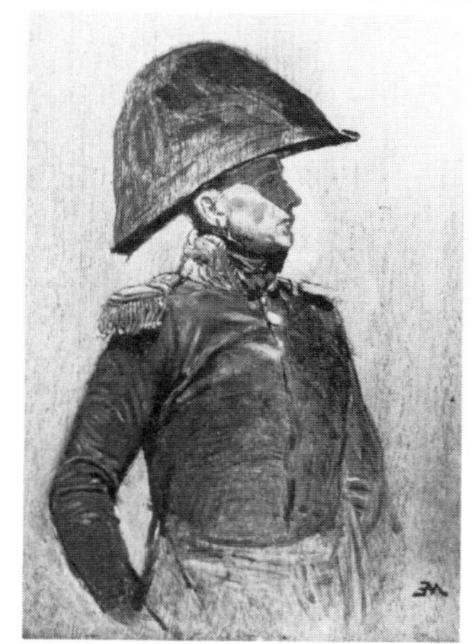

ADVANCE GUARD OF AN ARMY

Oil on panel
11·5 × 20·5 ($4\frac{1}{2} \times 8\frac{1}{16}$)
s(brc): *EM* (mon)
Assheton-Bennett bequest (1979.534)

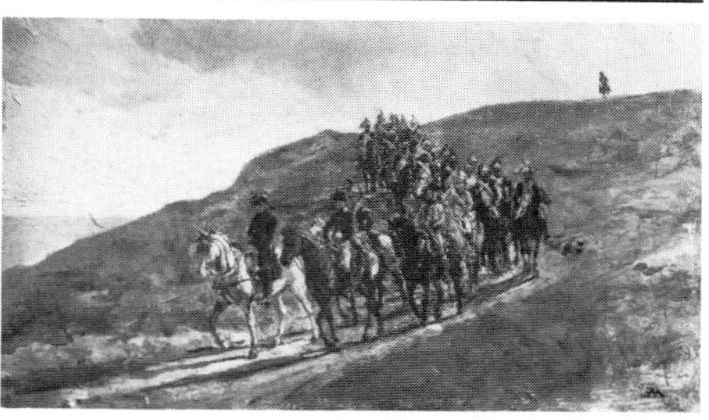

Charles-August Mengin
1853–1933 French

SAPPHO
1877

Oil on canvas
230·7 × 151·5 ($90\frac{7}{8} \times 59\frac{5}{8}$)
s(brc): *A. MENGIN 1877*
T. Lloyd gift (1884.5)

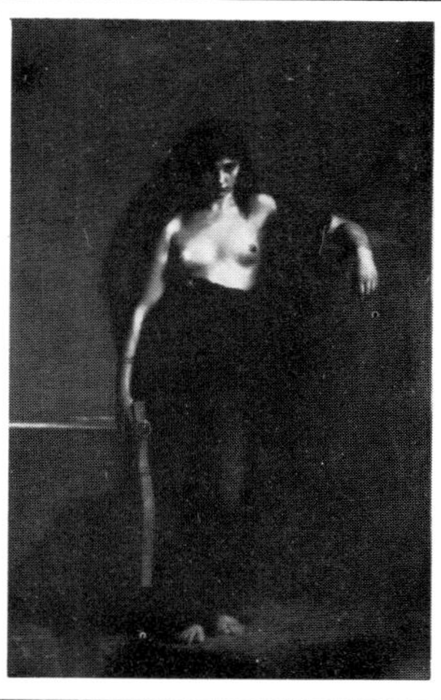

Anton Raphael Mengs
1728–1779 German

ST. EUSEBIUS CARRIED TO HEAVEN
c. 1757

Oil on canvas
73·3 × 36·5 ($28\frac{7}{8} \times 14\frac{3}{8}$)
Unsigned
Purchased (1966.49)

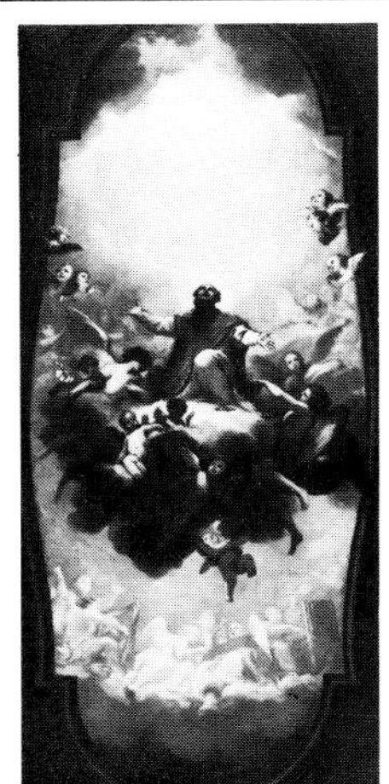

Attributed to Gabriel Metsu
1629–1667 Dutch

A WOMAN SEATED SMOKING A PIPE

Oil on panel
19·8 × 16·6 ($7\frac{13}{16} \times 6\frac{9}{16}$)
inscr(bl, on back of chair): *G Metsu.*
Assheton-Bennett bequest (1979.472)

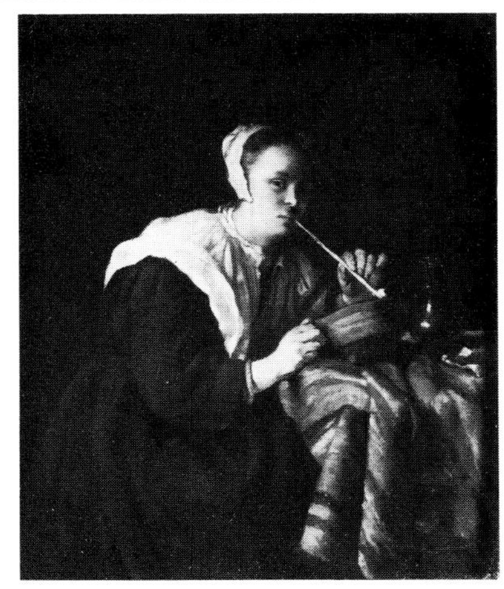

Theobald Michau
1676–1765 Flemish

FARMYARD SCENE: REAPING

Oil on panel
18·3 × 28·2 ($7\frac{1}{4} \times 11\frac{1}{8}$)
s(br): *T.M.*
Assheton-Bennett bequest (1979.473)

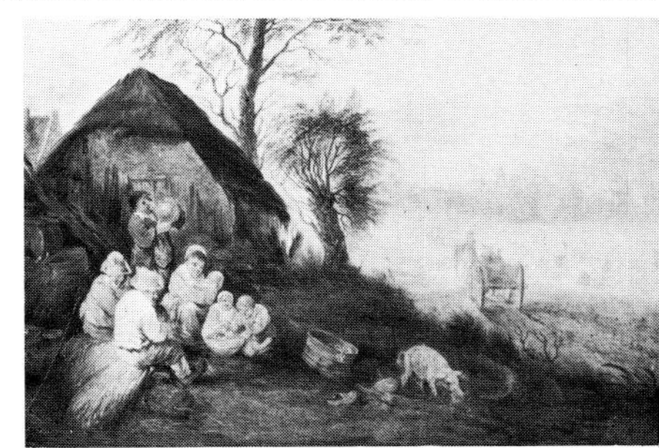

FARMYARD SCENE: THE VINTAGE

Oil on panel
18·6 × 28 ($7\frac{5}{16} \times 11\frac{1}{16}$)
Unsigned
Assheton-Bennett bequest (1979.474)

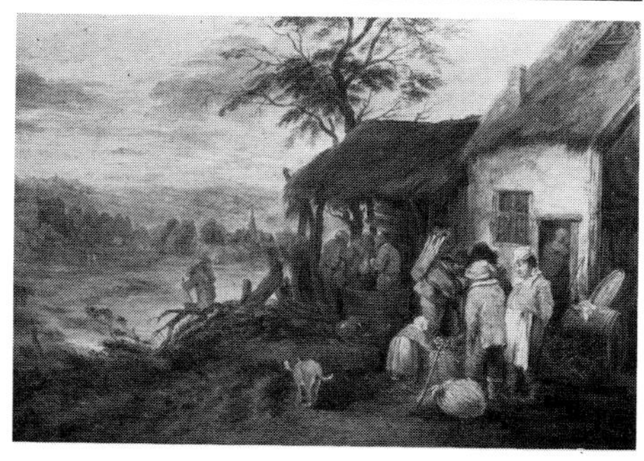

Georges Michel
1763–1843 French

LANDSCAPE

Oil on canvas
63·8 × 80 ($25\frac{1}{8} \times 31\frac{1}{2}$)
Unsigned
Purchased (1958.14)

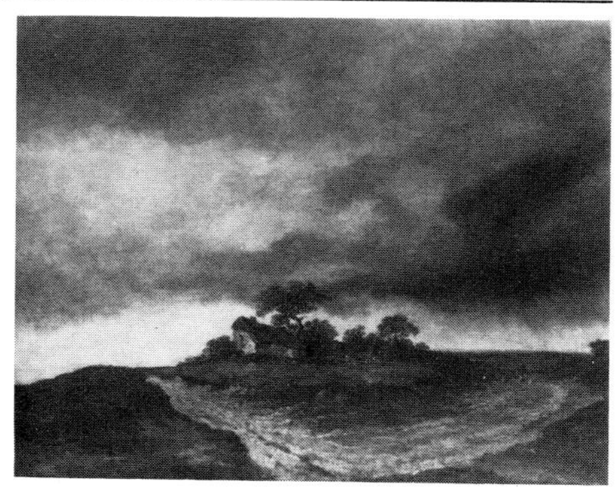

Michiel Jansz. van Miereveld
1567–1641 Dutch

PORTRAIT OF A LADY AGED FIFTY-EIGHT
1636

Oil on panel
69·2 × 59 ($27\frac{1}{4} \times 23\frac{1}{4}$)
s(r): *AE 58 / A° 1636 / M. Miereveld*
G. Beatson Blair bequest, 1941
(1947.144)

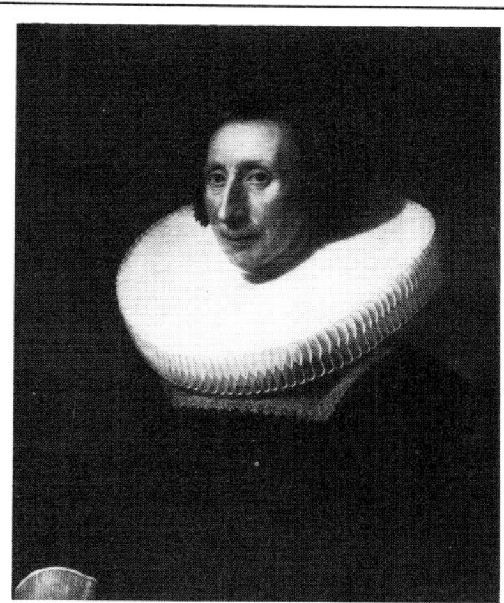

After Michiel Jansz. van Miereveld

PORTRAIT OF LUBBERT GERRITSZ (1535–1612)
Mennonite minister in Amsterdam

Oil on canvas
68·4 × 52·2 ($26\frac{15}{16} \times 20\frac{9}{16}$)
Unsigned
Miss M. E. Gaskell bequest (1914.3)

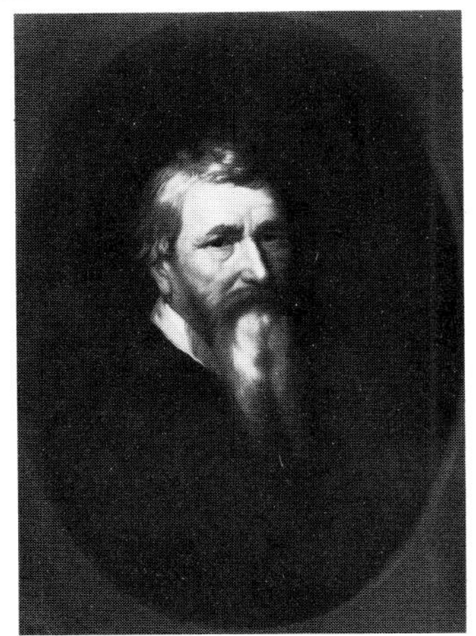

Willem van Mieris
1662–1747 Dutch

A LADY SEATED HOLDING A SMALL DOG

Oil on panel
16 × 12·5 ($6\frac{1}{4} \times 4\frac{7}{8}$)
Unsigned
Assheton-Bennett bequest (1979.475)

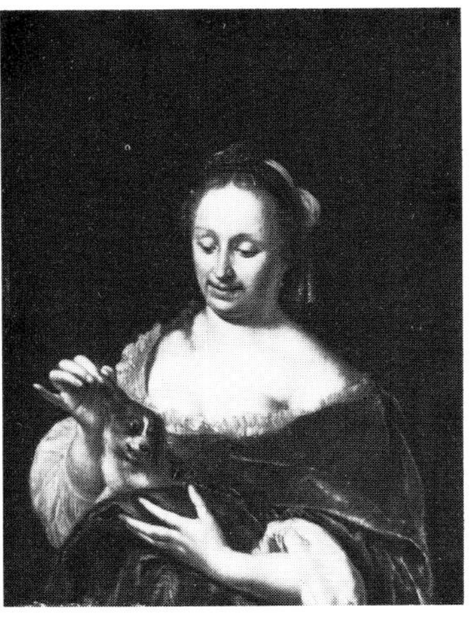

INTERIOR WITH A CAVALIER AND LADY
1685

Oil on panel
24·7 × 20·6 ($9\frac{3}{4} \times 8\frac{1}{16}$)
s(bl): . . . (illegible) / *Mieris / Fct A 1685*
Assheton-Bennett bequest (1979.476)

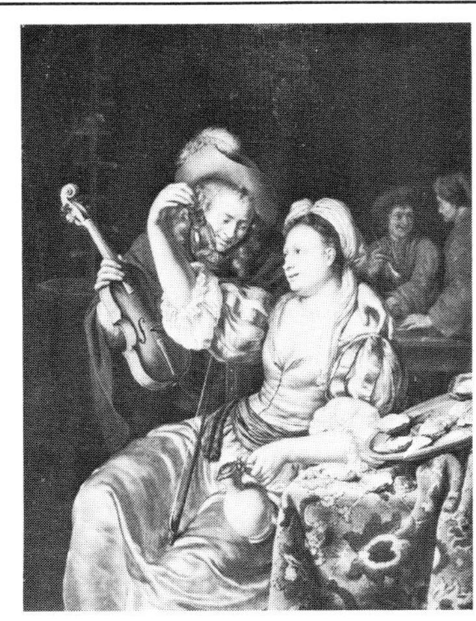

Willem van Mieris
See also Laureys Goubau

Manner of Jean-François Millet
1814–1875 French

PEASANT GIRL

Oil on canvas laid down on panel
30·3 × 21·9 ($11\frac{15}{16} \times 8\frac{5}{8}$)
inscr(blc): *J·F·Millet*
Purchased (1919.18)

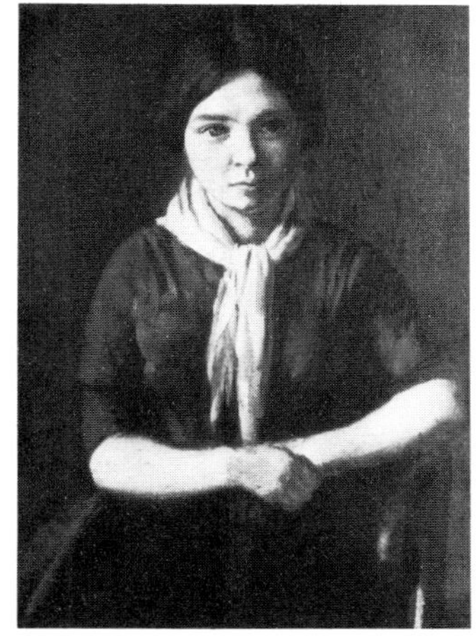

Jan Miensz. Molenaer
c. 1610–1668 Dutch

INTERIOR WITH PEASANTS AND SCHOOL CHILDREN

Oil on panel
33·8 × 42·7 ($13\frac{5}{16} \times 16\frac{7}{8}$)
Unsigned
Assheton-Bennett bequest (1979.478)

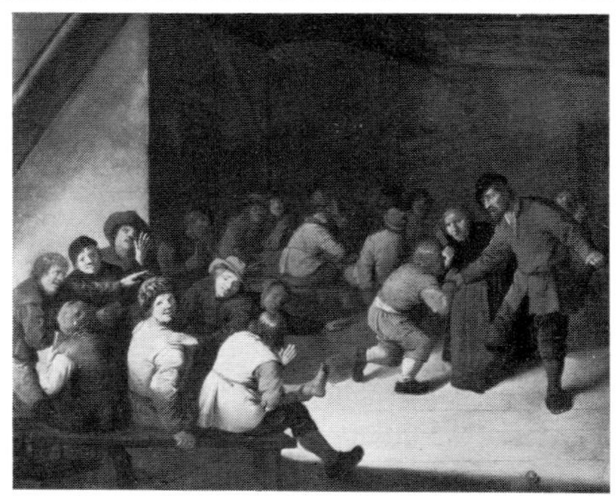

Klaes Molenaer
1620–1676 Dutch

SKATING SCENE: FIGURES ON THE ICE NEAR THE WALLS OF A TOWN

Oil on panel
33·3 × 41·5 ($13\frac{1}{8} \times 16\frac{3}{8}$)
s(blc): *K. Molenaer.*
Assheton-Bennett bequest (1979.479)

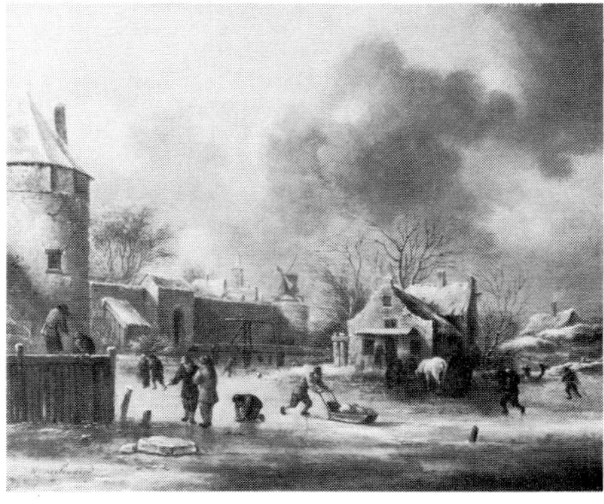

Francesco Monti
1685–1768 Italian

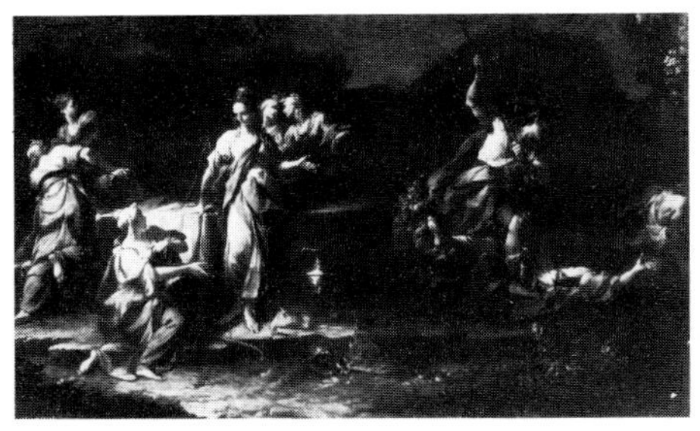

MOSES AND THE DAUGHTERS OF JETHRO

Oil on canvas
62·7 × 104·5 ($24\frac{11}{16} \times 41\frac{1}{8}$)
Unsigned
Dr. M. Gamble gift (1928.39)

Adolphe Monticelli
1824–1886 French

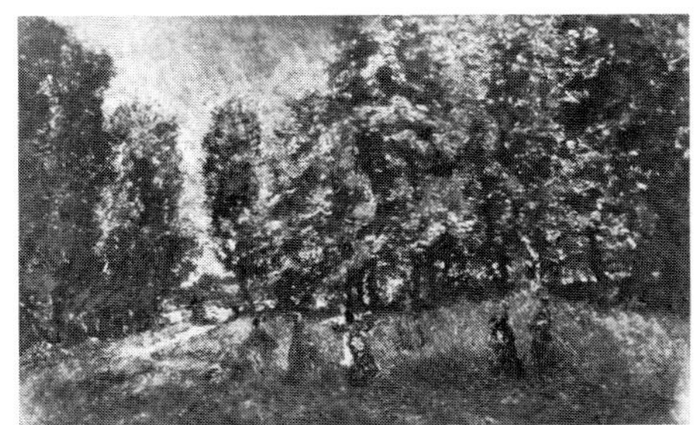

A WOODLAND GLADE

Oil on panel
48·2 × 79·3 ($19 \times 31\frac{3}{16}$)
s(blc) : *Monticelli*
Purchased (1910.10)

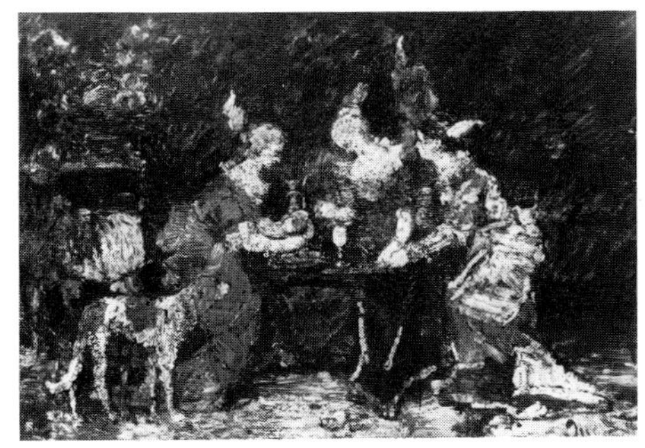

LADIES ON A TERRACE

Oil on panel
47·2 × 69·4 ($18\frac{9}{16} \times 27\frac{5}{16}$)
s(brc) : *Monticelli*
Purchased (1931.1)

Henry Moret
1856–1913 French

FISHING BOATS AT DOUÉLAN

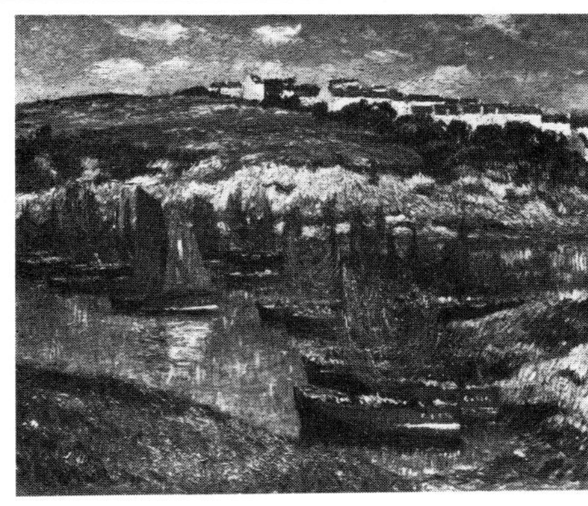

Oil on canvas
60·3 × 73 ($23\frac{3}{4} \times 28\frac{3}{4}$)
s(blc): *Henry Moret* . . . (followed by illegible date)
Presented by Messrs. Durand-Ruel and Sons, Paris (1908.5)

Christian Ernst Bernhard Morgenstern
1805–1867 German

BAVARIAN HIGHLANDS

Oil on canvas
92·5 × 140·2 ($36\frac{7}{8} \times 55\frac{3}{16}$)
s(blc): *Chr. Morgenstern*
H. F. Kessler bequest (1927.2)

Joseph Munsch
1832–1896 Austrian

THE ANTIQUARIES

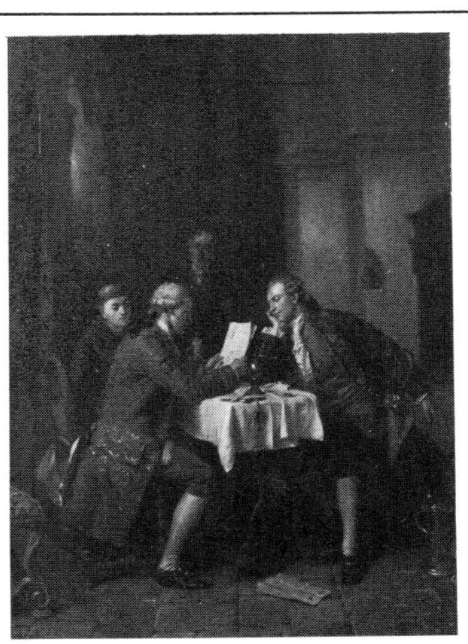

Oil on panel
41 × 30·5 ($16\frac{1}{8} \times 12$)

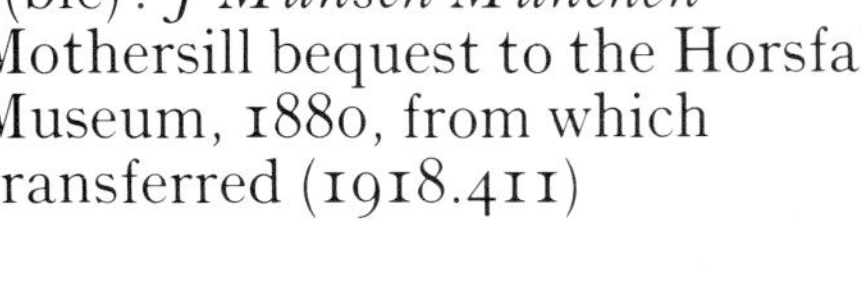

s(blc): *J Munsch München*
Mothersill bequest to the Horsfall Museum, 1880, from which transferred (1918.411)

Francesco de Mura
called Franceschiello
1696–1782 Italian

THE DEATH OF VERGINIA

Oil on canvas
90·5 × 144 (35½ × 56¾)
Unsigned
Purchased with the aid of a grant from the Victoria and Albert Museum (1971.52)

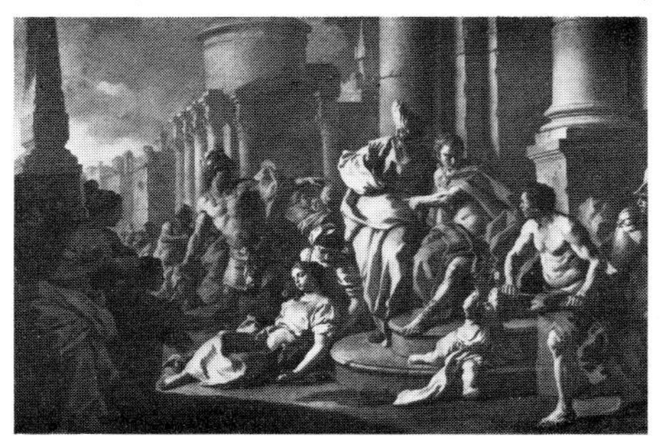

Frank Mura
1861–1913 or later, French

HAYRICKS

Oil on canvas
54·5 × 85·1 (21 7/16 × 33½)
s(brc): *Mura*
Purchased (1914.63)

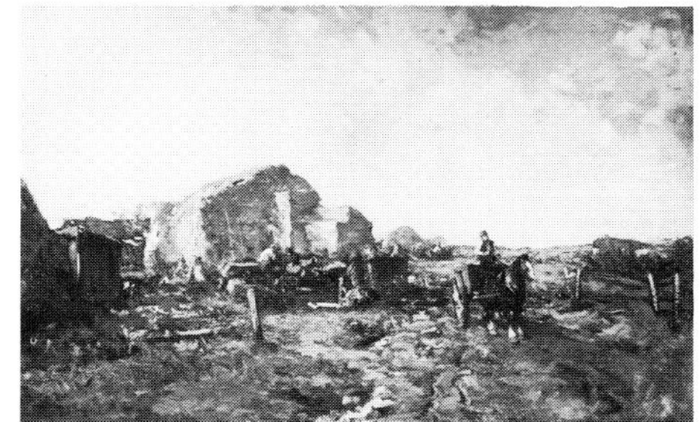

VILLAGE SCENE

Oil on canvas
61·1 × 50·5 (24 1/16 × 19⅞)
s(blc): *F Mura*
Purchased (1919.6)

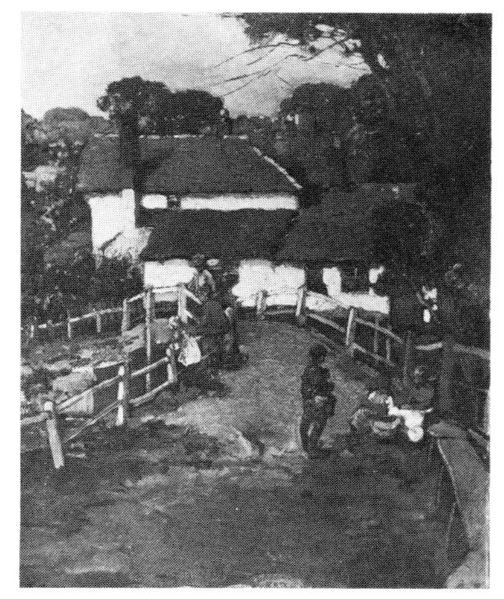

IN WEST MERSEA: ESSEX
1901

Oil on panel
54·1 × 85·2 (21 5/16 × 33 9/16)
s(brc): *F. Mura / 1901.*
Purchased (1924.34)

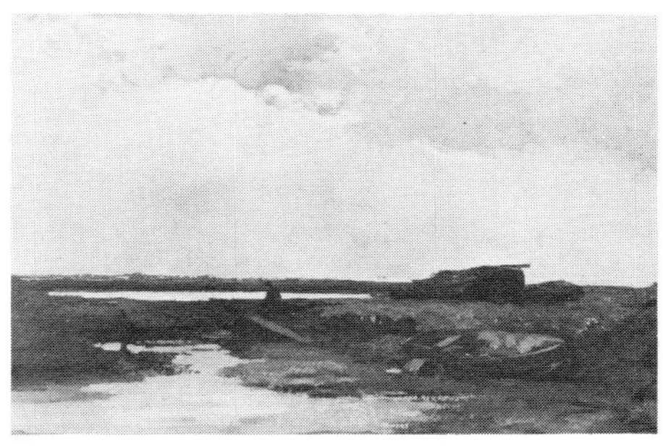

Aert van der Neer
1603/4–1677 Dutch

SKATING SCENE: FIGURES ON A RIVER FLOWING THROUGH A VILLAGE

Oil on canvas
52·3 × 73 (20 9/16 × 28 3/4)
s(brc): *AVN* (mon)
Assheton-Bennett bequest (1979.480)

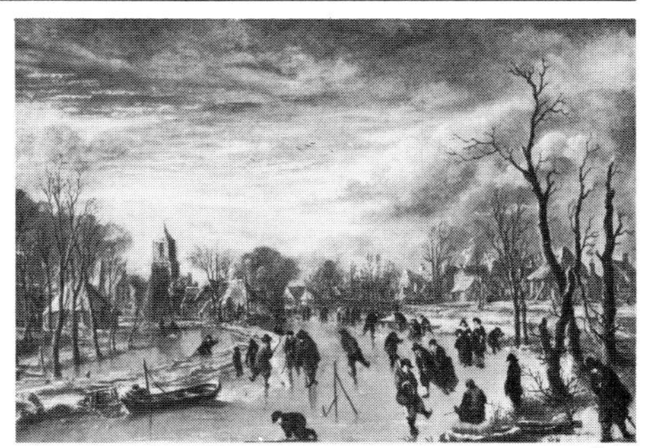

North Netherlandish, 17th century
(formerly attributed to Jacob Duck)

THE CARD PLAYERS

Oil on copper
37·5 × 42·9 (14 3/4 × 16 7/8)
Unsigned
Mrs. Robert Hatton gift (1908.35)

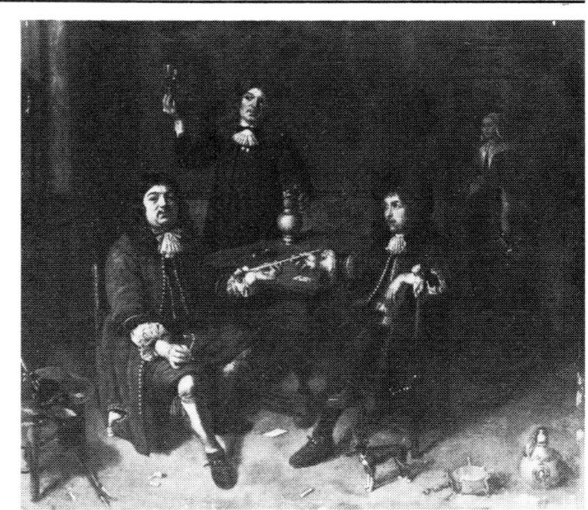

North Netherlandish, 17th century (formerly attributed to Caspar Netscher)

A LADY SEATED HOLDING A SMALL DOG

Oil on canvas
25·3 × 21·7 ($9\frac{15}{16} \times 8\frac{9}{16}$)
Unsigned
Assheton-Bennett bequest (1979.481)

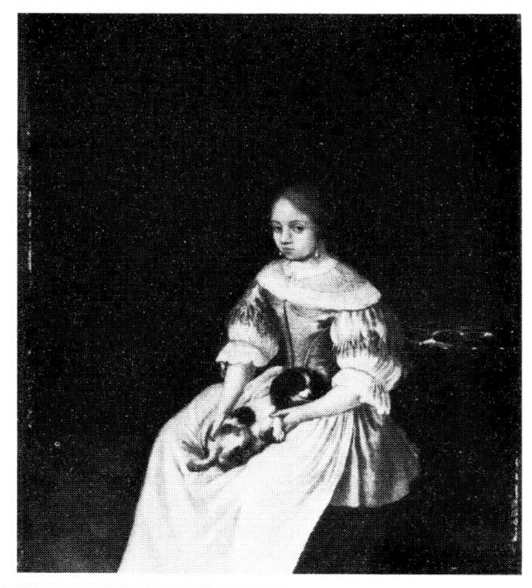

North Netherlandish, 17th century (formerly attributed to Adam Willaerts)

EGMOND-AAN-ZEE

Oil on panel
27·5 × 70·6 ($10\frac{7}{8} \times 27\frac{13}{16}$)
Unsigned
Assheton-Bennett bequest (1979.515)

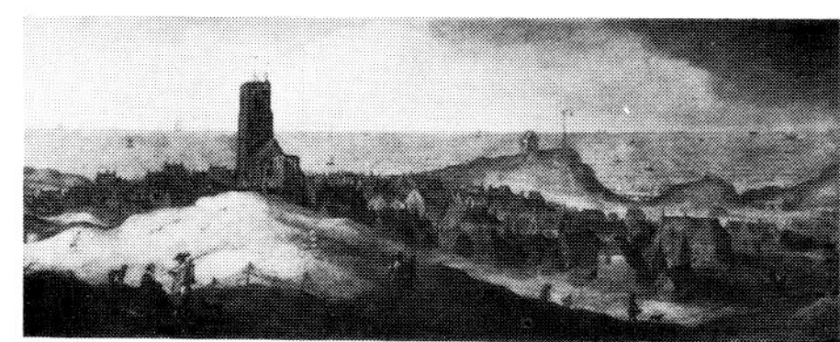

?North Netherlandish, 18th century
See Patrick Nasmyth (1947.90), British School Catalogue, Vol. I

South Netherlandish, 15th century?

A FEMALE SAINT

Oil on panel
59 × 47 ($23\frac{1}{4} \times 18\frac{1}{2}$)
Unsigned
James Blair bequest (1917.168)

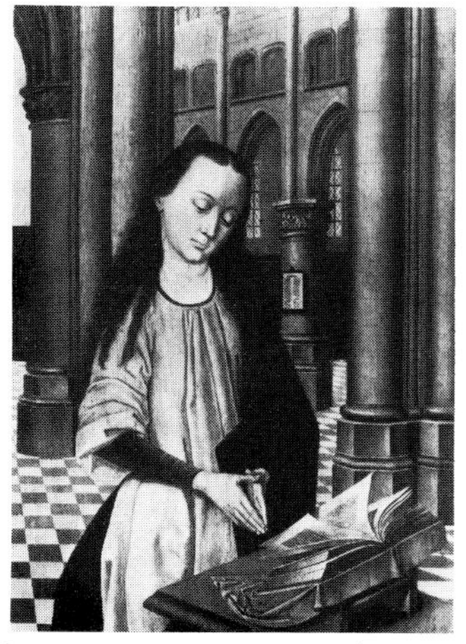

South Netherlandish, *c.* 1600, after **Bassano**

CHRIST IN THE HOUSE OF MARY, MARTHA AND LAZARUS

Oil on canvas
01·9 × 120 ($40\frac{1}{8} \times 47\frac{1}{2}$)
Unsigned
Provenance unknown (1979.613)

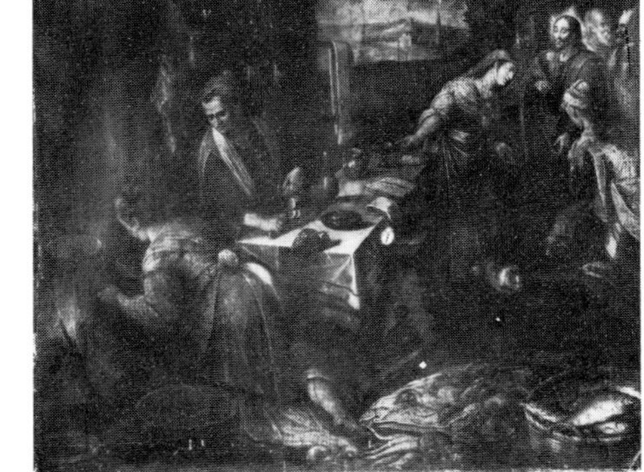

Caspar Netscher
See North Netherlandish, 17th century

Jacob Ochtervelt
1634–1682 Dutch

MERRY COMPANY

Oil on canvas
52·2 × 42 ($20\frac{9}{16} \times 16\frac{1}{2}$)
Unsigned
Purchased (1926.11)

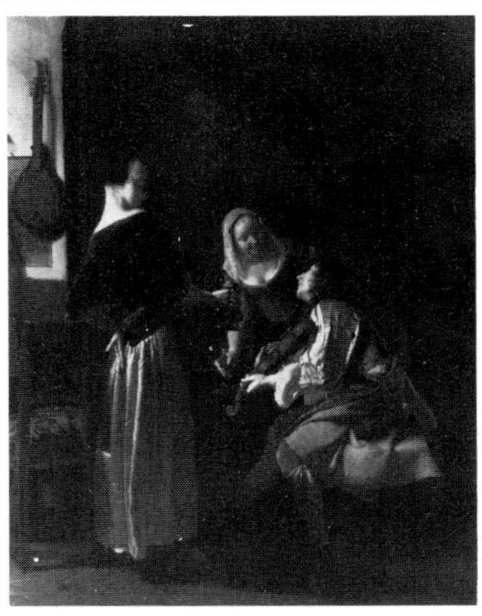

THE EMBRACING CAVALIER

Oil on panel
44·6 × 35·6 ($17\frac{5}{8} \times 13\frac{15}{16}$)
Unsigned
Assheton-Bennett bequest (1979.482)

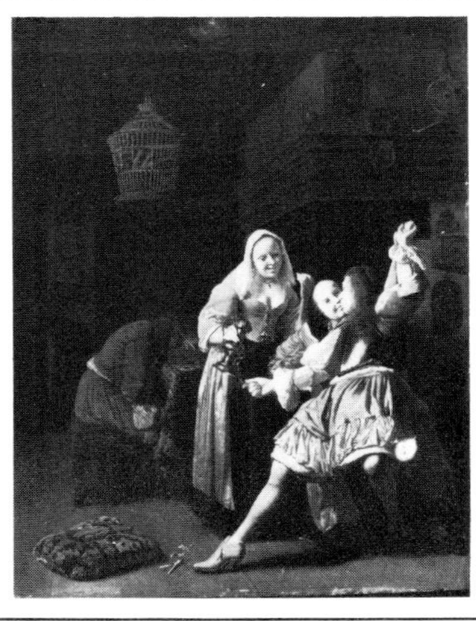

THE SLEEPING CAVALIER

Oil on panel
46 × 37·7 (18$\frac{1}{8}$ × 14$\frac{13}{16}$)
Unsigned
Assheton-Bennett bequest (1979.483)

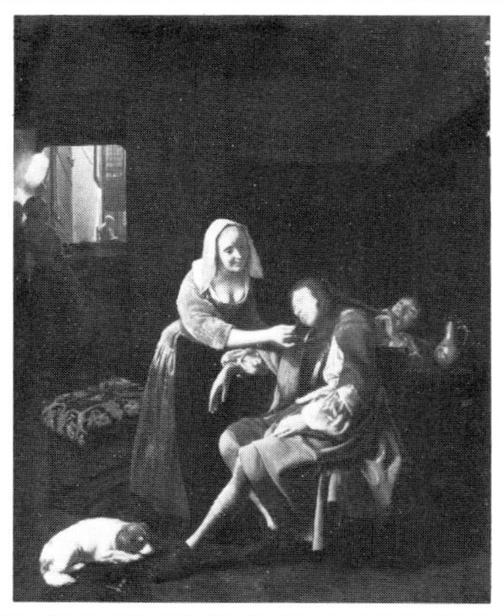

THE DOCTOR'S VISIT

Oil on canvas
65 × 51·8 (25$\frac{5}{8}$ × 20$\frac{3}{8}$)
Unsigned
Assheton-Bennett bequest (1979.536)

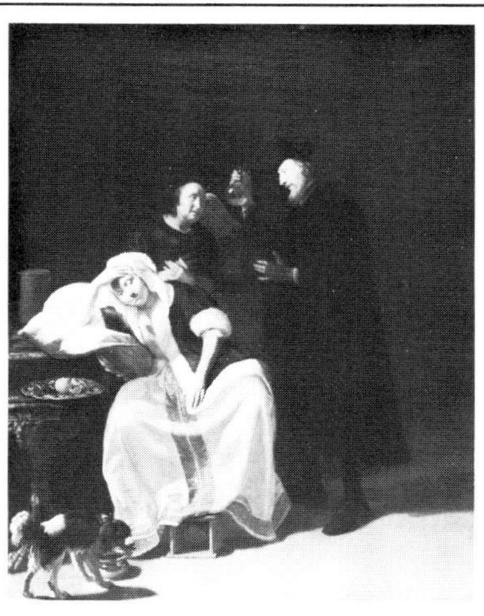

Takanori Oguiss

b. 1901 Japanese

PARIS LANDSCAPE
1928

Oil on canvas
50 × 61 (19$\frac{11}{16}$ × 24)
s(trc): *Oguiss / 1928*
Eric C. Gregory gift (1946.36)

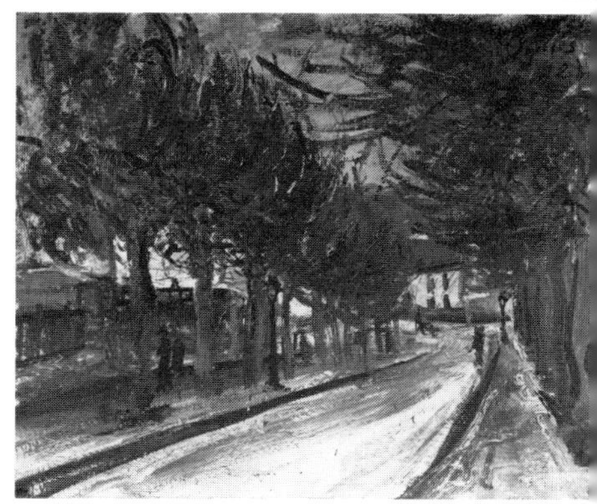

Balthasar Paul Ommeganck
755–1826 Flemish

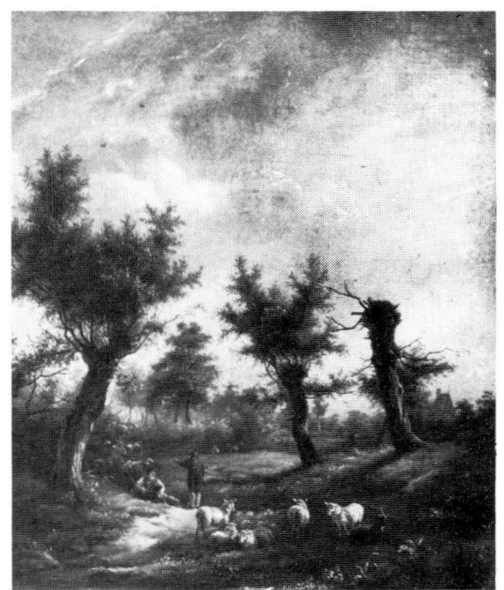

PASTORAL LANDSCAPE
797
Oil on canvas
4·5 × 38·4 ($17\frac{1}{2} \times 15\frac{1}{8}$)
S(blc): *B. P. Ommeganck . f . 1797*
Lt. Col. R. H. Antrobus gift
(1971.107)

Jan van Os
744–1808 Dutch

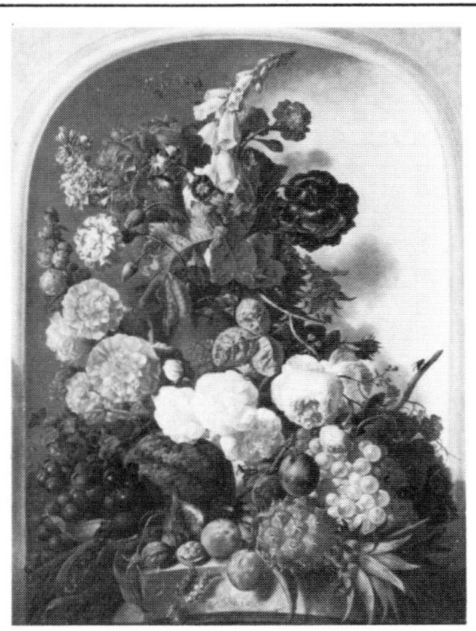

STILL LIFE: FLOWERS AND FRUIT
Oil on panel
72·3 × 55·5 ($28\frac{1}{2} \times 21\frac{7}{8}$)
S(b, centre): *J. Van Os fecit.*
Assheton-Bennett bequest (1979.484)

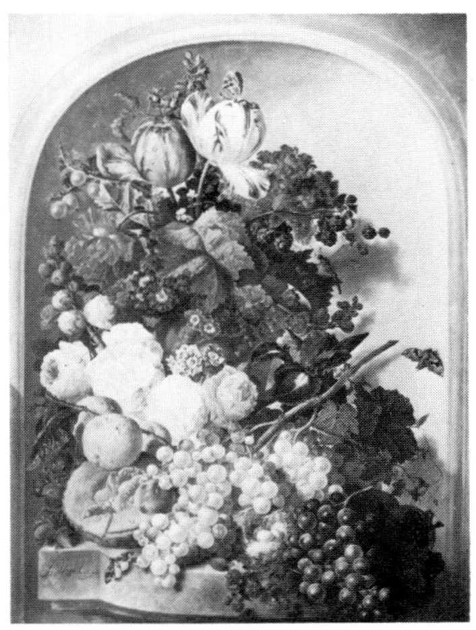

STILL LIFE: FLOWERS AND FRUIT
Oil on panel
72·1 × 55·6 ($28\frac{7}{16} \times 21\frac{7}{8}$)
S(blc): *J: Van Os fecit.*
Assheton-Bennett bequest (1979.485)

Adriaen van Ostade
1610–1685 Dutch

TWO PEASANTS SMOKING

Oil on panel
18·1 × 15·4 ($7\frac{1}{16} \times 6\frac{1}{16}$)
s(tlc): *A V Ostade* (AV in mon)
Assheton-Bennett bequest (1979.486)

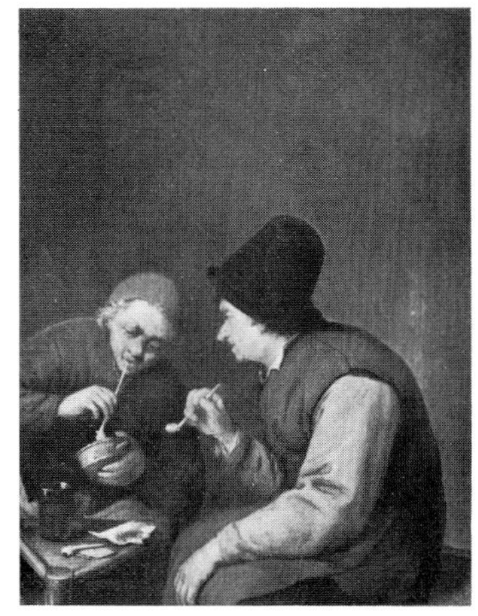

Attributed to Adriaen van Ostade

INTERIOR OF A BARN WITH TWO PEASANTS FIGHTING
1658

Oil on panel
22·4 × 27·2 ($8\frac{3}{4} \times 10\frac{11}{16}$)
s(br, on overturned bench): *A V OSTADE 1658* (AV in mon)
Assheton-Bennett bequest (1979.488)

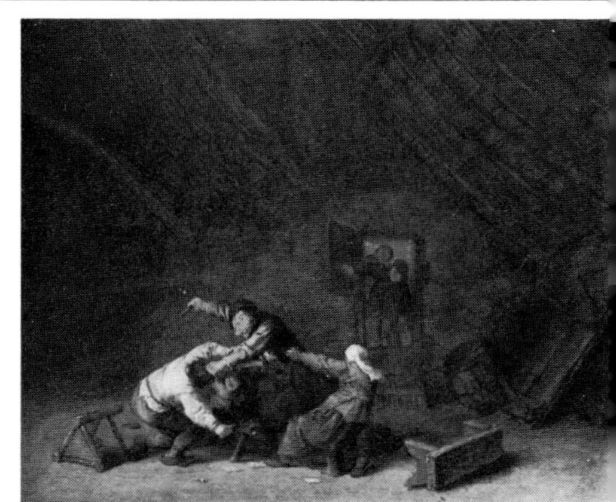

Follower of Adriaen van Ostade

AN ITINERANT MUSICIAN PLAYING THE HURDY-GURDY TO A GROUP OF CHILDREN OUTSIDE AN INN DOOR

Oil on panel
33 × 23·2 ($13 \times 9\frac{1}{8}$)
inscr(br): *A : ostade.*
Assheton-Bennett bequest (1979.487)

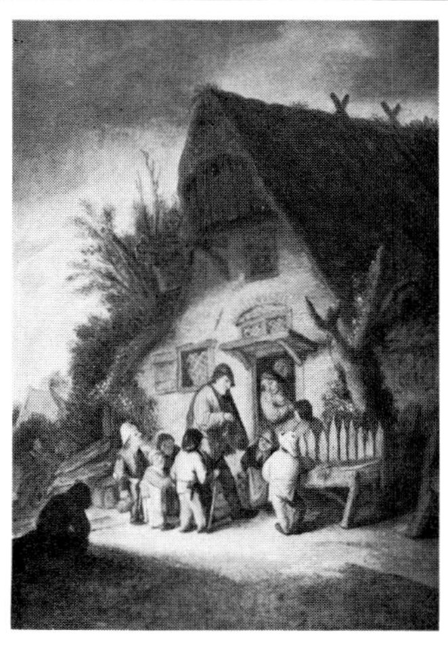

Isack van Ostade
1621–1649 Dutch

SCENE ON THE SHORE AT SCHEVENINGEN(?)

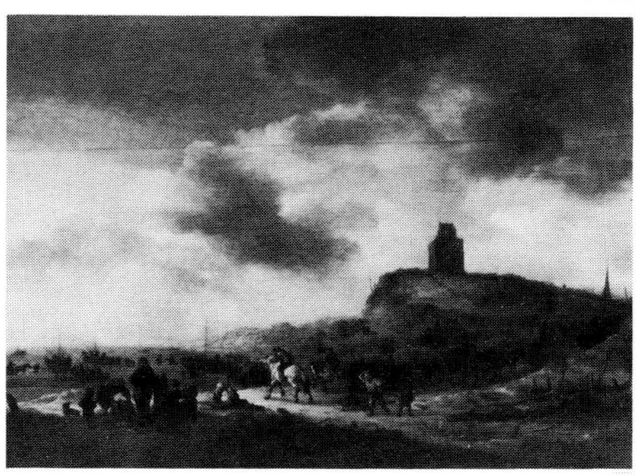

Oil on panel
74·2 × 110·1 ($29\frac{3}{16}$ × $43\frac{5}{16}$)
s(brc): *Isack . Ostade*
Mrs. E. Wood bequest (1908.20)

INTERIOR OF A BARN WITH AN OLD WOMAN AT A DISTAFF

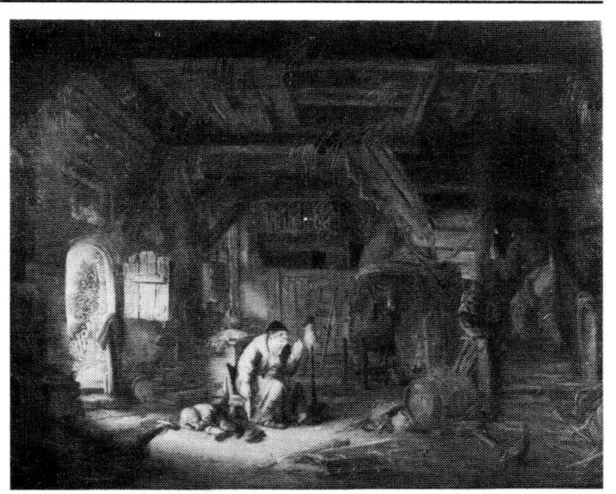

Oil on panel
41·6 × 53·2 ($16\frac{5}{16}$ × $20\frac{15}{16}$)
s(br): *Isack van Ostade 1646.*
Assheton-Bennett bequest (1979.490)

Attributed to Isack van Ostade

WINTER SCENE, WITH FIGURES ON A FROZEN RIVER IN FRONT OF A WALLED TOWN
1642

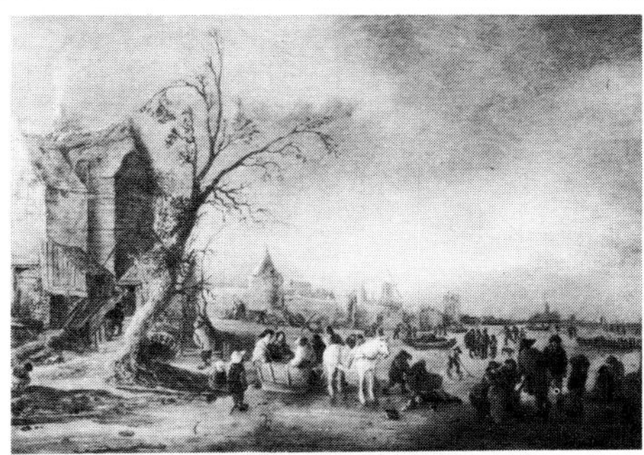

Oil on panel
39·9 × 61 ($15\frac{11}{16}$ × $23\frac{15}{16}$)
s(bl): *Isack van Ostade 1642.*
Assheton-Bennett bequest (1979.489)

Follower of Giovanni Paolo Pannini
1691/2–1765 Italian

ROMAN RUINS WITH FIGURES

Oil on canvas
118·7 × 160·8 ($46\frac{3}{4} \times 63\frac{5}{16}$)
Unsigned
Presented by the Manchester Education Committee (1903.18)

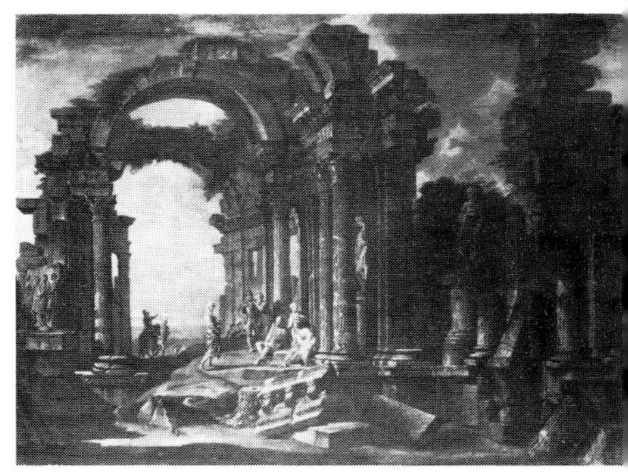

Alberto Pasini
1826–1899 Italian

A CAVALCADE OF ARABS
1869

Oil on canvas
55·6 × 46·4 ($21\frac{7}{8} \times 18\frac{1}{4}$)
s(brc): *A. Pasini 1869*
Mothersill bequest to the Horsfall Museum, 1880, from which transferred (1918.407)

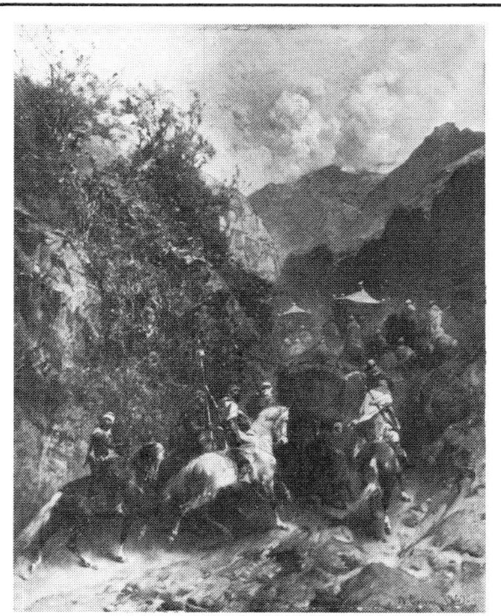

Attributed to Bartolommeo Passerotti
1529–1592 Italian

DOMENICO GIULIANI AND HIS SERVANT
1579

Oil on canvas
121 × 92·2 ($47\frac{5}{8} \times 36\frac{1}{4}$)
dated (on letter): *1579* and inscr (on envelope): *Al Mag* . . . [illeg.] *Giuliani / Napoli*
Purchased (1959.114)

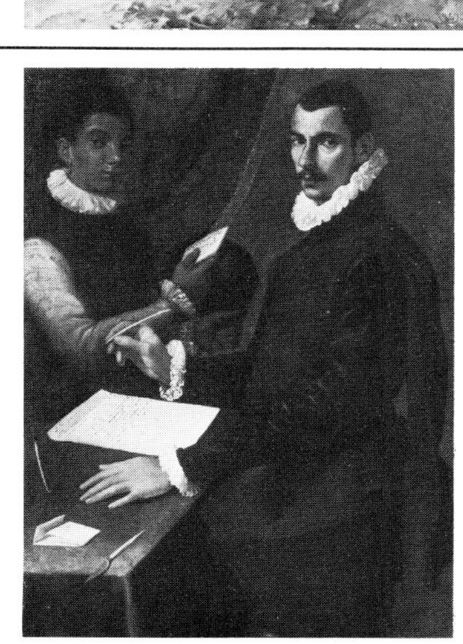

Bonaventura Peeters
1614–1652 Flemish

A YACHT IN A CHOPPY SEA

Oil on panel
40·7 × 36·2 (16 × 14½)
s(br, on large yacht): *B.P.*
Assheton-Bennett bequest (1979.491)

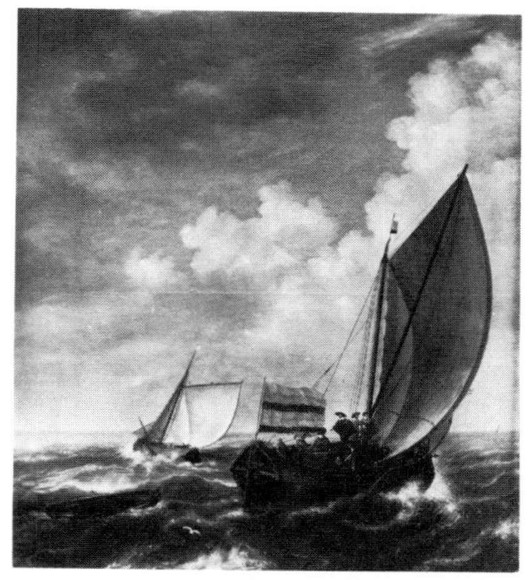

Léon Bazile Perrault
1832–1908 French

MEDITATION
1870

Oil on canvas
92·4 × 73·4 (36⅜ × 28⅞)
s(blc): *L Perrault . 70 .*
J. Cottrill gift (1911.29)

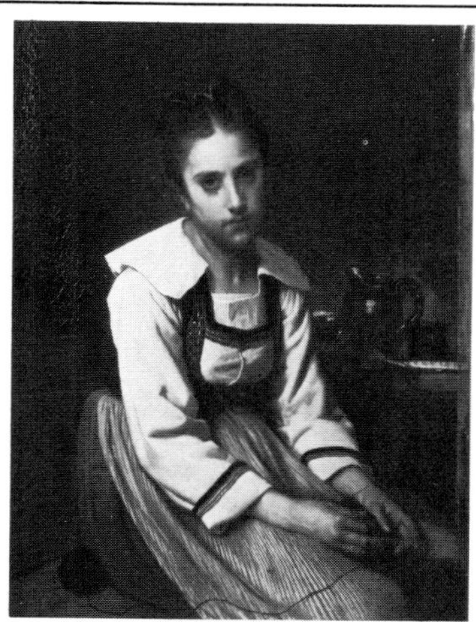

Karel Frans Phlippeau
1825–1897 Dutch

PLAYING CARDS

Oil on panel
33·7 × 46·3 (13⅝ × 18¼)
s(blc): *Phlippeau ft.*
Transferred from the Horsfall Museum (1918.409)

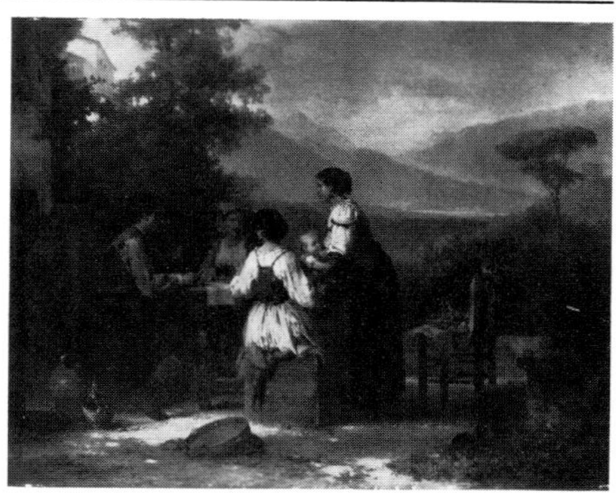

SPINNING: ITALIAN SCENE

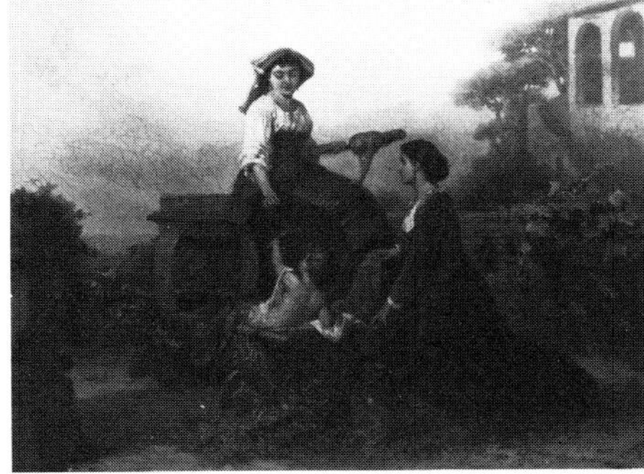

Oil on panel
29·5 × 40·1 ($11\frac{5}{8} \times 15\frac{13}{16}$)
s(brc): *Phlippeau Fe*
Transferred from the Horsfall Museum (1918.420)

Piero di Cosimo
See Ridolfo Ghirlandaio

Pietro da Cortona
See Berrettini

Antoine Piot
active 19th century, French

AN ITALIAN LADY

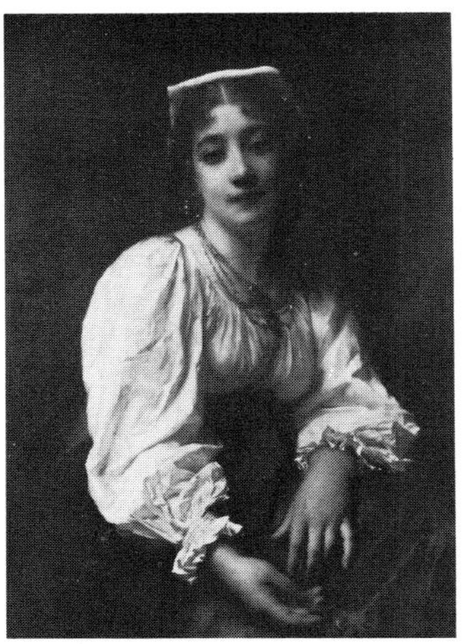

Oil on canvas
89·5 × 65·4 ($35\frac{1}{4} \times 25\frac{3}{4}$)
s(br): *Antoine Piot / Ft* (?)
Mothersill bequest to the Horsfall Museum, 1880, from which transferred (1918.408)

Camille Pissarro
1830–1903 French

OLD BRIDGE AT BRUGES
1903

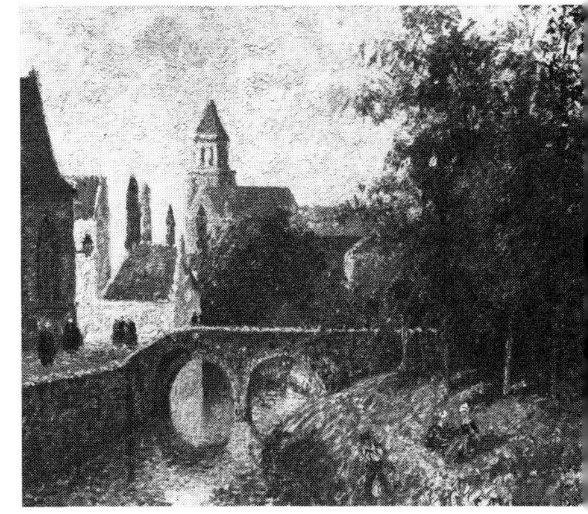

Oil on canvas
46·4 × 55·2 ($18\frac{1}{4} \times 21\frac{3}{4}$)
s(brc): *C. Pissarro . 1903*
Mrs. Lucien Pissarro gift (1946.69)

A VILLAGE STREET, LOUVECIENNES
1871

Oil on canvas
46 × 55·5 ($18\frac{1}{8} \times 21\frac{7}{8}$)
s(blc): *C Pissarro 1871*
Purchased with the aid of a grant from the Victoria and Albert Museum (1969.67)

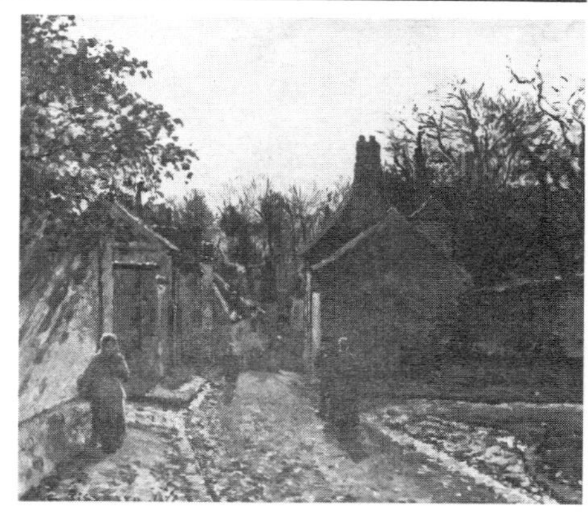

Felix Pissarro
1874–1897 French

THE BONFIRE

Oil on canvas
46·2 × 55·1 ($18\frac{1}{8} \times 21\frac{3}{4}$)
Unsigned
Mrs. Lucien Pissarro gift (1951.62)

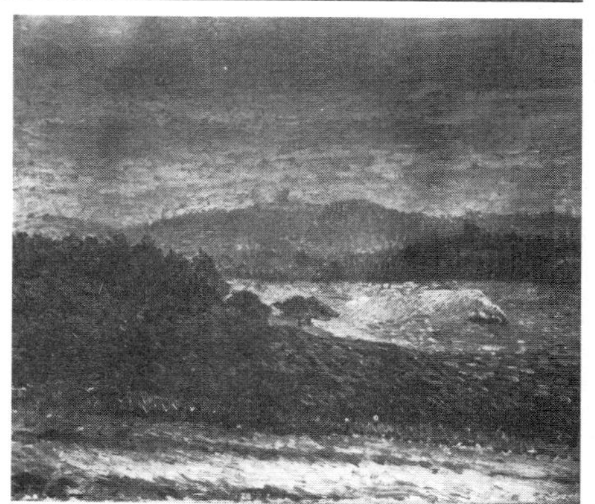

Lucien and Orovida Pissarro
See British School Catalogue, Vol. II

Egbert van der Poel
1621–1664 Dutch

SKATING SCENE WITH A TENT AND NUMEROUS FIGURES ON A WIDE RIVER

Oil on panel
39 × 51·1 ($15\frac{5}{16} \times 20\frac{1}{8}$)
s(b, centre to l, on wooden stake): *P 1661* (?)
Assheton-Bennett bequest (1979.492)

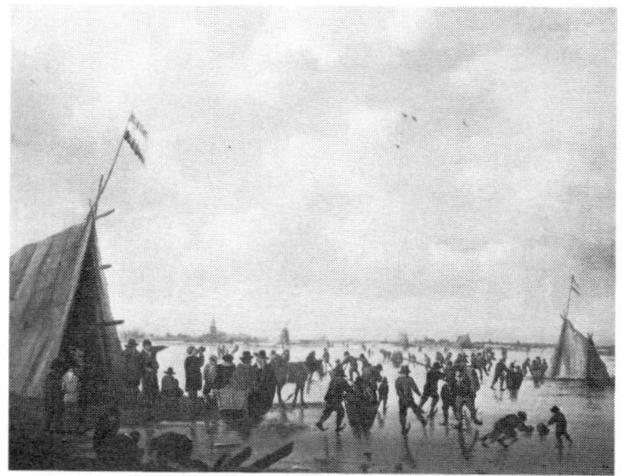

Cornelis van Poelenburgh
See ?German, 18th century

Paulus Potter
1625–1654 Dutch

EVENING LANDSCAPE WITH CATTLE AND WITH PEASANTS DANCING TO THE SOUND OF A PIPE
1649

Oil on panel
37·5 × 50·3 ($14\frac{3}{4} \times 19\frac{13}{16}$)
s(bl, on hut, above opening): *paulus. potter / 1649.*
Assheton-Bennett bequest (1979.493)

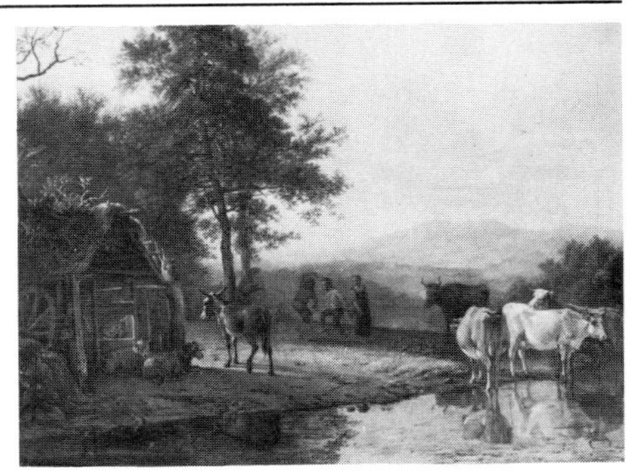

Frans Pourbus the Elder
1545–1581 Flemish
(formerly attributed to Adriaen Thomasz. Key)

PORTRAIT OF AN OLD MAN (HUBERTUS LANGETUS?)
1580

Oil on panel
40·6 × 30·4 ($16 \times 11\frac{15}{16}$)
inscr(tl): *1580*
Purchased (1950.298)

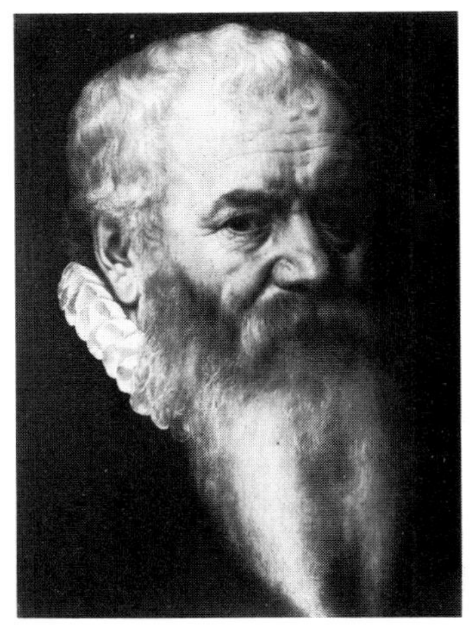

Benito Quinquella Martin
b. 1890 Argentinian

MORNING SUN, BUENOS AIRES
1930

Oil on canvas
201·2 × 165·1 ($79\frac{3}{16} \times 65$)
s(brc): *Quinquella MARTIN*
Sir Joseph Duveen gift (1931.4)

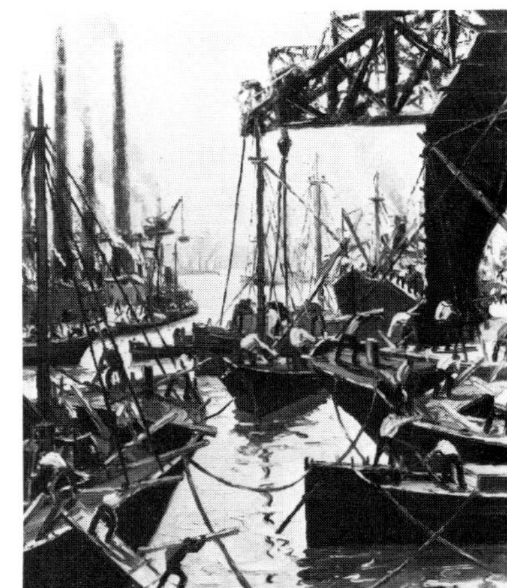

Rembrandt
See Samuel van Hoogstraten

Guido Reni
1575–1642 Italian

ST. CATHERINE

Oil on canvas
102 × 83·6 ($40\frac{1}{8} \times 33\frac{7}{8}$)
Unsigned
Purchased with the aid of grants from the National Art-Collections Fund and the Victoria and Albert Museum (1974.88)

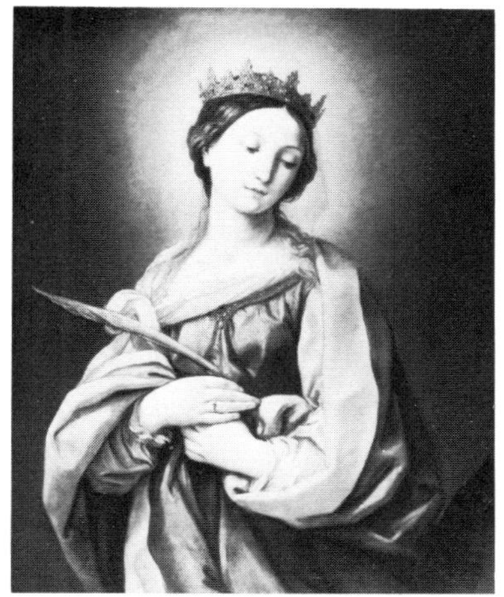

Pierre-Auguste Renoir
1841–1919 French

SEATED WOMAN

Oil on canvas
55·2 × 46·5 ($21\frac{11}{16} \times 18\frac{5}{16}$)
s(brc): *Renoir*
G. Beatson Blair bequest, 1941 (1947.164)

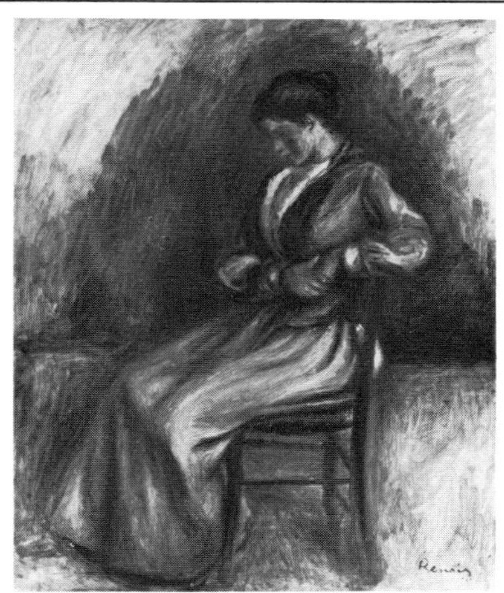

SEATED NUDE

Oil on canvas
40·1 × 33·8 ($15\frac{1}{2} \times 13\frac{1}{4}$)
s(blc): *Renoir*.
Presented by the Trustees of the will of the late Lady Marks of Broughton (1972.90)

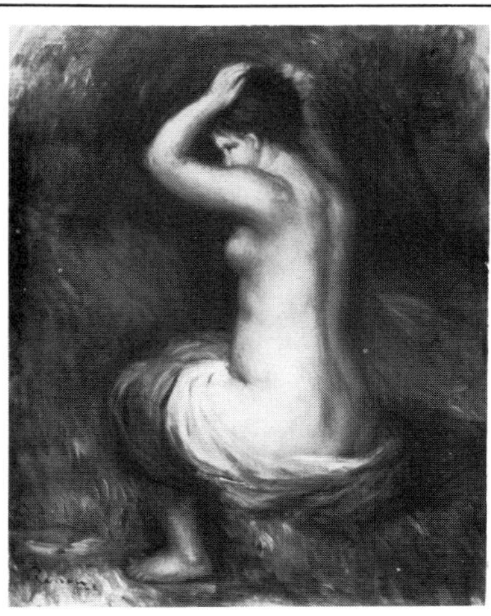

Attributed to Marco Ricci
1676–1730 Italian

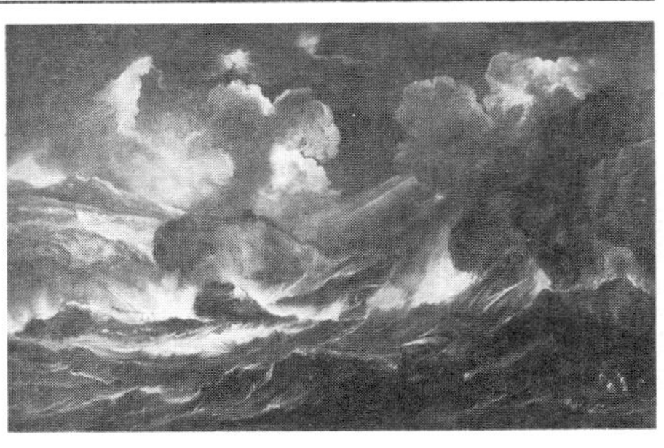

A STORM AT SEA

Oil on canvas
96·3 × 154 ($37\frac{7}{8} \times 60\frac{5}{8}$)
Unsigned
Purchased with the aid of a grant from the Victoria and Albert Museum (1966.335)

Studio of Sebastiano Ricci
1659–1734 Italian

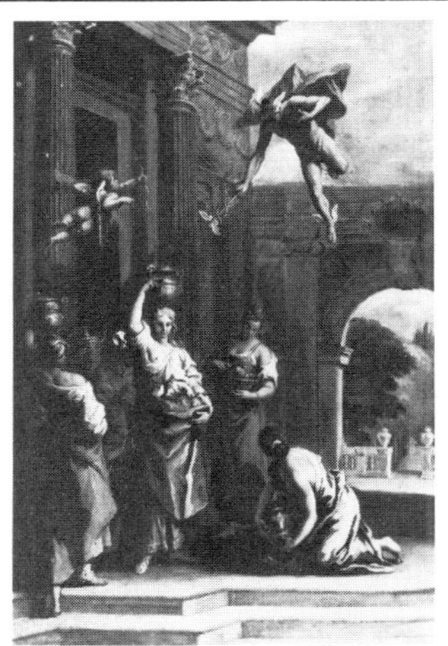

MERCURY, HERSE AND AGLAUROS

Oil on canvas
88·5 × 58·8 ($34\frac{13}{16} \times 23\frac{1}{8}$)
Unsigned
Presented by the National Art-Collections Fund (1954.903)

Jan Claes Rietschoof
1652–1719 Dutch

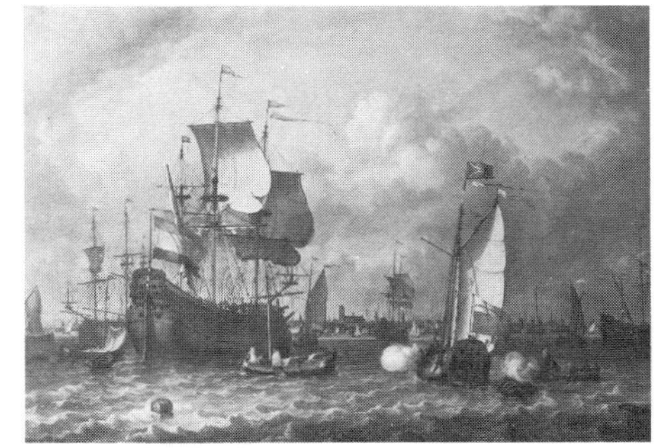

MASSED SHIPPING ANCHORED IN THE FOREGROUND: A VIEW OF ROTTERDAM BEYOND
1706

Oil on panel
47·8 × 68·2 ($18\frac{13}{16} \times 26\frac{7}{8}$)
s(brc, on plank): *J C R* (mon)
dated (bl, on stern of large merchantman): *ANNO 1706*
Assheton-Bennett bequest (1979.495)

Willem Roelofs
1822–1897 Dutch

FERME SOUS LES ARBRES

Oil on canvas laid down on panel
29·9 × 41·4 ($11\frac{3}{4} \times 16\frac{5}{16}$)
Unsigned
Lady Mary Boyd Dawkins bequest
(1979.616)

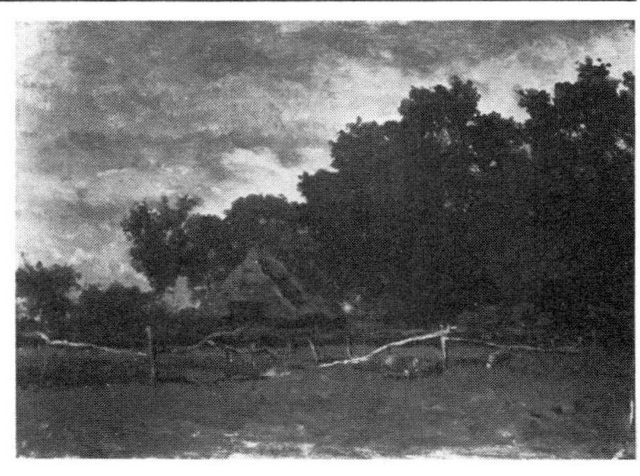

Gino Romiti
b. 1881 Italian

AN OLD TUSCAN ROAD
1908

Oil on canvas
60 × 80 ($23\frac{5}{8} \times 31\frac{1}{2}$)
s(brc): *·GINO·ROMITI·1908*
Alderman E. F. M. Sutton gift
(1930.80)

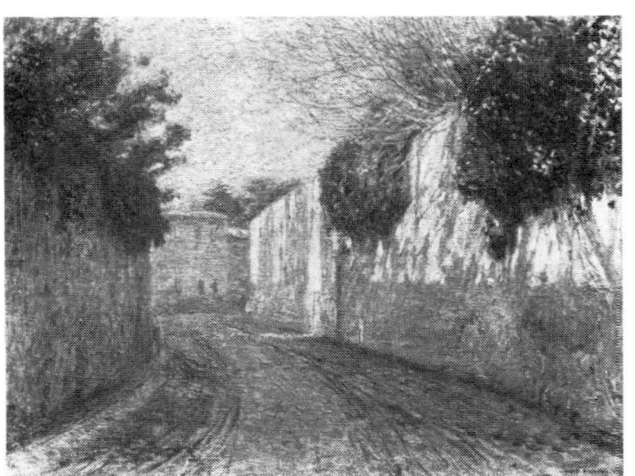

Salvator Rosa
See Italian, *c.* 1700

Jan Albertsz. Rotius
1624–1666 Dutch

PORTRAIT OF A BOY WITH A DOG (A PRINCE OF ORANGE?)
1660

Oil on canvas
114·6 × 88 ($45\frac{1}{8} \times 34\frac{11}{16}$)
s(blc): *AEtatis. 1 - 1660 - / JA* (mon) *- Rotius - fe -*
Miss C. Scott bequest (1930.54)

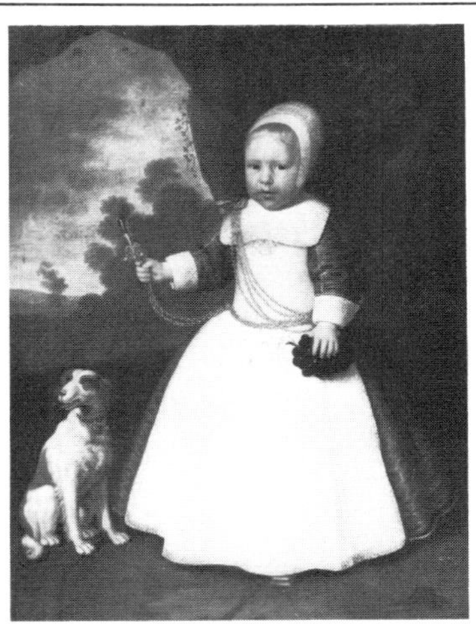

Circle of Jan Albertsz. Rotius

A LADY WITH GLOVES

Oil on canvas
101·3 × 81·5 ($39\frac{7}{8} \times 32\frac{1}{8}$)
Unsigned
G. Beatson Blair bequest, 1941
(1947.143)

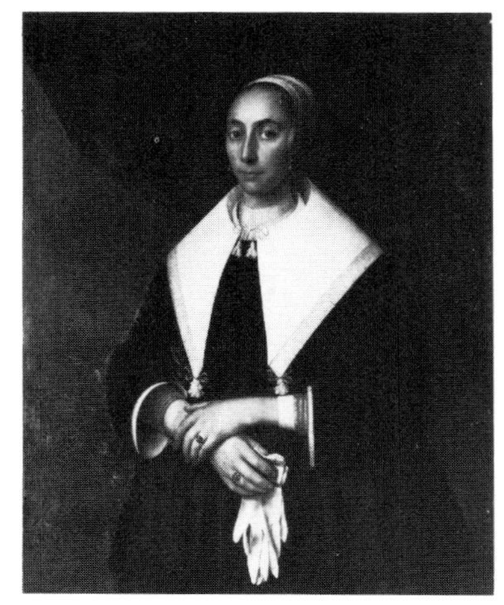

Reuven Rubin
b. 1893 Israeli

BETHLEHEM

Oil on canvas
60 × 73 ($23\frac{5}{8} \times 28\frac{3}{4}$)
s(blc): *Riki / Rubin*
Lt. Col. C. Beddington gift (1938.538)

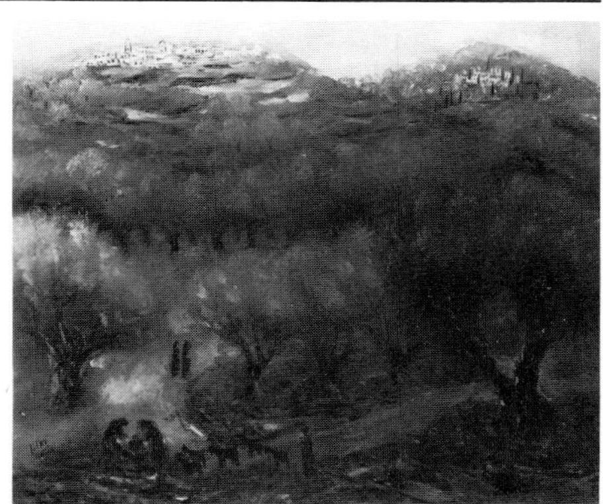

Jacob Isaacksz. van Ruisdael
1628/9–1682 Dutch

A STORM OFF THE DUTCH COAST

Oil on canvas
85·3 × 100·4 ($33\frac{5}{8} \times 39\frac{9}{16}$)
s(brc): *Ruisdael*
Presented by the National Art-Collections Fund from the E. E. Cook collection (1955.124)

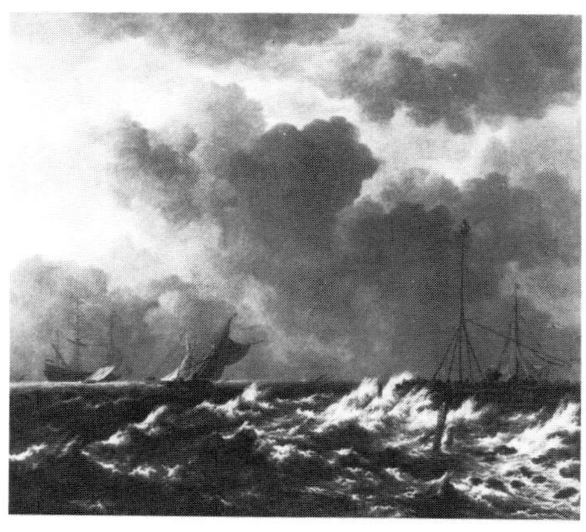

LANDSCAPE WITH A WOMAN AND CHILD WALKING ALONG A WOODED COUNTRY LANE
1649

Oil on panel
25·9 × 21·4 ($10\frac{3}{16} \times 8\frac{7}{16}$)
s(blc): *JVR* (mon) *1649*.
Assheton-Bennett bequest (1979.496)

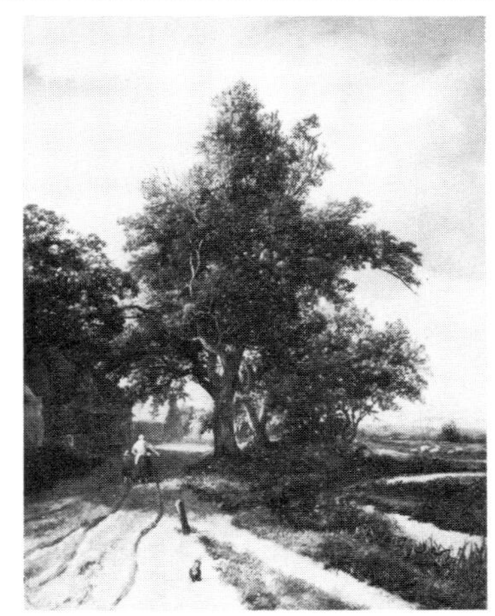

Salomon van Ruysdael
1600/3–1670 Dutch

WINTER SCENE WITH SLEDGES AND SKATERS ON A RIVER; A TOWN AT THE RIGHT
1656

Oil on panel
39·6 × 59·1 ($15\frac{5}{8} \times 23\frac{1}{4}$)
s(bl, on sledge): *S. v Ruysdael / 1656*.
Assheton-Bennett bequest (1979.497)

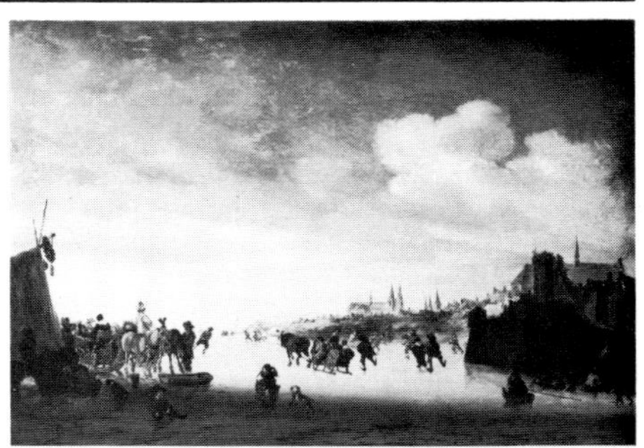

RIVER SCENE WITH SAILING BOATS UNLOADING AT THE SHORE

Oil on panel
42·2 × 59·7 ($16\frac{5}{8} \times 23\frac{7}{16}$)
s(b, centre, on rowing boat): *SVR* (mon)
Assheton-Bennett bequest (1979.498)

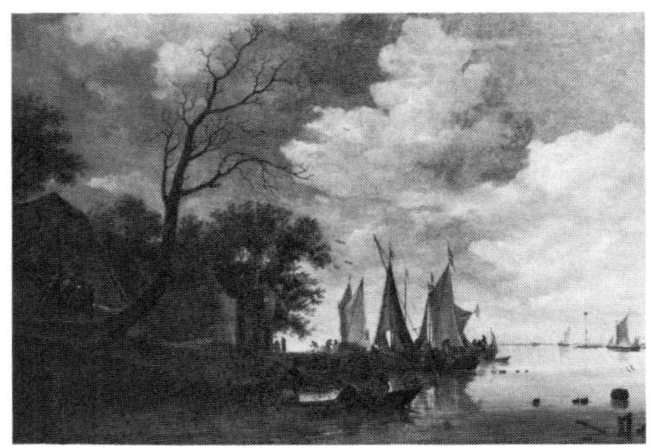

Pieter Andries Rysbrack
1690–1748 Flemish

DEAD GAME
1740

Oil on canvas
72·2 × 91·7 ($28\frac{7}{16} \times 36\frac{1}{8}$)
s(b, centre): *P. Rysbrack 1740*
Mrs. R. Hatton gift (1908.36)

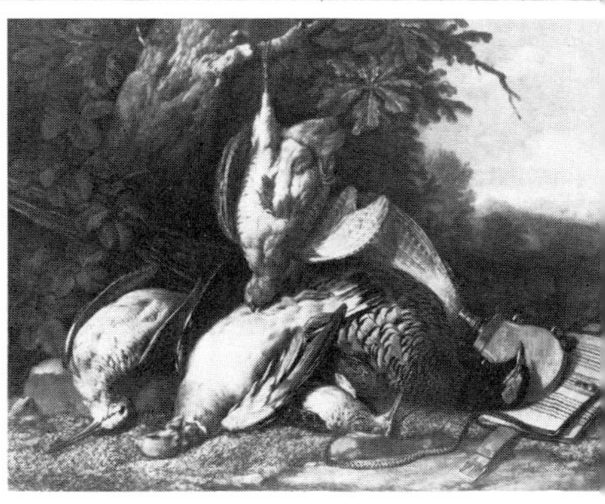

Eugénie Marie Salanson
active 1864–1892 French

LA FRANCINE DE GRANDVILLE

Oil on canvas
55·2 × 46·2 ($21\frac{3}{4} \times 18\frac{3}{16}$)
s(brc): *E. SALANSON*
James Blair bequest (1917.218)

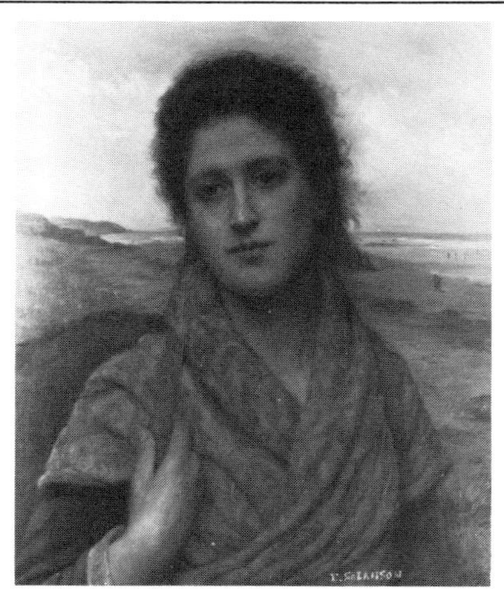

HEAD OF A GIRL

Oil on canvas
41 × 33 ($16\frac{1}{8} \times 13$)
s(trc): *E. Salanson*
James Blair bequest (1917.219)

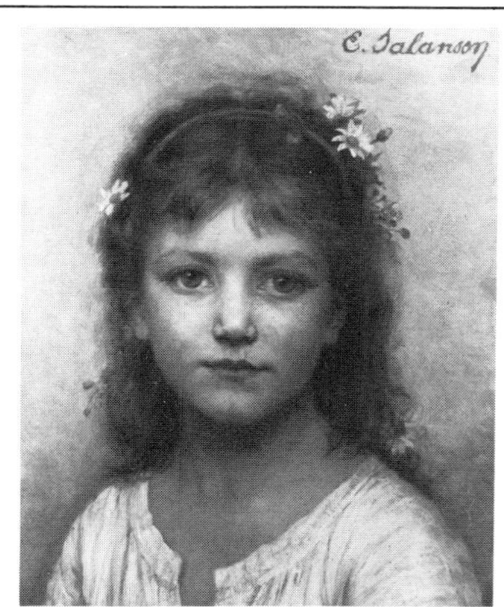

Rubens Santoro
1859–1896 Italian

BASKET-MAKERS IN NAPLES
1878

Oil on canvas
64·1 × 37·5 (25¼ × 14¾)
s(brc): *Rubens Santoro '78 | - Napoli -*
Mothersill bequest to the Horsfall Museum, 1880, from which transferred (1918.400)

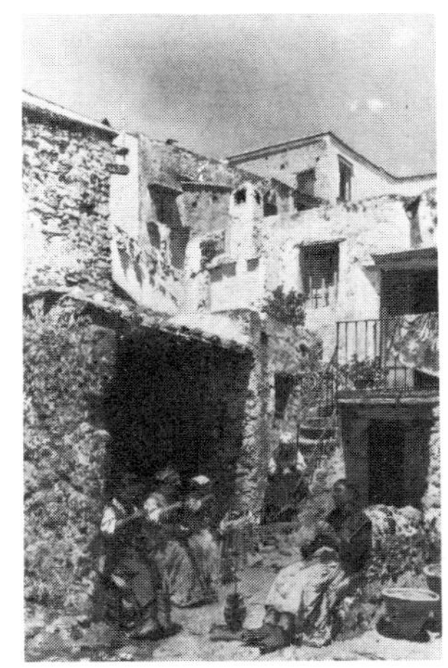

A SIESTA IN SUNSHINE
1878

Oil on canvas
35·5 × 61·9 (14 × 24⅜)
s(brc): *Rubens Santoro - 78 | - Napoli -*
Mothersill bequest, 1880, to the Horsfall Museum, from which transferred (1918.405)

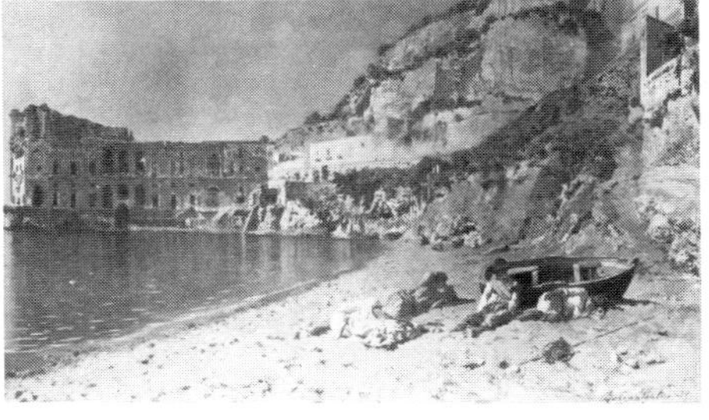

John Singer Sargent
See British School catalogue, vol. II

Ary Scheffer
1795–1858 French

THE HOLY WOMEN AT THE SEPULCHRE
1845

Oil on panel
108·8 × 86 (42⅞ × 33⅞)
s(blc): *Ary Scheffer 1845*
Lord Ashton of Hyde gift (1924.17)

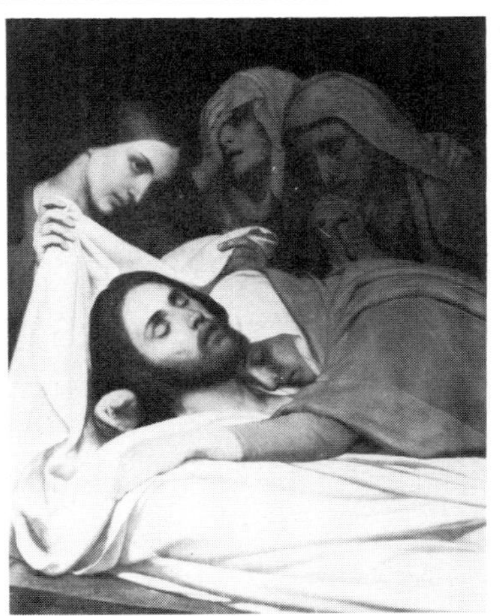

Floris van Schooten
active 1612–1655 Dutch

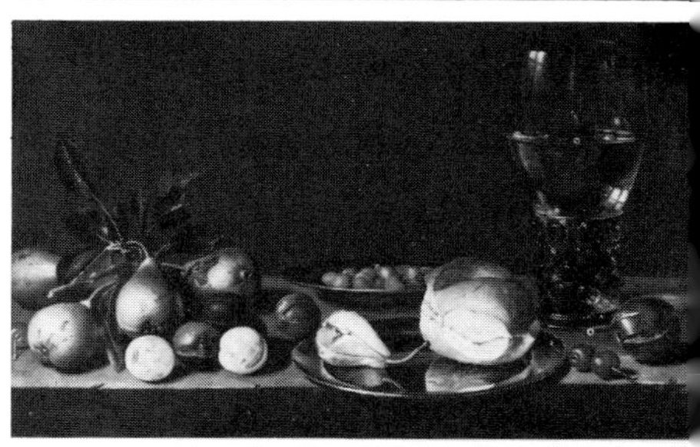

STILL LIFE: FRUIT, BREAD AND A GOBLET ON A TABLE

Oil on panel
34·2 × 55·5 ($13\frac{7}{16} \times 21\frac{7}{8}$)
s(b, centre to left, on edge of table): *FVS.*
Assheton-Bennett bequest (1979.499)

Adolphe Schreyer
1828–1899 German

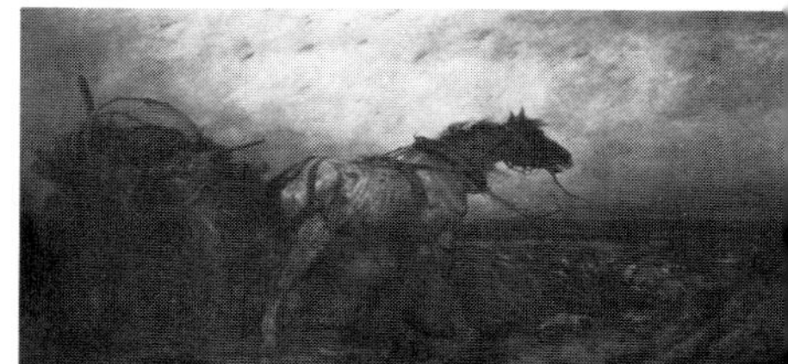

ABANDONED

Oil on canvas
130 × 250 ($51\frac{3}{16} \times 98\frac{1}{2}$)
s(blc): *Ad. Schreyer*
Purchased (1888.3)

Adolf Schweitzer
1847–1914 German

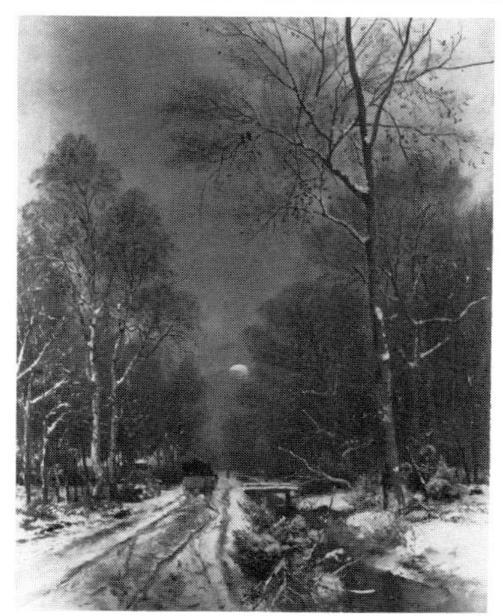

THE OLD DILIGENCE IN WINTER
1877

Oil on canvas
106·6 × 77·6 ($42 \times 30\frac{9}{16}$)
s(blc): *Adolf Schweitzer 18* (?) *.77.*
Mothersill bequest to the Horsfall Museum, 1880, from which transferred (1918.402)

Émile Eisman Semenowsky
active *c.* 1880 French

AUTUMN

Oil on panel
56·1 × 37·8 ($22\frac{1}{8} \times 14\frac{7}{8}$)
s(brc): *PARIS. / Eisman - Semenowsky*
James Blair bequest (1917.211)

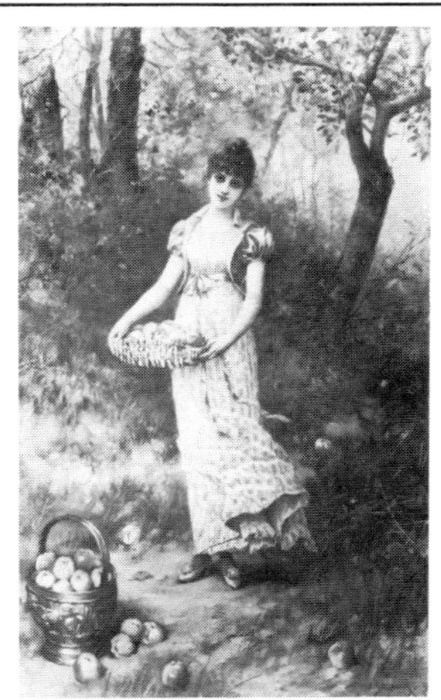

Frans van Severdonck
1809–1889 Belgian

DOMESTIC FOWL IN A LANDSCAPE
1867

Oil on panel
17·8 × 24 ($7 \times 9\frac{7}{16}$)
s(blc): *F. Van Severdonck Pt 1867*
Presented by C. A. Clarke in memory of J. Ernest Phythian (1938.504)

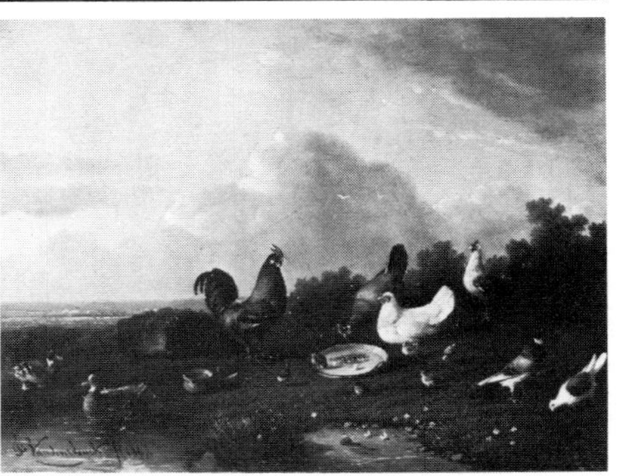

Circle of Girolamo Siciolante da Sermoneta
1521–*c.* 1580 Italian

ST. MATTHEW

Oil on copper
22·4 × 17 ($8\frac{13}{16} \times 6\frac{11}{16}$) irregular oval
Unsigned
Purchased (1979.60)

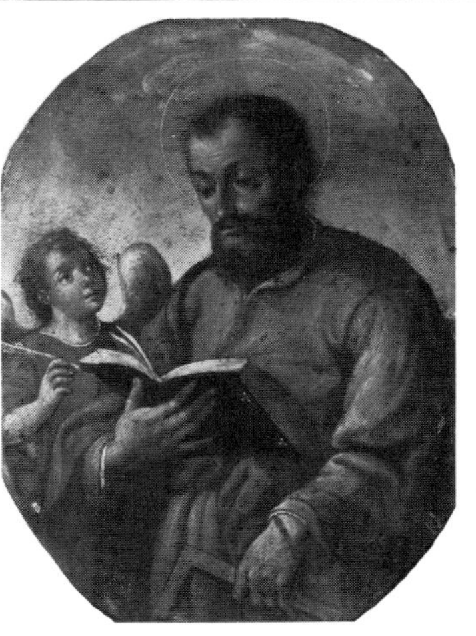

ST. MARK

Oil on copper
22·1 × 17·3 ($8\frac{11}{16} \times 6\frac{13}{16}$) irregular oval
Unsigned
Purchased (1979.61)

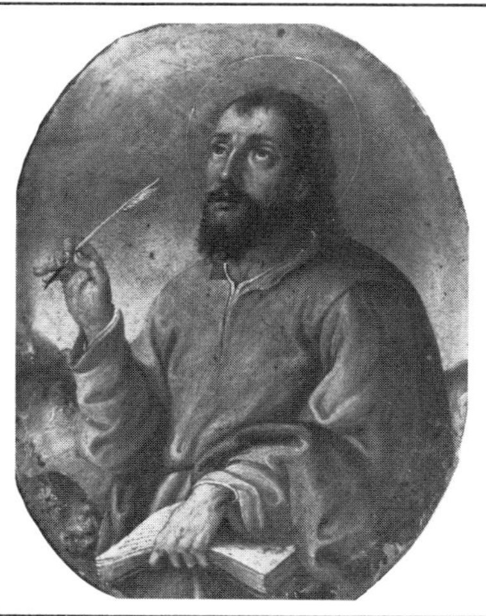

Arthur Siefert
b. 1858 German

DEVOTION

Oil on panel
35 × 27·2 ($13\frac{13}{16} \times 10\frac{3}{4}$)
s(brc): *A. Siefert*
James Blair bequest (1917.240)

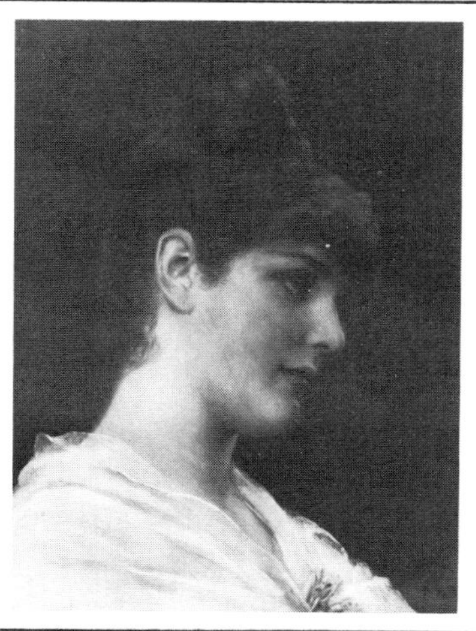

J. Simon
active 20th century Israeli

ISRAELI SCENE WITH FIGURES

Oil on hardboard
35·2 × 44·8 ($13\frac{7}{8} \times 17\frac{5}{8}$)
s in Hebrew
Presented by the Leonard Cohen Fund (1968.153)

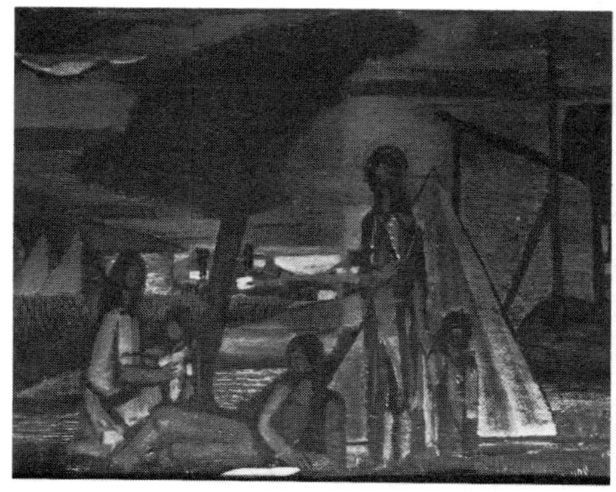

Alfred Sisley
1839–1899 French

A NORMANDY FARM
1874

Oil on canvas
49·6 × 59·8 (19 9/16 × 23 9/16)
s(brc): *Sisley . 74*
Purchased (1927.19)

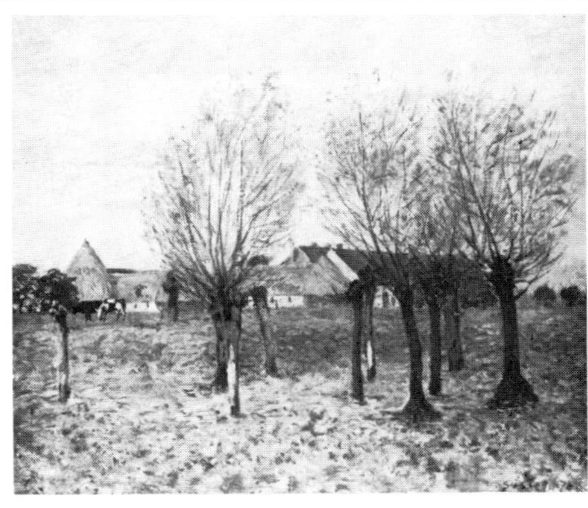

School of Frans Snyders
1579–1657 Flemish

THE LEOPARDS

Oil on canvas
117·5 × 165·4 (46 1/4 × 65 1/8)
Unsigned
Mrs. E. Wood bequest (1908.19)

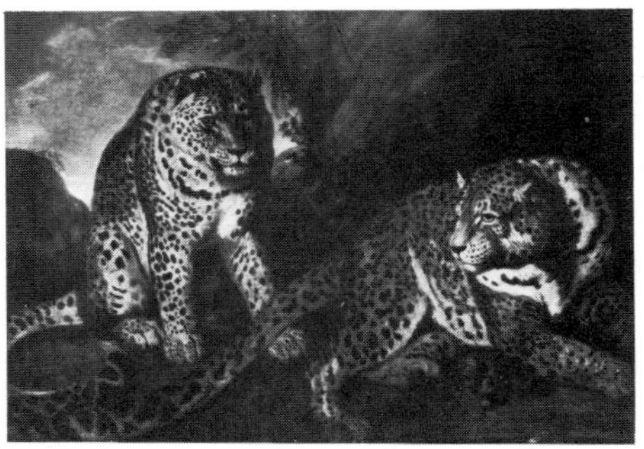

Attributed to Jan Soens
1547/8–1611/14 *N. Netherlandish*

THE HOLY FAMILY WITH THE INFANT BAPTIST

Oil on canvas
158·3 × 110·8 (62 5/16 × 43 5/8)
Unsigned
Purchased (1961.74)

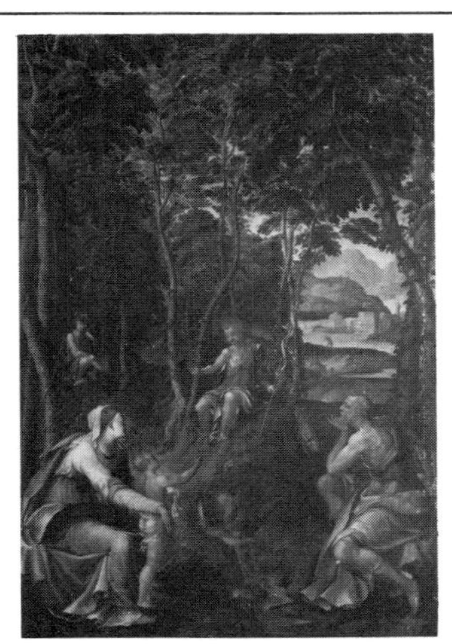

Gerard Soest
See English School Catalogue, Vol. II, Appendix I

Hendrick Martensz. Sorgh
1610/11–1670 Dutch

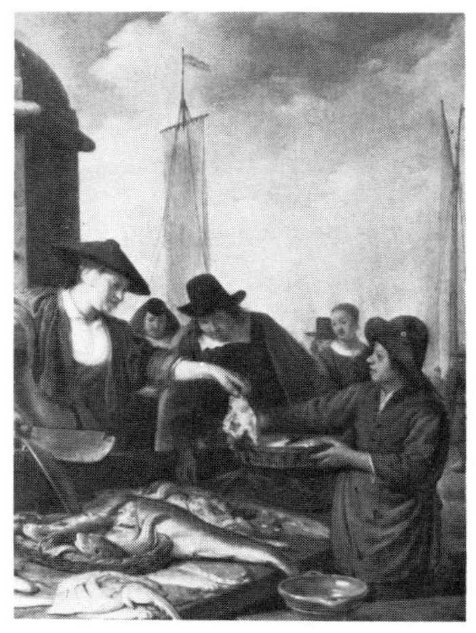

A FISH STALL BY A HARBOUR

Oil on panel
31·2 × 26·2 ($12\frac{5}{16} \times 10\frac{5}{16}$)
Unsigned
Assheton-Bennett bequest (1979.500)

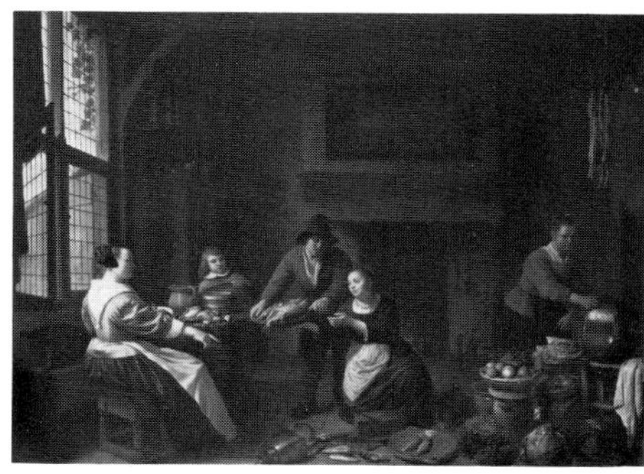

KITCHEN INTERIOR WITH A MAN BRINGING FISH FOR SALE
1657

Oil on panel
47 × 62·9 ($18\frac{1}{2} \times 24\frac{3}{4}$)
s(bl, on bench): *H. Sorgh 1657.*
Assheton-Bennett bequest (1979.501)

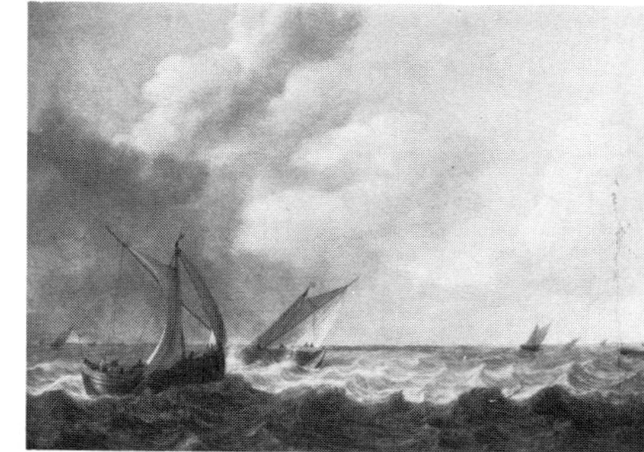

FISHING BOATS IN A CHOPPY SEA
1666

Oil on panel
35·7 × 49·6 ($14\frac{1}{16} \times 19\frac{1}{2}$)
s(br, on piece of wood below sailing boat): *Sorgh 1666.*
Assheton-Bennett bequest (1979.502)

Paul Constant Soyer
1823–1903 French

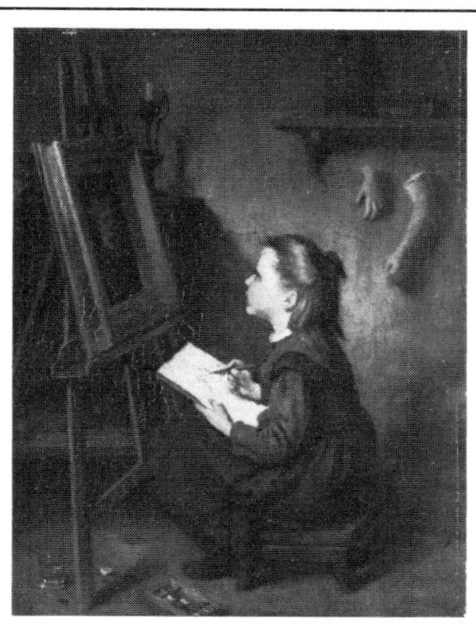

A YOUNG ARTIST

Oil on canvas
22·7 × 18 ($8\frac{15}{16} \times 7\frac{1}{16}$)
s(brc): *PAUL SOYER*
Mothersill bequest to the Horsfall Museum, 1880, from which transferred (1918.421)

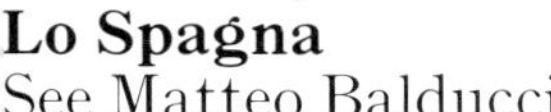

Lo Spagna
See Matteo Balducci

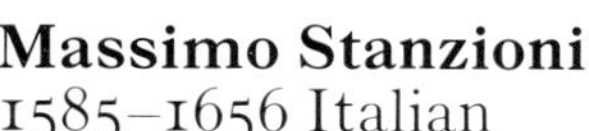

Massimo Stanzioni
1585–1656 Italian

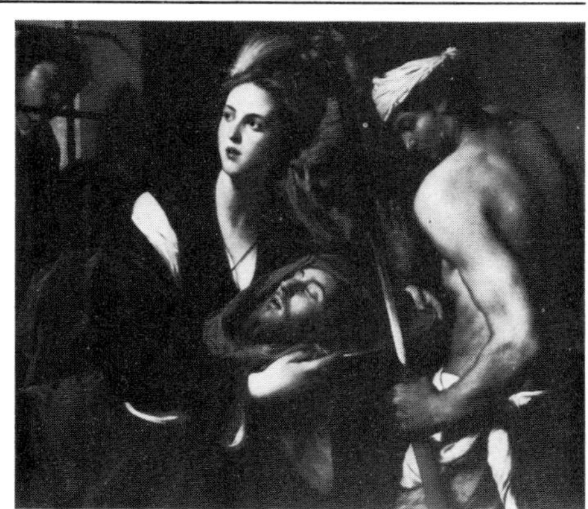

SALOME WITH THE HEAD OF THE BAPTIST

Oil on canvas
106 × 126·9 ($41\frac{3}{4} \times 49\frac{15}{16}$)
Unsigned
Purchased (1958.1007)

Jan Steen
1625/6–1679 Dutch

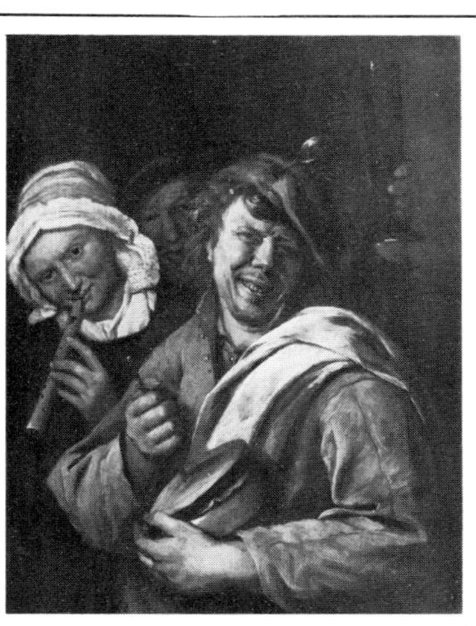

THE ROMMELPOT: INTERIOR WITH THREE FIGURES

Oil on panel
32·8 × 26·1 ($12\frac{15}{16} \times 10\frac{1}{4}$)
s(trc): *J Steen* (JS in mon)
Assheton-Bennett bequest (1979.503)

Abraham Storck
1644–after 1704 Dutch

SHIPPING OFF AMSTERDAM

Oil on canvas
28·7 × 33·5 ($11\frac{5}{16} \times 13\frac{3}{16}$) original canvas; enlarged to 29·3 × 34·5 ($11\frac{9}{16} \times 13\frac{9}{16}$)
Unsigned
Presented by Mrs. R. Hatton (1908.31)

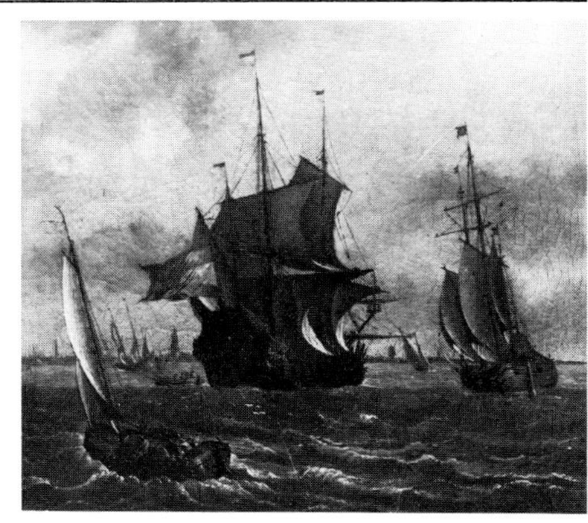

COAST SCENE WITH SHIPPING ANCHORED OFF-SHORE AND FIGURES ON A BEACH IN THE FOREGROUND

Oil on panel
36·4 × 49·1 ($14\frac{3}{8} \times 19\frac{5}{16}$)
s(blc): *A. STORCK.*
Assheton-Bennett bequest (1979.504)

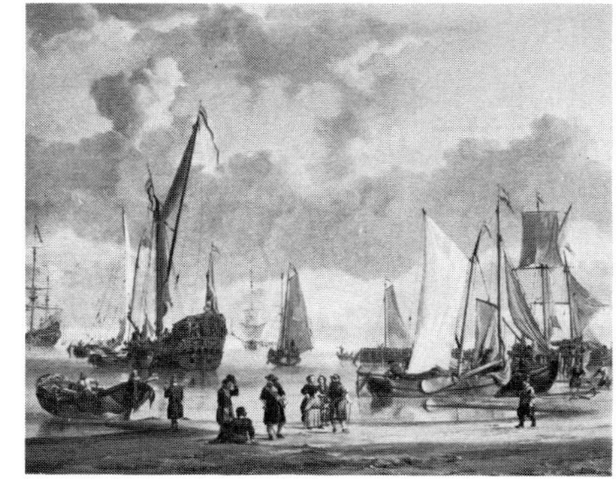

Antoni van Stralen
c. 1594–1641 Dutch

SKATING SCENE WITH NUMEROUS FIGURES ON THE ICE AND AN ISLAND FORT

Oil on panel
23·7 × 35·8 ($9\frac{3}{8} \times 14\frac{1}{16}$)
Unsigned
Assheton-Bennett bequest (1979.505)

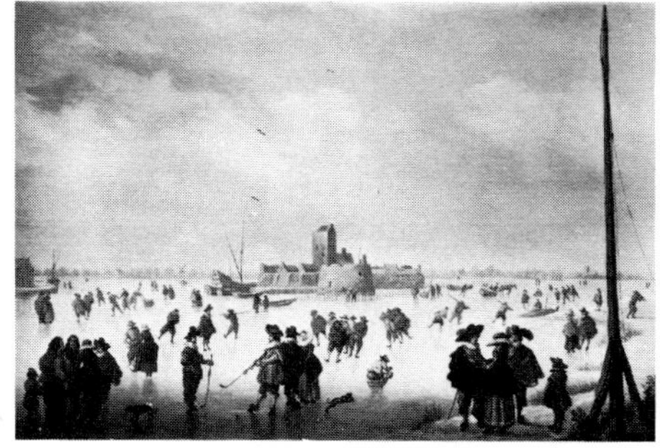

School of Bernardo Strozzi
1581–1644 Italian
(formerly attributed to Carlo Bononi)

ALLEGORY OF THE ARTS

Oil on canvas
134 × 75 ($52\frac{3}{4} \times 29\frac{1}{2}$)
Unsigned
Purchased (1964.285)

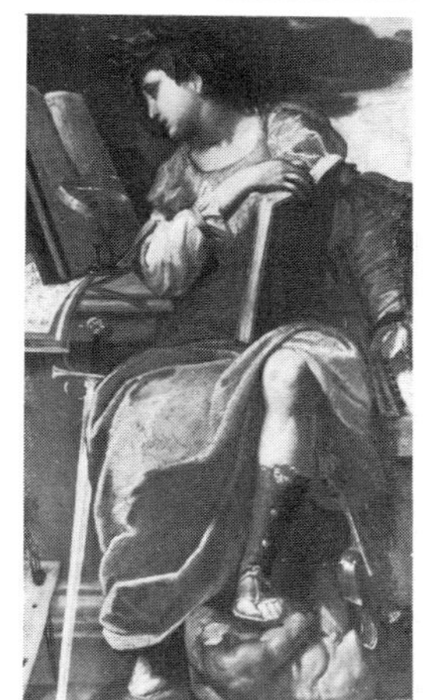

?Swiss, 18th century

LANDSCAPE WITH BATHERS

Oil on canvas
29·3 × 36 ($11\frac{9}{16} \times 14\frac{3}{16}$)
Unsigned
G. Beatson Blair bequest, 1941
(1947.69)

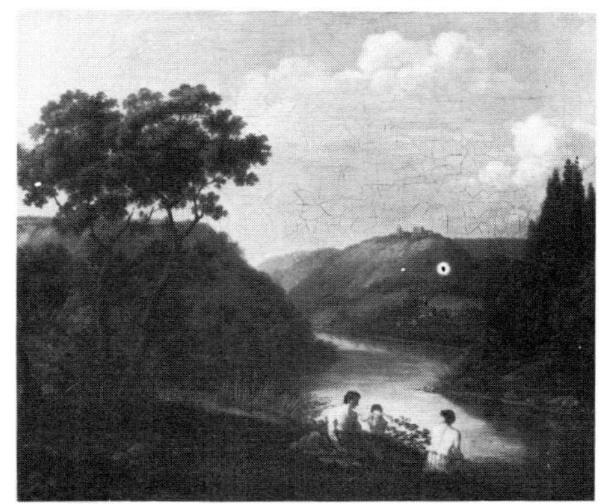

Pierre Louis Corentin Jacob, called Tal-coat
b. 1905 French

FRENCH VILLAGE
1933

Oil on canvas laid down on board
49·9 × 60·8 ($19\frac{5}{8} \times 23\frac{15}{16}$)
s(*verso*): *Tal-coat 1933*
Sir Thomas Barlow gift (1952.6)

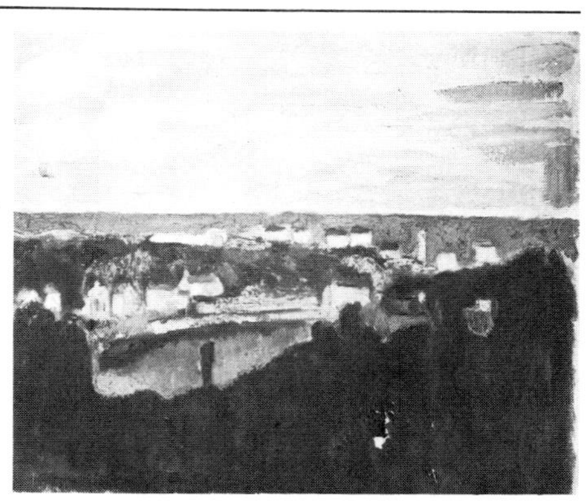

LANDSCAPE WITH RAINBOW
1933

Oil on canvas
53·8 × 64·8 (21⅛ × 25½)
Unsigned
Sir Thomas Barlow gift (1952.7)

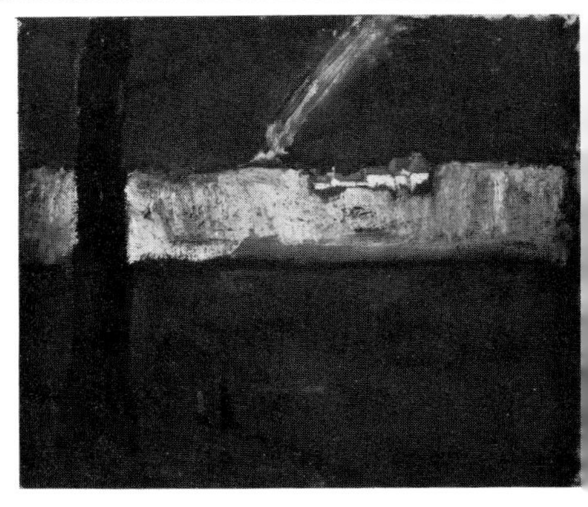

David Teniers the Younger
1610–1690 Flemish

COTTAGE IN A LANDSCAPE

Oil on panel
24·3 × 35 ($9\frac{9}{16}$ × 13¾)
Unsigned
Mrs. E. Wood bequest (1908.21)

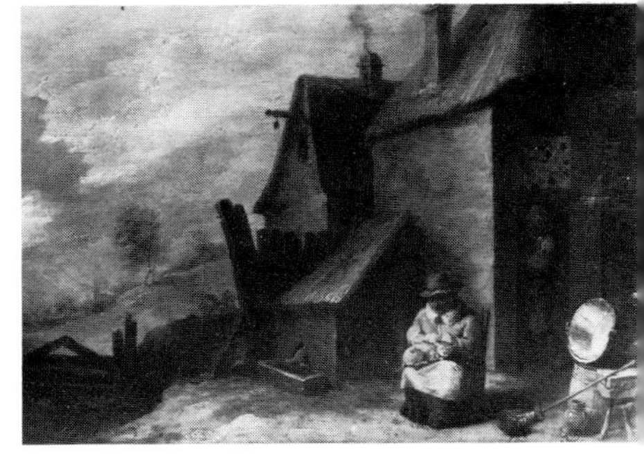

THE DENTIST
1652

Oil on panel
32·7 × 46·8 (12⅞ × $18\frac{7}{16}$)
s(brc): *D. TENIERS FEC*
dated (centre, on picture on wall): *A°. 1652.*
Assheton-Bennett bequest (1979.506)

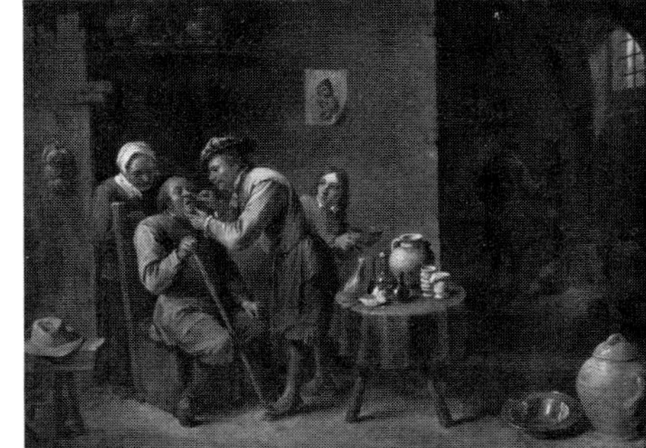

PEASANTS PLAYING CARDS AND SKITTLES IN A YARD

Oil on panel
27·8 × 37·3 ($10\frac{15}{16} \times 14\frac{3}{16}$)
s(brc): *D TENIERS. FEC.*
Assheton-Bennett bequest (1979.507)

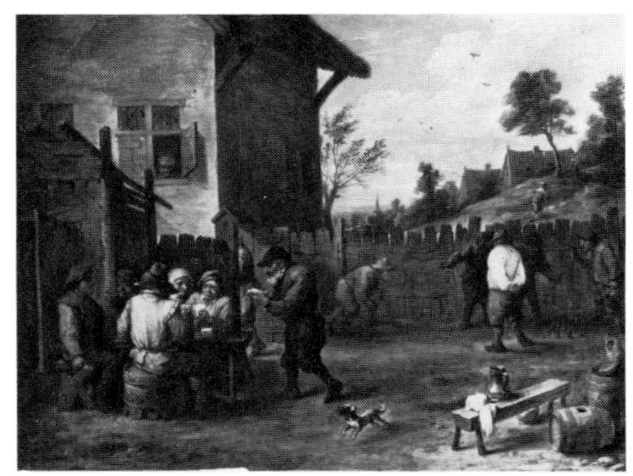

Jacques Joseph Tissot
See British School Catalogue, Vol. I

Troin
active 20th century, French

FRENCH LANDSCAPE

Oil on canvas
49·3 × 61·6 ($19\frac{3}{8} \times 24\frac{1}{4}$)
s(brc): *Troin*
Eric C. Gregory gift (1946.45)

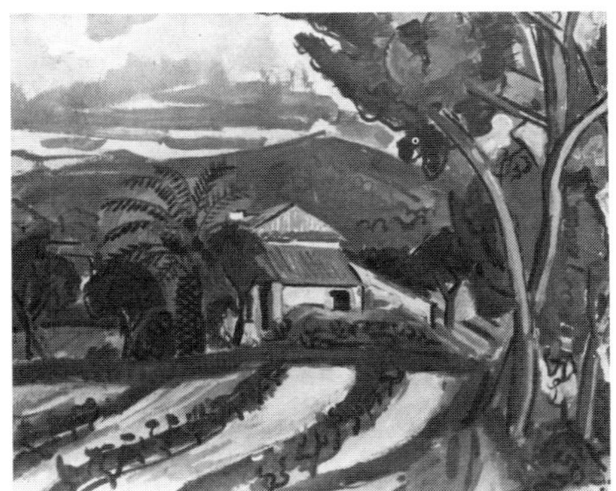

Constant Troyon
1810–1865 French

A PASTURE IN NORMANDY

Oil on canvas
54 × 73·1 ($21\frac{1}{4} \times 28\frac{3}{4}$)
s(brc): *C. Troyon*
Purchased (1911.17)

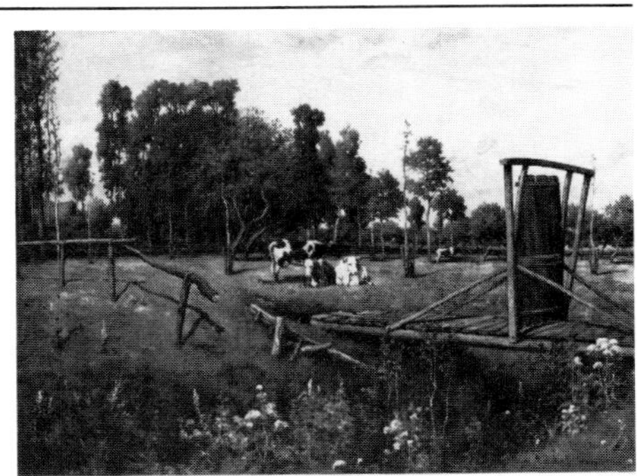

Alessandro Turchi
1578–1649 Italian

THE FLIGHT INTO EGYPT

Oil on canvas
307·5 × 180 ($121\frac{1}{8} \times 70\frac{7}{8}$)
Unsigned
Purchased (1978.259)

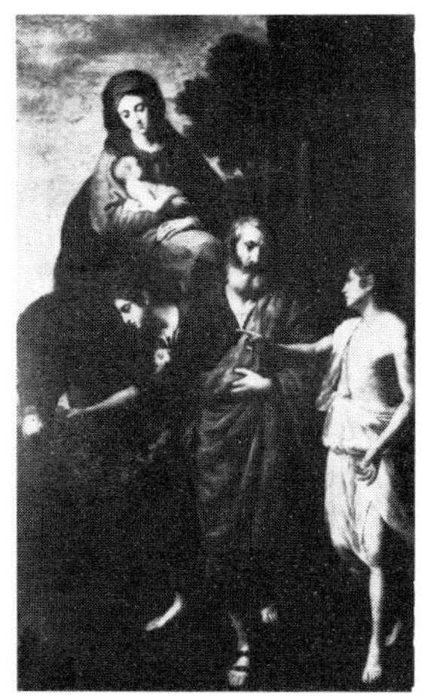

Maurice Utrillo
1883–1955 French

CHURCH AT ANET

Oil on panel
65 × 50·2 ($25\frac{9}{16} \times 19\frac{3}{4}$)
s(brc): *Maurice.Utrillo.V*
Purchased (1935.188)

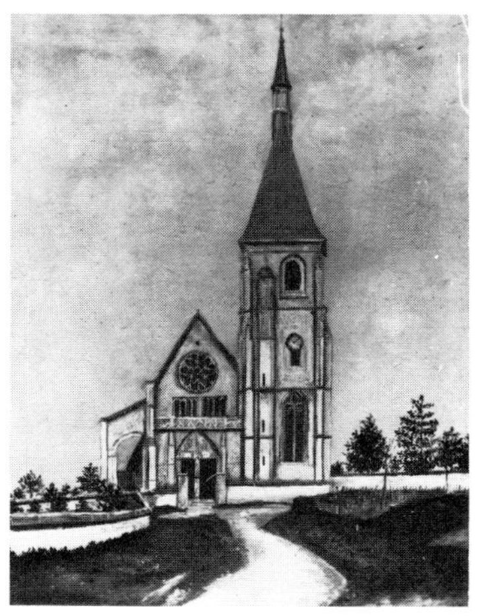

CHAPELLE À ROSCOFF

Oil on canvas
62 × 81·5 ($23\frac{11}{16} \times 32\frac{1}{16}$)
s(brc): *Maurice Utrillo.V.*
Mrs. S. R. Macnair bequest (1974.93)

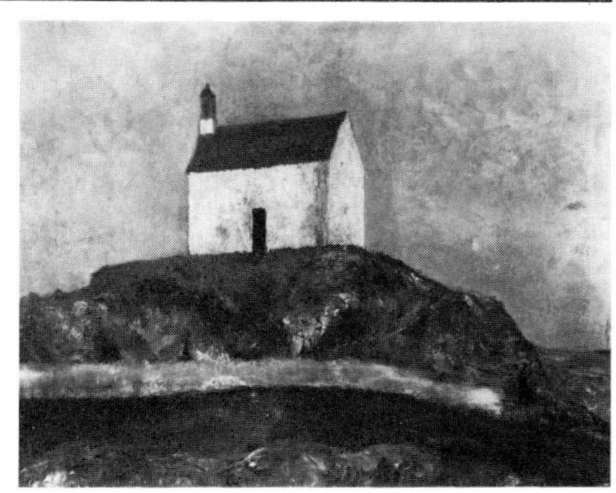

Adriaen van de Velde
1636–1672 Dutch

WINTER SCENE WITH A GROUP OF GOLFERS ON A FROZEN RIVER

Oil on panel
22·4 × 28·4 ($8\frac{7}{8} \times 11\frac{3}{16}$)
Unsigned
Assheton-Bennett bequest (1979.508)

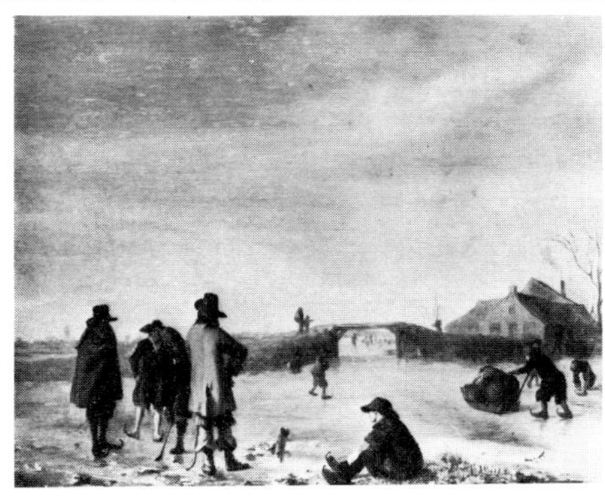

Esaias van de Velde
c. 1590–1630 Dutch

LANDSCAPE WITH RIDERS IN A CARRIAGE PASSING A CHURCH
1623

Oil on panel
40 × 68·8 ($15\frac{3}{4} \times 27\frac{1}{8}$)
s(b, centre to right, in front of horses): *E. V. VELDE. 1623.*
Assheton-Bennett bequest (1979.509)

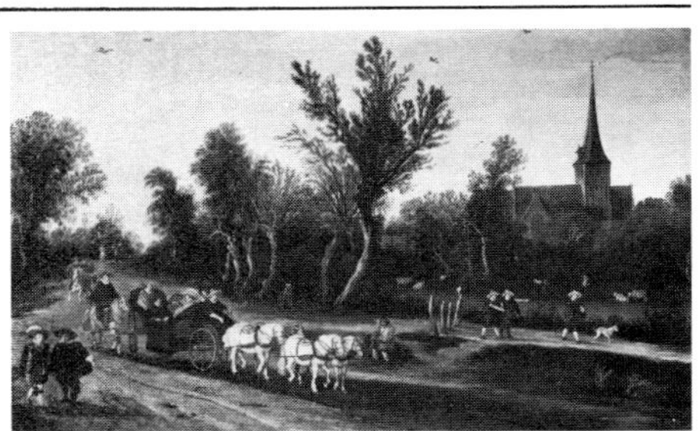

Studio of
Willem van de Velde the Elder
1611–1693 Dutch

SAILING VESSELS PASSING A COAST OF SAND DUNES
1657

Oil on canvas laid down on panel
30·8 × 40·1 ($12\frac{1}{8} \times 15\frac{3}{4}$)
s(brc): *W.V.V. 1657.*
Assheton-Bennett bequest (1979.510)

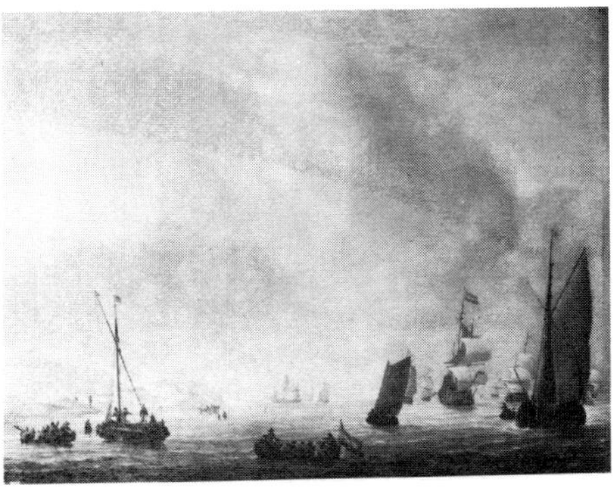

Willem van de Velde the Younger
1633–1707 Dutch

SEASCAPE: WITH A YACHT SAILING UNDER A RAINY SKY

Oil on panel
19·2 × 15·2 ($7\frac{9}{16} \times 5\frac{15}{16}$)
s(bl): *W.V.V.*
Assheton-Bennett bequest (1979.511)

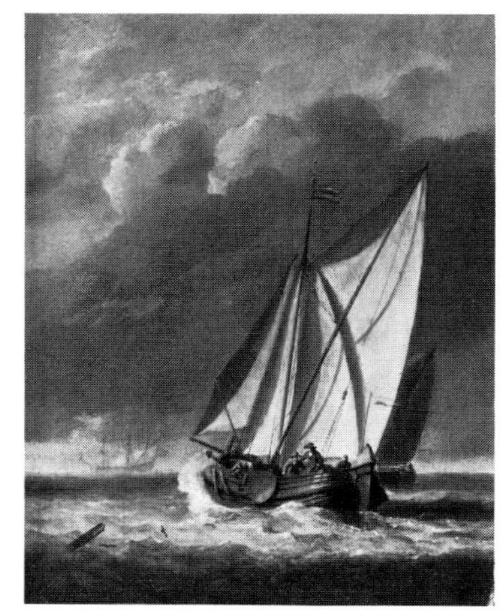

MEN OF WAR AT ANCHOR IN A CALM

Oil on canvas
64·4 × 80·5 ($25\frac{5}{16} \times 31\frac{3}{4}$)
Unsigned
Assheton-Bennett bequest (1979.512)

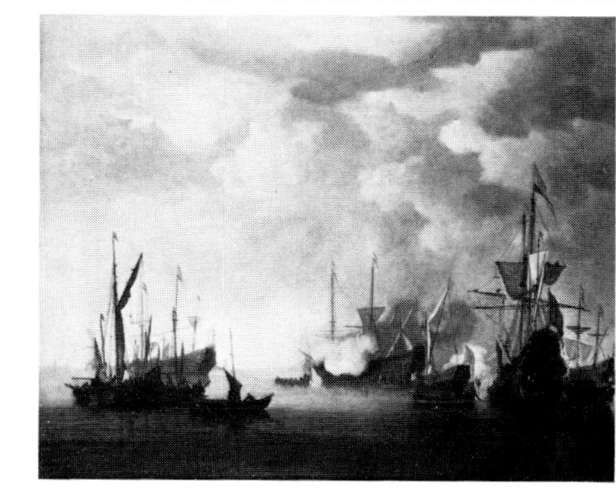

Follower of Willem van de Velde the Younger

SEASCAPE WITH YACHTS MOORED IN A CALM

Oil on canvas
33·7 × 41 ($13\frac{5}{16} \times 16\frac{1}{8}$)
indistinctly signed (bl)
Assheton-Bennett bequest (1979.513)

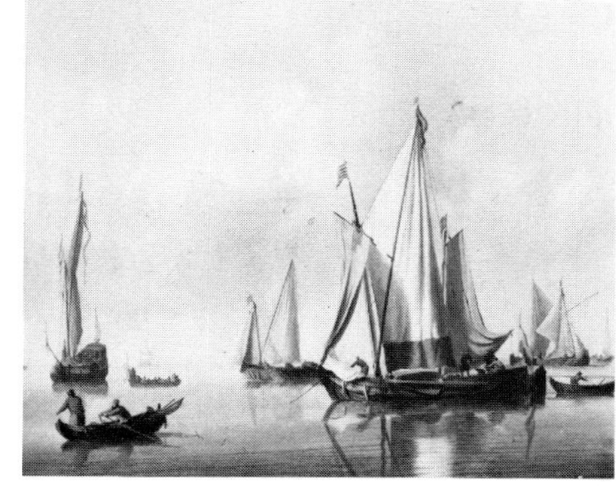

Claude Venard

b. 1913 French

STILL LIFE WITH GREEN APPLE

Oil on canvas
73 × 59·9 (28¾ × 23 9/16)
s(brc): *C VENARD*
Purchased (1956.4)

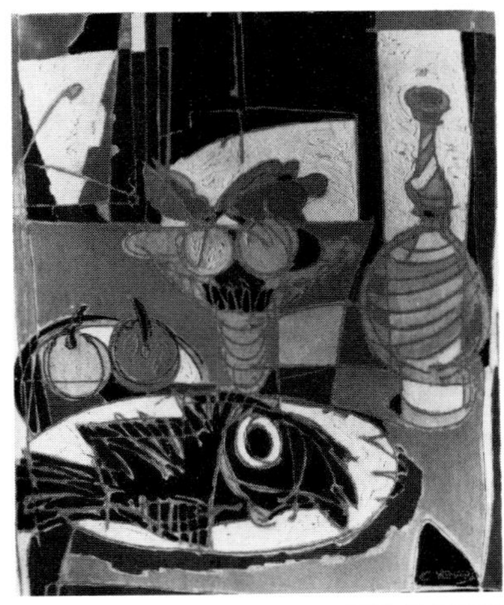

Eugène Joseph Verboeckhoven
1798–1881 Belgian

SHEEP AND DOGS
1861

Oil on canvas
77·5 × 58·4 (30½ × 23)
s(blc): *Eugène Verboeckhoven Ft. 1861.*
James Blair bequest (1917.187)

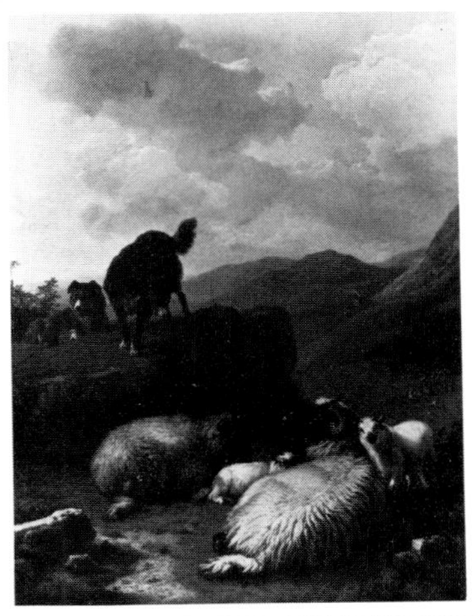

CATTLE NEAR A LAKE
1842

Oil on panel
18·6 × 27·2 (7 5/16 × 10 11/16)
s(blc): *Eugène Verboeckhoven / f. 1842. Roma*
John E. Yates bequest (1934.396)

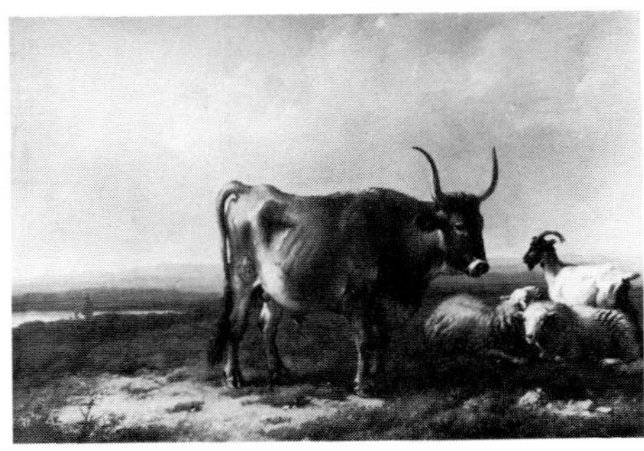

STARTLED
1864

Oil on panel
72 × 100·4 ($28\frac{5}{16} \times 39\frac{1}{2}$)
s(blc): *Eugène Verboeckhoven f*[t] *1864*
John E. Yates bequest (1934.399)

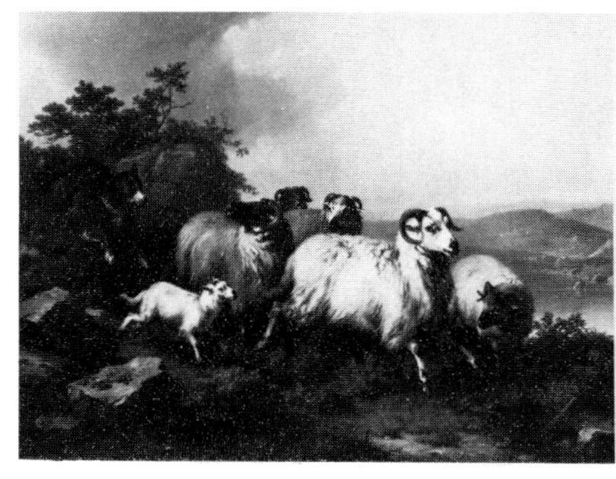

Claude-Joseph Vernet
1714–1789 French

COAST SCENE WITH A BRITISH MAN OF WAR
1766

Oil on canvas
81·8 × 131·2 ($32\frac{3}{16} \times 51\frac{11}{16}$)
s(brc): *Joseph Vernet / f.1766*
Purchased (1977.53)

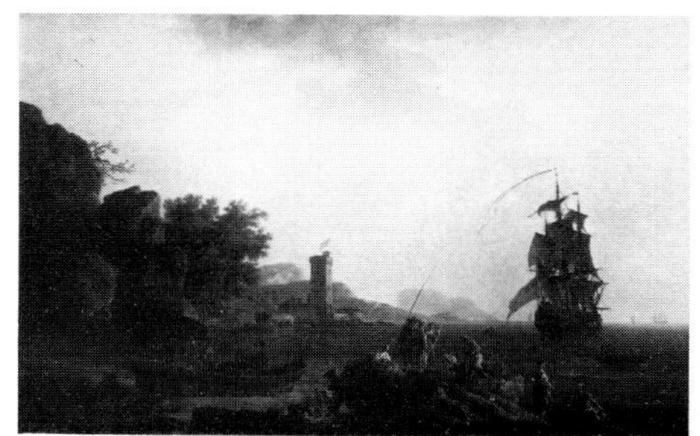

Antoni Verstraelen
See Antoni van Stralen

Salomon Leonardus Verveer
1813–1876 Dutch

VILLAGE WITH A CHURCH

Oil on panel
14·3 × 30·5 ($5\frac{5}{8} \times 12$)
s(blc): *S L Verveer*
Lady Mary Boyd Dawkins bequest (1979.617)

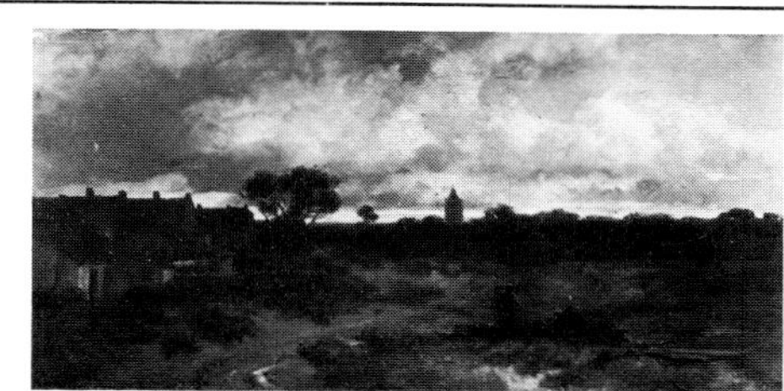

Jules Jacques Veyrassat
1828–1893 French

RETURNING HOME

Oil on canvas
22·2 × 35·2 ($8\frac{3}{4} \times 13\frac{13}{16}$)
s(br): *Veyrassat*
James Blair bequest (1917.220)

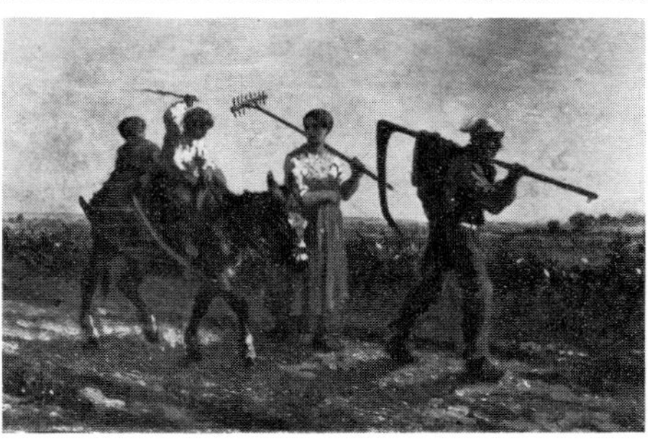

Maurice de Vlaminck
1876–1958 French

ROAD THROUGH TREES

Oil on canvas
60 × 73 ($23\frac{5}{8} \times 28\frac{3}{4}$)
s(brc): *Vlaminck*
Purchased (1949.101)

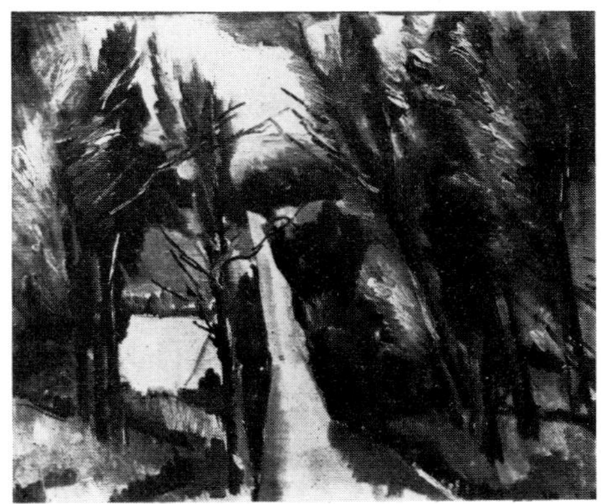

Simon de Vlieger
c. 1600–1653 Dutch

RIVER ESTUARY WITH SHIPPING ON A WINDY DAY

Oil on panel
30 × 38·9 ($11\frac{13}{16} \times 15\frac{5}{16}$)
Unsigned
Assheton-Bennett bequest (1979.514)

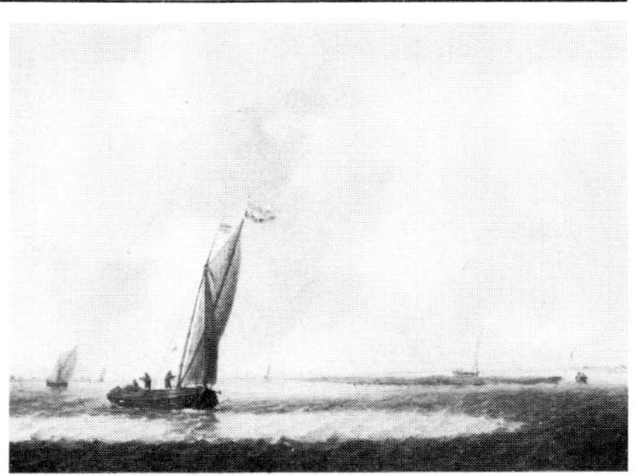

Hendrick Cornelisz. van der Vliet
1612–1675 Dutch

PORTRAIT OF A MAN
1661

Oil on canvas
100·5 × 91·7 ($39\frac{9}{16} \times 36\frac{1}{8}$)
s(bl): *Aetat.26.A° 1661 / H. van. Vliet.*
Sir Thomas Thornhill Shann gift
(1909.34)

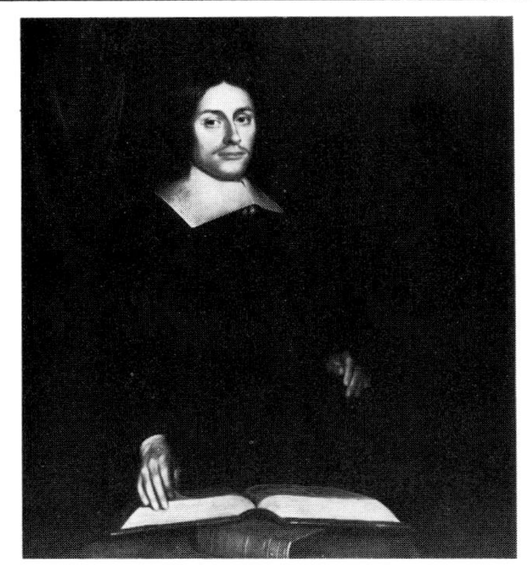

PORTRAIT OF A YOUNG WOMAN
1661

Oil on canvas
100·9 × 91·3 ($39\frac{3}{4} \times 35\frac{15}{16}$)
s(blc): *Aetat.19.A° 1661 / H. van Vliet*
Sir Thomas Thornhill Shann gift
(1909.35)

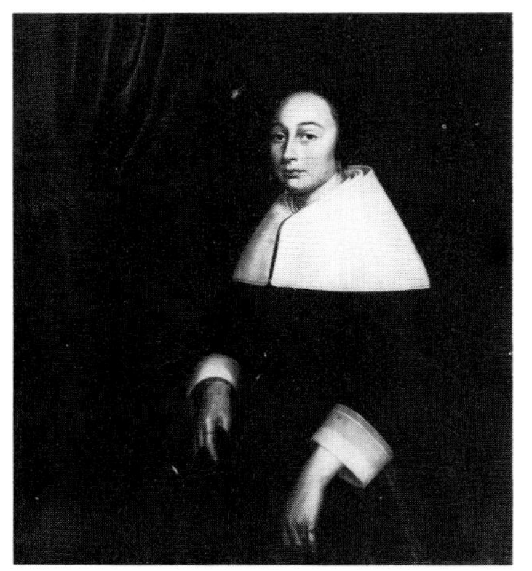

After Hendrick Cornelisz. van der Vliet

INTERIOR OF THE OUDE KERK AT DELFT

Oil on canvas
77 × 69 ($30\frac{5}{16} \times 27\frac{1}{8}$)
Unsigned
Purchased (1953.207)

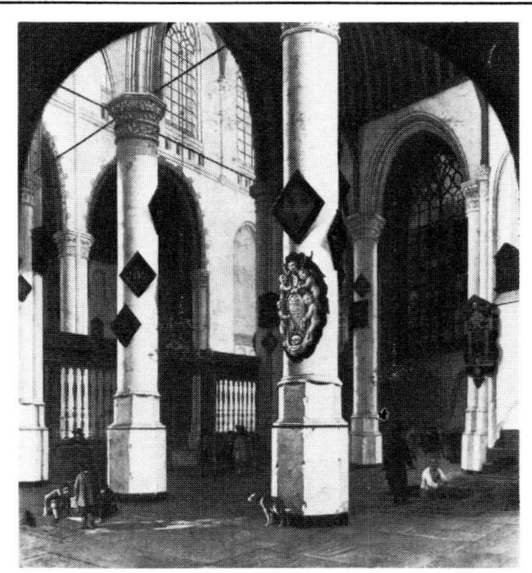

Antoine Vollon
1833–1900 French

STRAWBERRIES

Oil on panel
32·5 × 40·6 ($12\frac{13}{16}$ × 16)
s(tlc): *A. Vollon*
Purchased (1914.64)

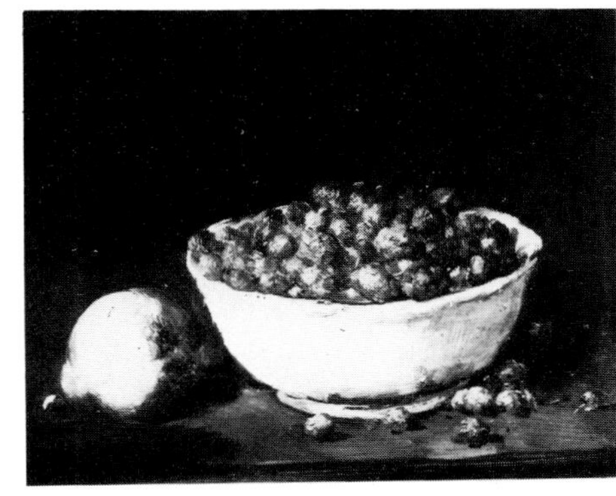

Friedrich Johann Voltz
1817–1886 German

CATTLE DRINKING
1875

Oil on panel
37·5 × 92·4 ($14\frac{3}{4}$ × $36\frac{3}{8}$)
s(brc): *Fr. Voltz. 75 / München*
Mothersill bequest to the Horsfall Museum, 1880, from which transferred (1918.939)

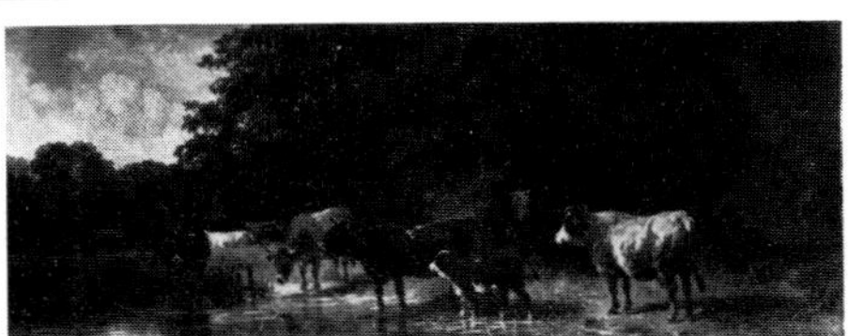

Attributed to Simon Vouet
1590–1649 French

APOLLO IN HIS CHARIOT WITH TIME

Oil on canvas
37·3 × 31·9 ($14\frac{11}{16}$ × $12\frac{9}{16}$)
Unsigned
Purchased (1966.295)

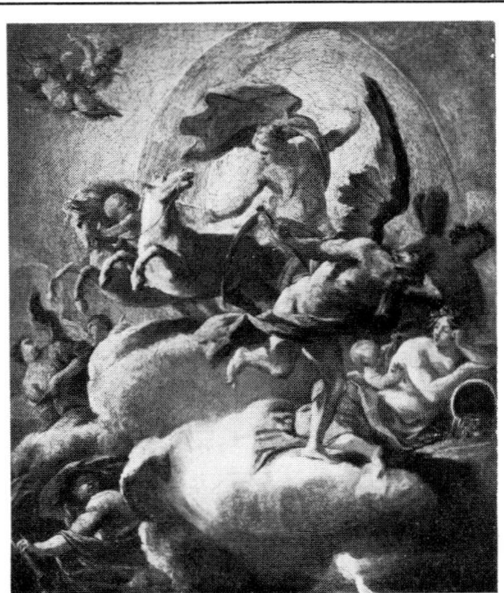

Alexander von Wagner
1838–1919 Hungarian

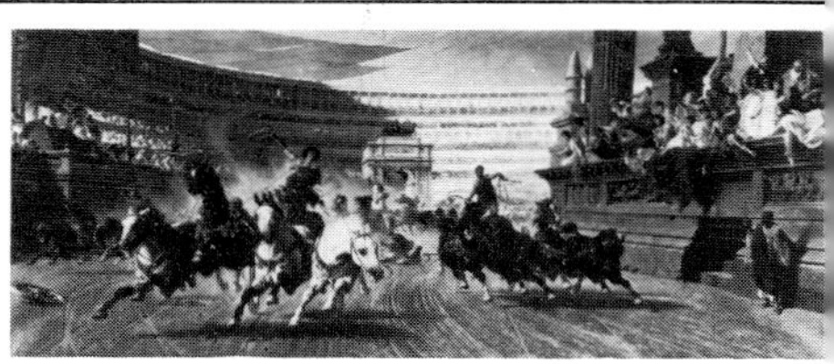

THE CHARIOT RACE

Oil on canvas
138·3 × 347 ($54\frac{7}{16}$ × $136\frac{9}{16}$)
s(brc): *A Wagner* (AW in mon)
Mrs. H. Higgins bequest (1898.12)

Philip Weber
b. 1849 German

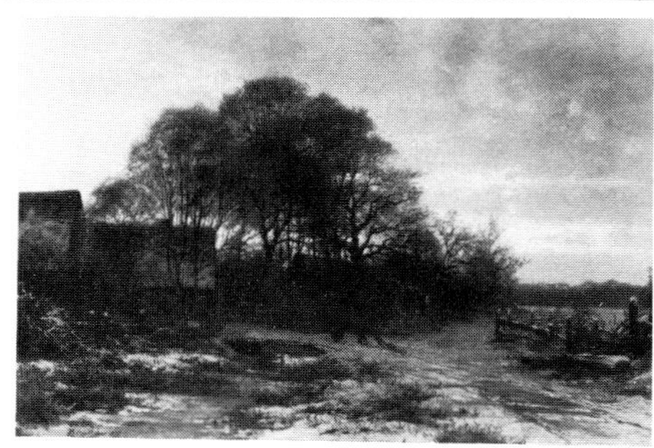

A WINTER EVENING
1873

Oil on canvas
61 × 101·5 (24 × $39\frac{15}{16}$)
s(blc): *Philip Weber 1873 / München*
Mothersill bequest to the Horsfall Museum, 1880, from which transferred (1918.1153)

Jan Wijnants
active 1643, d. 1684 Dutch

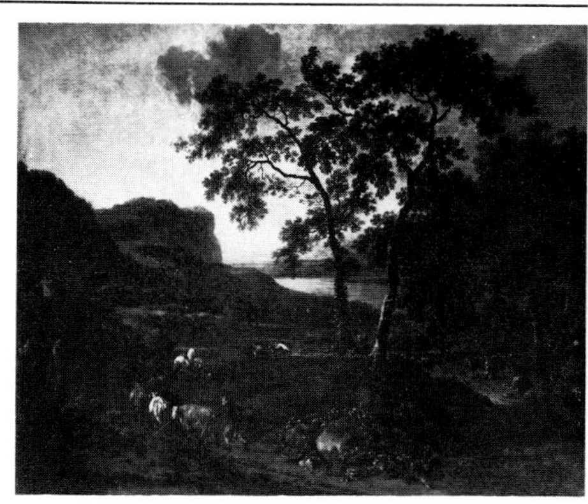

LANDSCAPE WITH CATTLE
1670

Oil on canvas
67·7 × 83·5 ($26\frac{11}{16}$ × $32\frac{7}{8}$)
s(bl): *J. Wijnants. f 1670*
Presented by Mrs. McConnel in memory of her late husband John W. McConnel (1923.15)

WOODED LANDSCAPE WITH FIGURES WALKING BY A SANDY BANK

Oil on canvas
26·7 × 30·7 ($10\frac{7}{16} \times 12\frac{1}{16}$)
s(br): *J. Wynants.*
Assheton-Bennett bequest (1979.517)

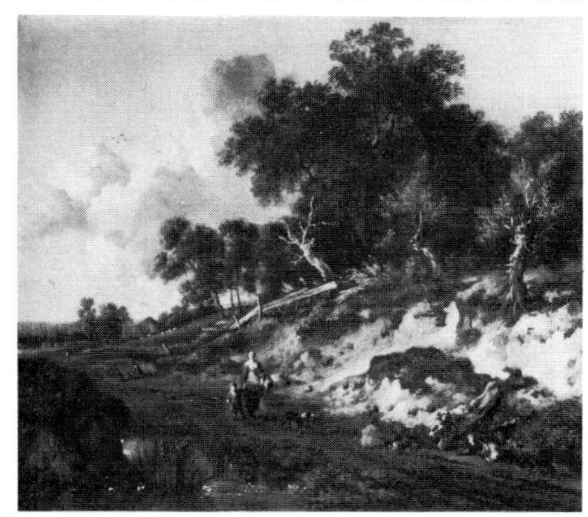

Adam Willaerts
See North Netherlandish

Studio of Willem Wissing
1653–1687 Dutch

QUEEN MARY, WIFE OF WILLIAM OF ORANGE (1662–1694)

Oil on canvas
122·8 × 99·8 ($48\frac{5}{16} \times 39\frac{5}{16}$)
Unsigned
James Blair bequest (1917.183)

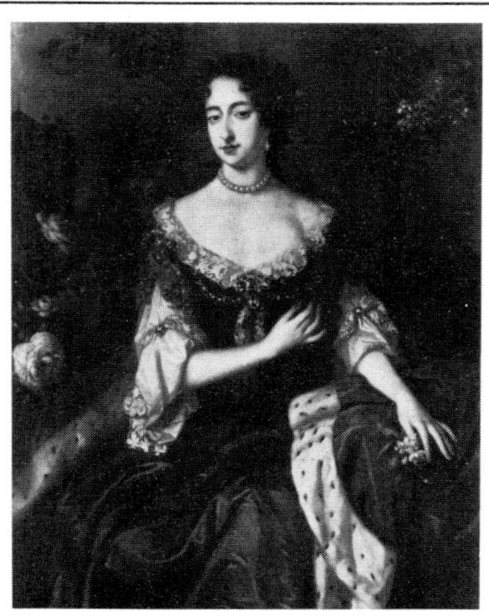

Jacob de Wit
1696–1754 Dutch

SKETCH FOR A CEILING: BACCHUS AND ARIADNE

Oil on canvas
48·2 × 61 (19 × 24)
Unsigned
Purchased with the aid of a grant from the Victoria and Albert Museum (1965.135)

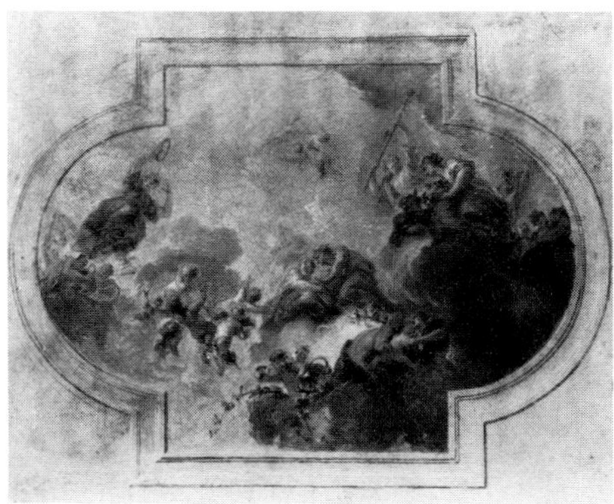

Philips Wouwermans
1619–1668 Dutch

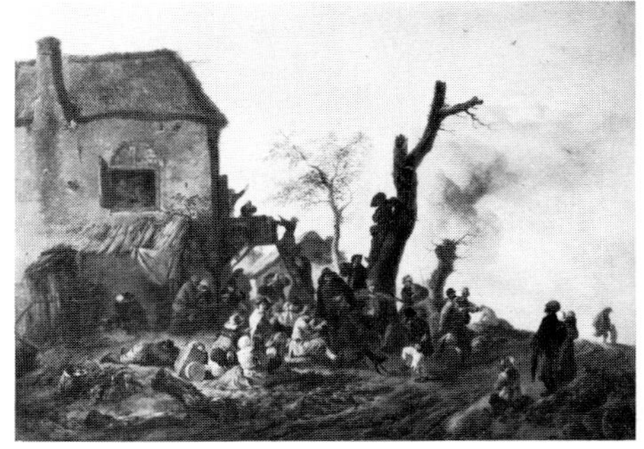

LANDSCAPE WITH A LARGE NUMBER OF PEASANTS MERRYMAKING IN FRONT OF A COTTAGE
1646

Oil on canvas
52·5 × 75·1 ($20\frac{11}{16} \times 29\frac{9}{16}$)
inscr(br): *PHLSWV* (mon) *1646*.
Assheton-Bennett bequest (1979.516)

Follower of Philips Wouwermans

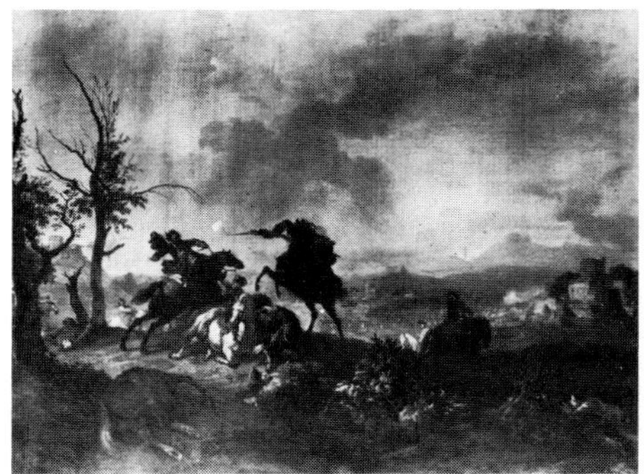

BATTLE SCENE

Oil on canvas
50·7 × 65·2 ($19\frac{15}{16} \times 25\frac{11}{16}$)
Unsigned
Presented by Mrs. E. F. Hickman in memory of her husband (1931.129)

Adolphe Yvon
1817–1893 French

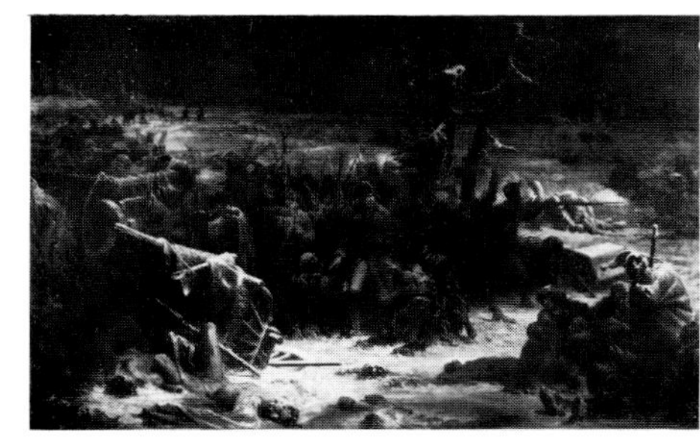

MARSHAL NEY SUPPORTING THE REAR GUARD DURING THE RETREAT FROM MOSCOW

Oil on canvas
179·8 × 301 ($70\frac{3}{4} \times 118\frac{1}{2}$)
s(brc): *Adᵉ. Yvon. 1850* (?)
Royal Manchester Institution, 1857, from which transferred (1882.7)

Januarius Zick
1730–1797 German

CHRIST HEALING THE SICK
1773

Oil on canvas
116·9 × 148·2 (46 × 58⅜)
s(bc): *jan: Zick inv: / et pinx: 1773 / convin*(?), and inscr(bl): *MAth Cap. 8*:v. *17 / Ph: J: de Loutherbourg Pinxit*
Presented by Manchester Y.M.C.A., 1961 (1979.612)

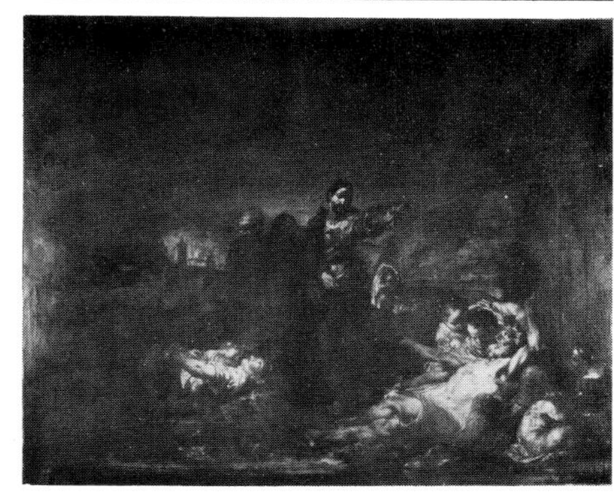

Johann Zoffany
See English School catalogue, Vol. I

Francesco Zuccarelli
1702–1788 Italian

CLASSICAL LANDSCAPE

Oil on canvas
59·8 × 84·5 (23½ × 33¼)
Unsigned
Presented by the Trustees of the will of the late Lady Marks of Broughton (1972.91)

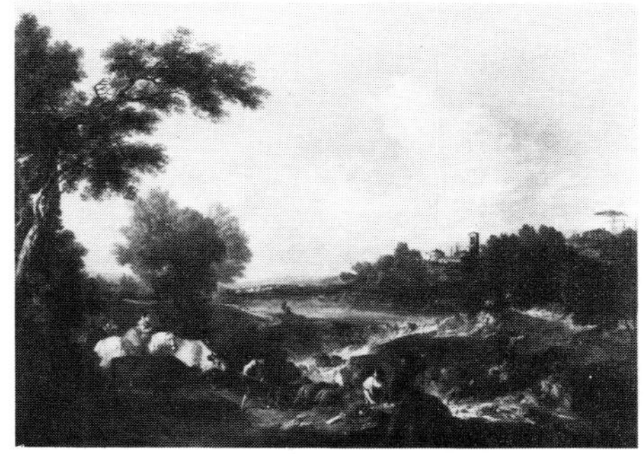

APPENDIX I

British Paintings acquired after, or not included in, publication of Vols. I and II

Francis Bacon
b. 1909

PORTRAIT OF HENRIETTA MORAES
1965

Oil on canvas
198 × 147 ($77\frac{15}{16} \times 57\frac{7}{8}$)
Unsigned
Purchased with the aid of the Wilfrid R. Wood Bequest Fund and a grant from the Victoria and Albert Museum
(1979.603)

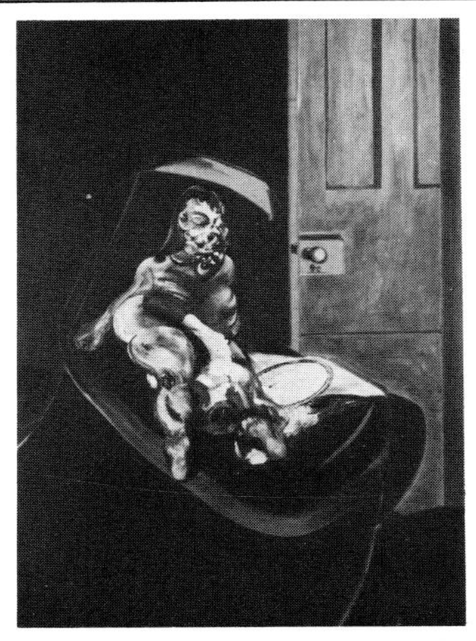

Richard Parkes Bonington
1802–1828

PAYS DE CAUX: TWILIGHT

Oil on canvas
31·1 × 41 ($12\frac{1}{4} \times 16\frac{1}{8}$)
Unsigned
Assheton-Bennett bequest (1979.529)

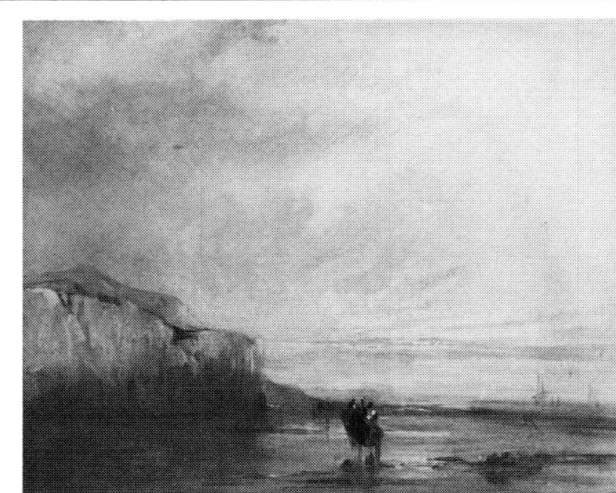

VIEW IN (?) BRITTANY: BRIDGE, COTTAGES AND WASHERWOMEN

Oil on panel
31·7 × 40·9 ($12\frac{7}{16} \times 16\frac{1}{8}$)
Unsigned
Assheton-Bennett bequest (1979.530)

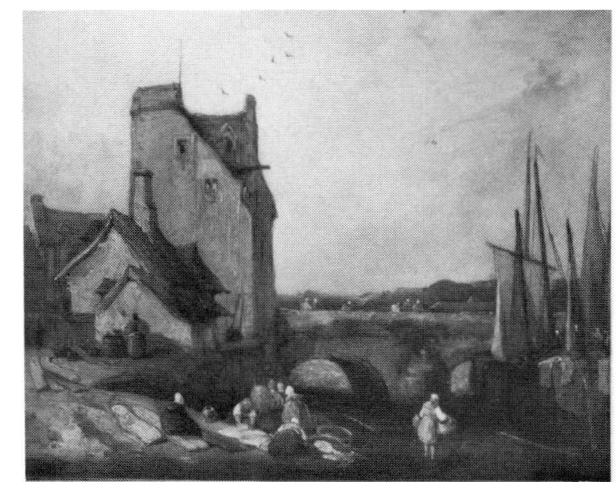

William Bradley
1801–1857

LADY WITH A DOG

Oil on canvas
77 × 64 ($30\frac{5}{16} \times 25\frac{3}{16}$)
Unsigned
Edwin K. Hilton gift (1979.599)

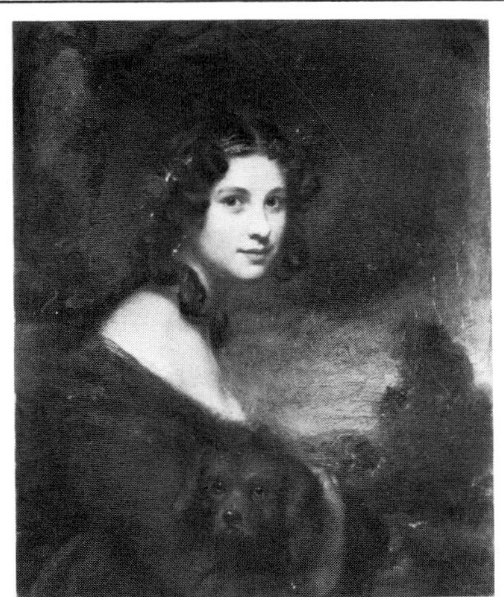

Guy Edward Broun-Morison
b. 1868

THE HARBOUR, PONT AVEN

Oil on panel
25·4 × 35·6 ($10 \times 14\frac{1}{16}$)
s(brc): *G. E. Broun-Morison*
Lady Mary Boyd Dawkins bequest (1979.604)

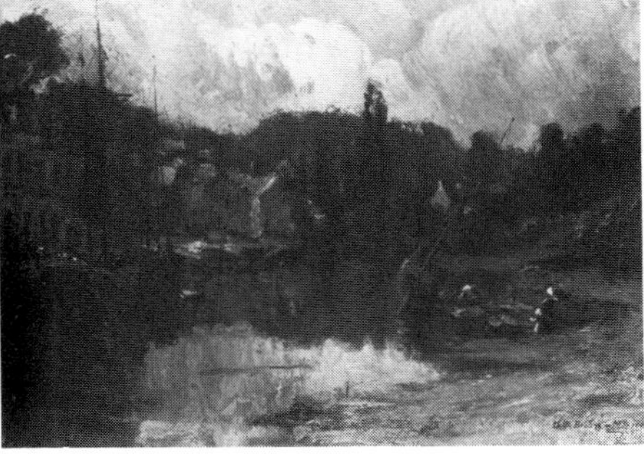

James Patchell Chettle
1871–1944

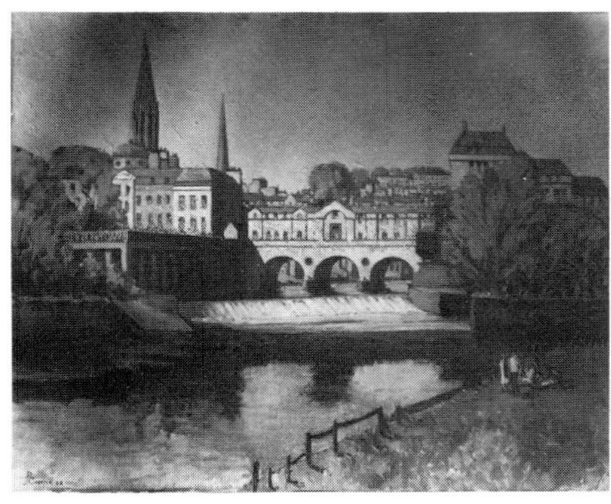

PULTENEY BRIDGE, BATH
1938

Oil on canvas
71 × 91·2 (28 × $35\frac{7}{8}$)
s(blc): *J P CHETTLE 38*
Provenance unknown (1979.605)

John Crome
1768–1821

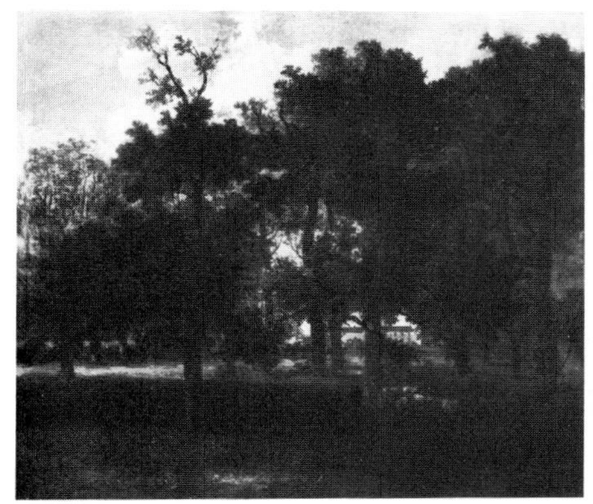

WOODLAND SCENE WITH SHEEP
(CHAPEL FIELDS)

Oil on canvas
64 × 76·3 ($25\frac{3}{16}$ × $30\frac{1}{16}$)
Unsigned
Purchased with the aid of a grant
from the Victoria and Albert Museum
(1979.547)

Francis H. Dodd
1874–1949

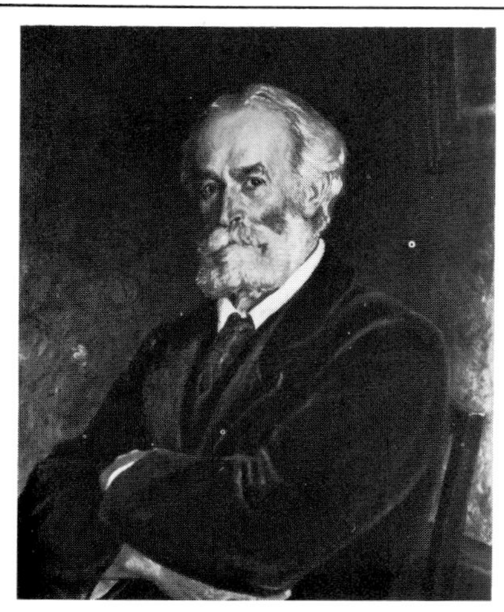

CHARLES PRESTWICH SCOTT
(1846–1932)
Editor of the Manchester Guardian
1872–1929
1916

Oil on canvas
76·2 × 63·5 (30 × 25)
s(brc): *Francis / Dodd. / 1916*
Mrs. Alice Olga Scott bequest
(1978.180)

English, *c.* 1915

BRENDA, COUNTESS OF WILTON
(1896–1930)
née Peterson, m. 6th Earl of Wilton, 1917

Oil on canvas
129·4 × 98·7 ($50\frac{15}{16} \times 38\frac{1}{2}$)
Unsigned
Presented by the Rt. Hon. The Earl of Wilton (1979.582)

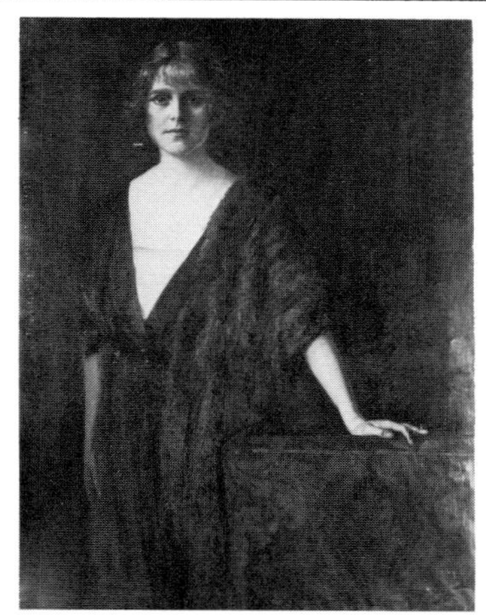

Stanhope Alexander Forbes
1857–1947

FARMYARD
1937

Oil on canvas
76·5 × 61 ($30\frac{1}{8} \times 24$)
s(blc): *Stanhope A. Forbes. / 1937.*
Provenance unknown (1979.133)

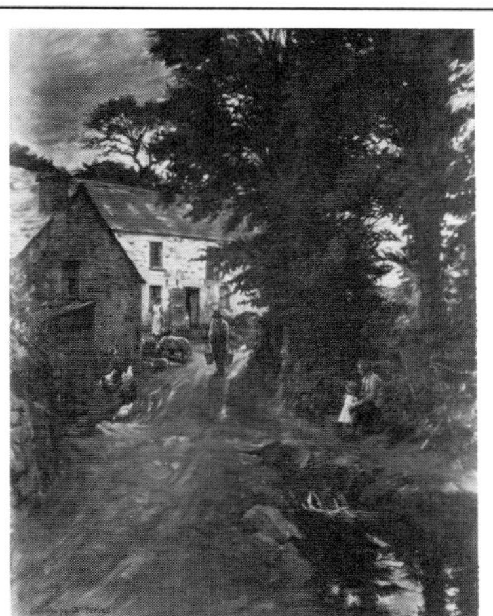

Thomas Gainsborough
1727–1788

A PEASANT GIRL GATHERING FAGGOTS IN A WOOD
1782

Oil on canvas
169 × 123 ($66\frac{1}{2} \times 48\frac{1}{2}$)
Unsigned
Purchased with the aid of grants from the Victoria and Albert Museum and the National Art-Collections Fund (1978.138)

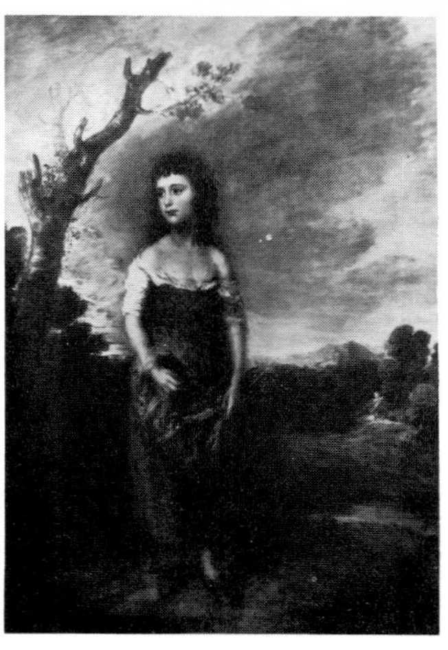

John Frederick Herring Senior
1795–1865

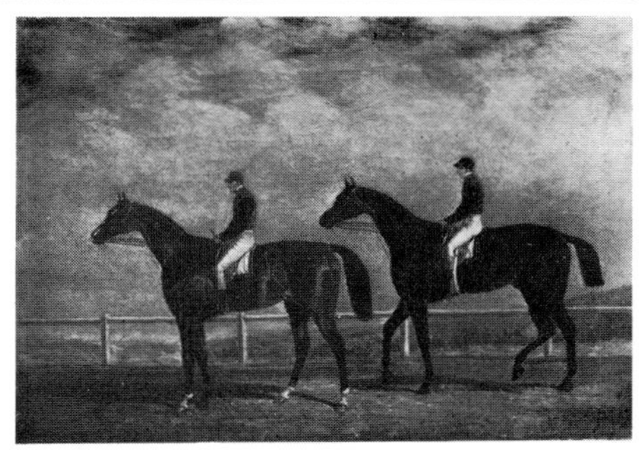

THE ASCOT CUP, 1829
The Earl of Chesterfield's 'Zinganee'.
The Duke of Rutland's 'Cadland'

Oil on canvas
20·6 × 30·2 ($8\frac{1}{8} \times 11\frac{7}{8}$)
s(brc): *J. F. Herring. 1829*
Assheton-Bennett bequest (1979.531)

Howard Hodgkin
b. 1932

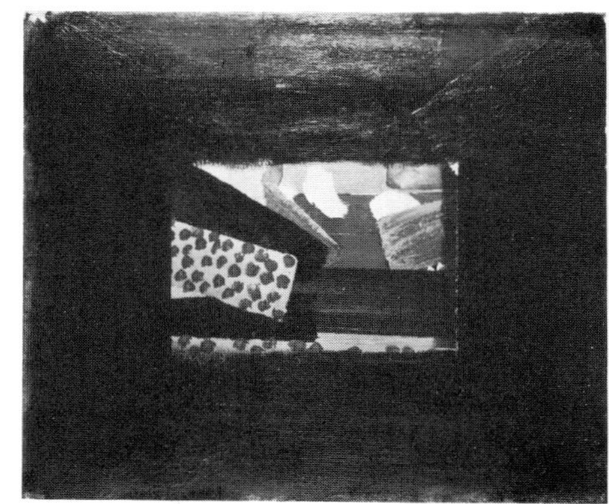

THE HOPES AT HOME
1973–77

Oil on plywood
91·3 × 106·7 (36 × 42)
Unsigned
Purchased with the Wilfrid R. Wood bequest (1978.71)

Frederick William Jackson
1859–1918

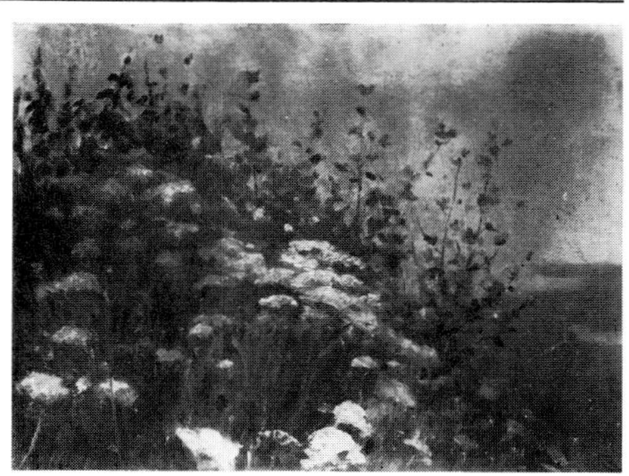

A FLOWERY BANK

Oil on canvas
25·2 × 35·3 ($9\frac{15}{16} \times 13\frac{7}{8}$)
s(brc): *F. W. JACKSON*
Ian Pringle gift (1979.573)

David James
active 1881–92

THE TIDE COMING IN, GERNARDS HEAD, CORNWALL
1889

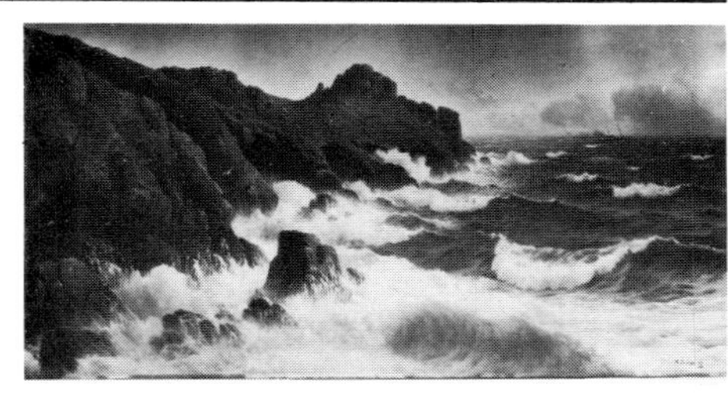

Oil on canvas
64 × 127·8 ($25\frac{3}{16} \times 50\frac{5}{16}$)
s(brc): *D. James 89*
Provenance unknown (1979.600)

Geoffrey Key
b. 1941

ALBERT SQUARE, MANCHESTER
1965

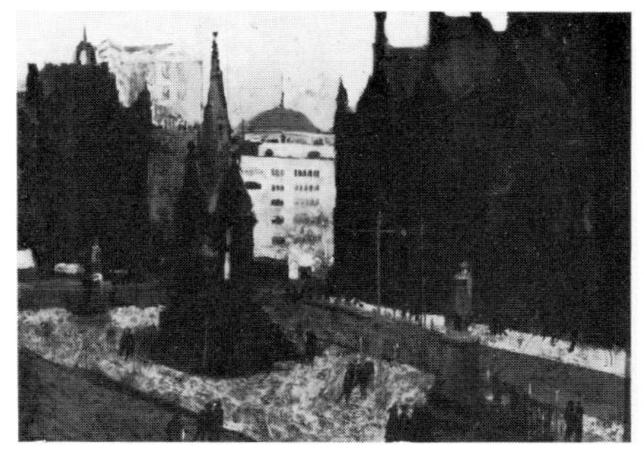

Oil on hardboard
34·7 × 49·9 ($13\frac{5}{8} \times 19\frac{5}{8}$)
s(blc): *G KEY 65*
Purchased from the artist (1979.50)

John William Buxton Knight
1842–1908

EVENING
?1904

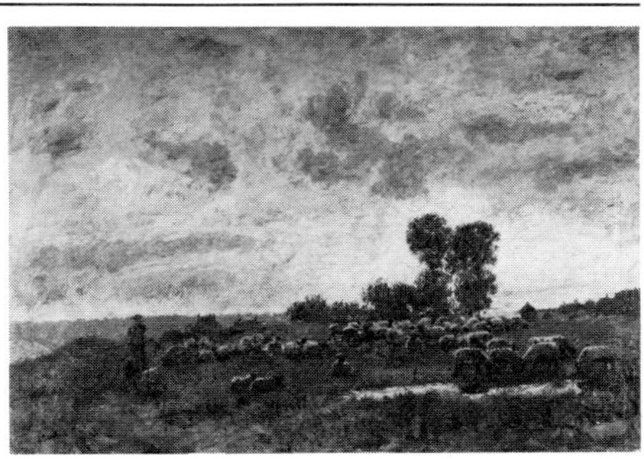

Oil on canvas
50·8 × 76·3 ($20\frac{11}{16} \times 30\frac{1}{16}$)
s(blc): *J Buxton Knight / 1904* (?)
Lady Mary Boyd Dawkins bequest (1979.606)

THE MILL, BASINGSTOKE, HAMPSHIRE

Oil on canvas
30·7 × 40·7 ($12\frac{1}{8} \times 16\frac{1}{16}$)
s(brc): *J. Buxton Knight*
Lady Mary Boyd Dawkins bequest
(1979.607)

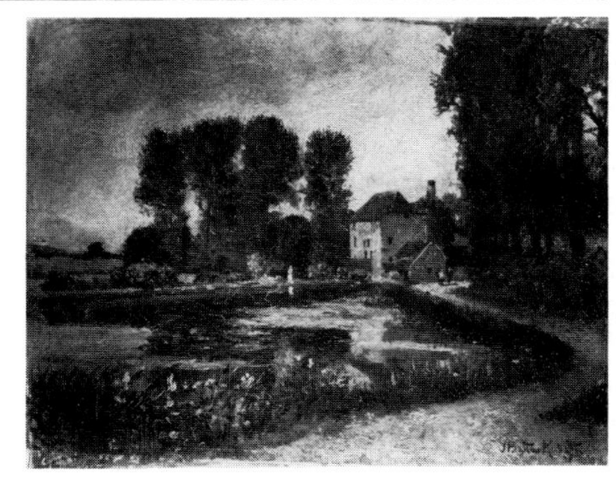

Henry Lamb
1883–1960

MARGARET ASHTON (1856–1937)
First woman councillor of the City of Manchester

Oil on canvas
112 × 86·3 ($44\frac{1}{16} \times 34$)
Unsigned
Gift of the Manchester University Women's Union (1979.601)

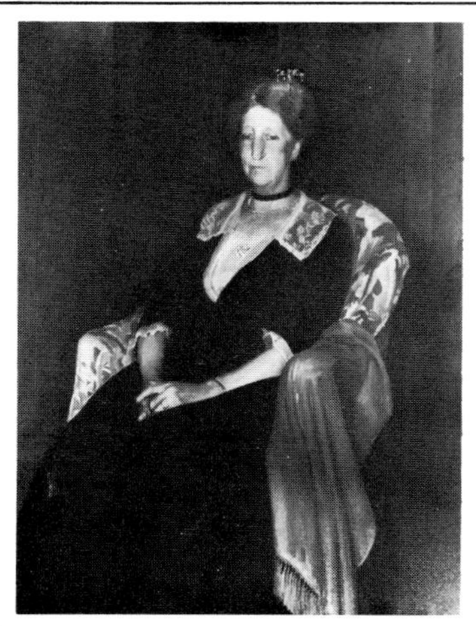

Peter Lanyon
1918–1964

BUILT UP COAST
1960

Ceramic tile, stained glass, wire, mirror and oil on masonite
60·4 × 41·3 ($23\frac{3}{4} \times 16\frac{1}{4}$)
Unsigned
Purchased (1978.89)

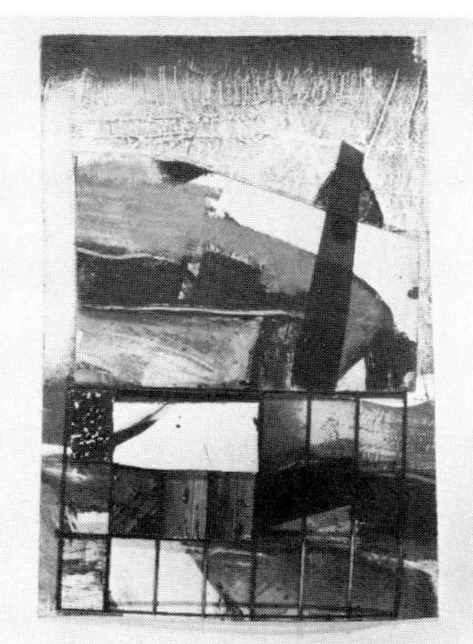

SILENT COAST
1957

Oil on masonite
122 × 93·6 (48 × $36\frac{7}{8}$)
s(blc): *Lanyon 57*
Purchased (1978.263)

Philippe-Jacques de Loutherbourg
See Januarius Zick

John Campbell Mitchell
1862–1922

AT THE CLOSE OF DAY
1903

Oil on canvas
51 × 62 ($20\frac{1}{8}$ × $24\frac{3}{16}$)
s(brc): *J. Campbell Mitchell 03*
Lady Mary Boyd Dawkins bequest (1979.608)

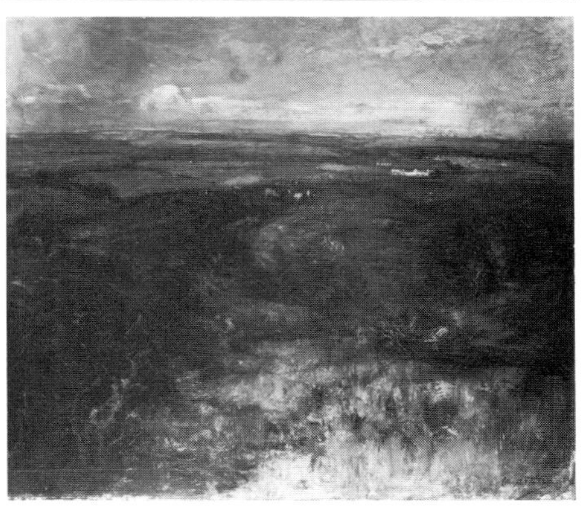

Thomas Saunders Nash
1891–1968

THE SERMON ON THE MOUNT

Oil on canvas
127·2 × 102·2 ($50\frac{1}{16}$ × $40\frac{1}{4}$)
Unsigned
Dr. Jane Walker bequest (1939.23)

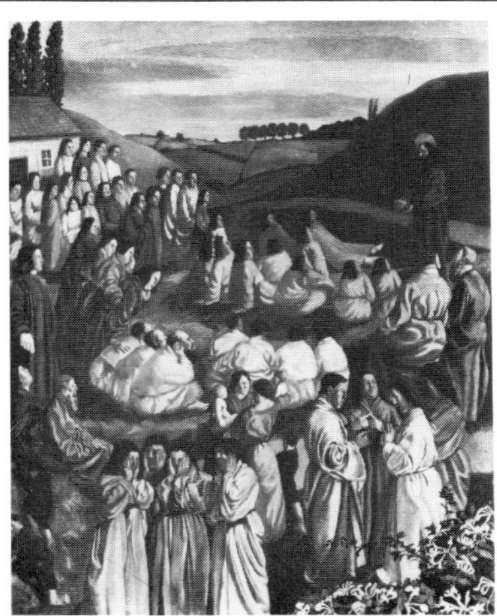

L. Spindler
active 1839–45

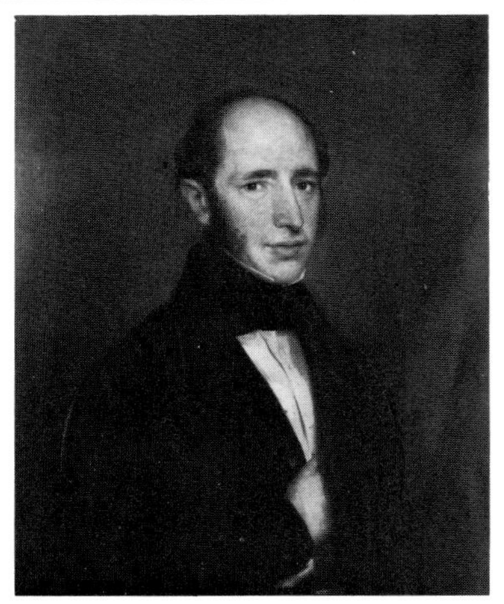

PORTRAIT OF WILLIAM CROSFIELD
(1805–1881)
Manchester merchant and Quaker
1843

Oil on canvas
77 × 64 ($30\frac{5}{16} \times 25\frac{3}{16}$)
s(tlc): *Spindler 1843*
N. Pearson gift (1971.62)

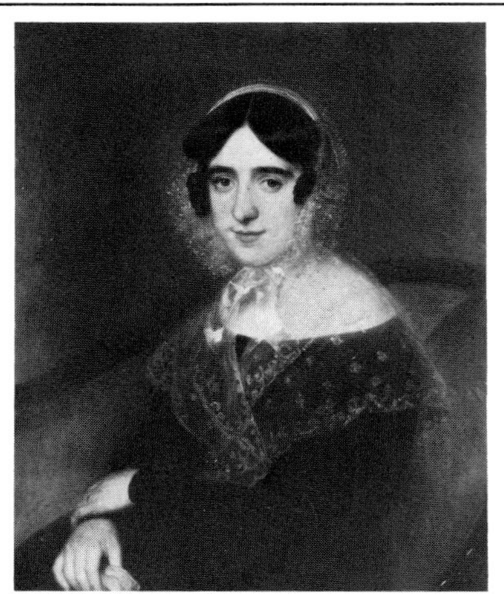

PORTRAIT OF ELIZA CROSFIELD
(1807–1886)
Wife of William Crosfield (above)
1843

Oil on canvas
76·1 × 63·2 ($29\frac{15}{16} \times 24\frac{7}{8}$)
s(trc): *Spindler | 1843*
N. Pearson gift (1971.63)

Thomas Stringer
fl. 1767–87

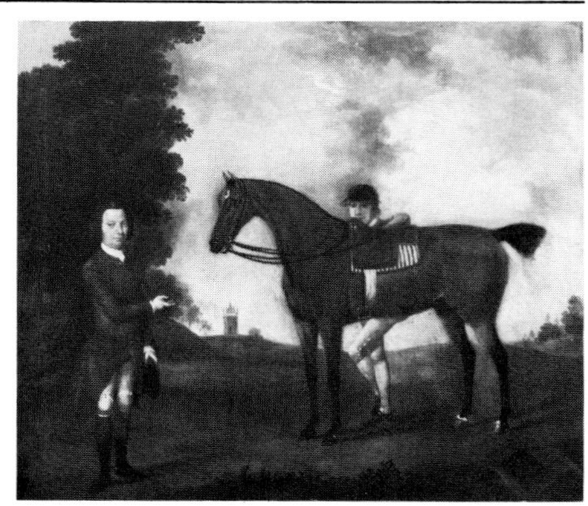

'DRIVER' WITH OWNER AND GROOM

Oil on canvas
63 × 75·3 ($24\frac{3}{4} \times 29\frac{1}{2}$)
inscr(brc): *DRIVER | Hunter | given by the Honble John | Grey | . . .* [illegible] *Cook*[*e*]
Transferred from the Parks Department (1979.609)

HUNTSMAN IN A LANDSCAPE

Oil on canvas
62 × 91 (24 7/16 × 35 5/8)
s(bc, on rock): *TS*
Transferred from the Parks Department (1979.610)

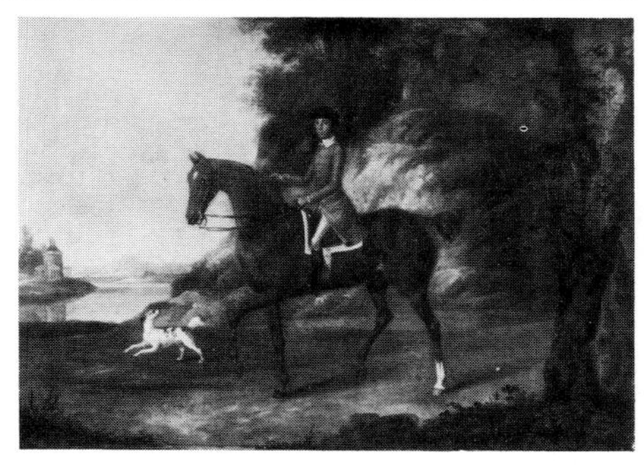

Joseph Mallord William Turner
1775–1851

THOMSON'S AEOLIAN HARP
1809

Oil on canvas
166·7 × 306 (65 5/8 × 120 1/2)
Unsigned
Allocated to Manchester by H.M. Treasury in lieu of Capital Transfer Tax from the Trustees of the Walter Morrison Picture Settlement (1979.7)

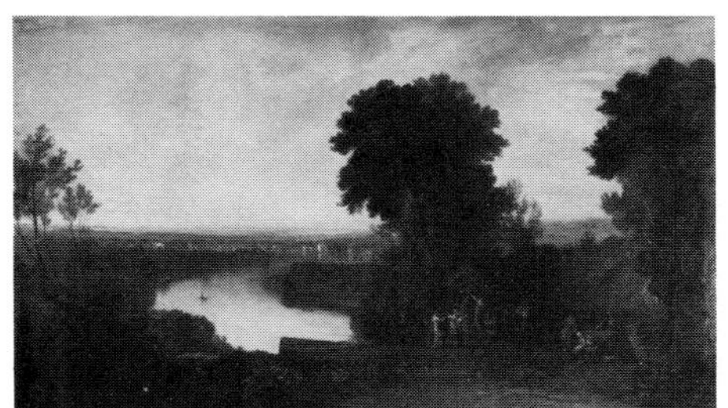

Phillip Westcott
1815–1878

CROMWELL'S PROTEST AGAINST THE PERSECUTION OF THE WALDENSIAN AMBASSADORS

Oil on canvas
144 × 212·5 (56 11/16 × 83 11/16)
Unsigned
Gift of the Manchester Grammar School (1979.602)

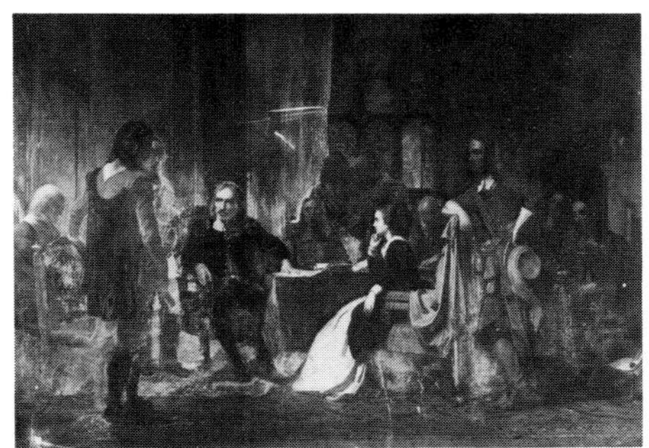

Henry Clarence Whaite
1828–1912

GIPSY CAMP, SUNRISE

Oil on canvas
86·3 × 152·6 (34 × 60$\frac{1}{16}$)
s(brc): *H. Clarence Whaite*
Mrs. Roberts gift (1979.611)

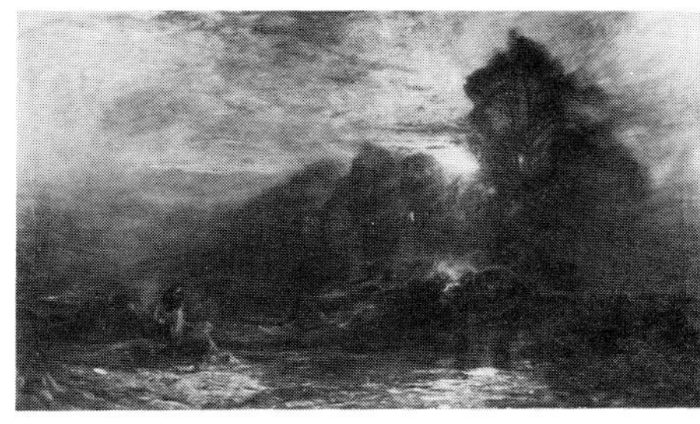

APPENDIX 2

Paintings from the collection of the Royal Manchester Institution

The Royal Manchester Institution was founded in 1823. Its collection was transferred to the City of Manchester in 1882 along with the R.M.I. building, to become the present City Art Gallery. This appendix lists firstly the mode and date of acquisition by the R.M.I. of works which fall within the scope of this volume. The other details are given in the body of the catalogue.

Henriette Browne (Mme Jules de Saux; née Sophie de Bouteillier)
A BROTHER OF THE CHRISTIAN SCHOOLS
R. N. Philips gift 1856

Attributed to Giovanni Francesco Guerrieri (as Follower of Honthorst)
LOT AND HIS DAUGHTERS
James Bradock gift 1832

Alphonse Legros
STUDY OF A HEAD (C. NAPIER HEMY)
Gift of the artist 1879

STUDY OF AN OLD MAN'S HEAD
Gift of the artist 1881

ST. JEROME
Gift of the artist 1881

Adolphe Yvon
MARSHAL NEY SUPPORTING THE REAR GUARD DURING THE RETREAT FROM MOSCOW
Purchased (?) 1857

Listed below are items transferred from the R.M.I. which have been sold or written off.

Fra Bartolommeo
VIRGIN AND CHILD
Rev. G. H. Bowers bequest. Sold 1931

Jan Both and Paul Bril
TOBIT AND THE ANGEL
Henry Bannermann, junr. Destroyed 1931

Christian-Wilhelm-Ernst Dietrich
ST. JOSEPH REPOSING
James Bradock gift, 1832. Sold 1931

Giulio Romano
HEAD OF ST. JOHN
James Bradock gift, 1832. Sold 1931

Guercino (Ribera ?)
ITALIAN BANDIT
James Bradock gift, 1832. Sold 1931

Gerrit van Honthorst
MARRIAGE OF ST. CATHERINE
James Bradock gift, 1832. Sold 1931

Girolano Muziano
ECCE HOMO
James Bradock gift, 1832. Destroyed 1931

Perino del Vaga
VIRGIN AND CHILD
James Bradock gift, 1832. Destroyed 1931

Pietro da Cortona
MOSES PRAYING THAT THE ISRAELITES MAY CONQUER
Charles O'Neil gift, *c.* 1832. Sold 1931

JOSHUA COMMANDING THE SUN AND MOON TO STAND STILL
Charles O'Neil gift, *c.* 1832. Sold 1931

SUSANNAH AND THE ELDERS
Provenance unknown. Sold 1931

School of Rembrandt
SURRENDER TO THE VICTOR (OFFERING A CROWN)
Provenance unknown. Sold 1931

Rubens
FIGURE STUDY (A SATYR?)
James Bradock gift? 1832. Sold 1931

GOING TO MARKET
Richard Holt gift, 1845. Sold 1931

Tintoretto
CRUCIFIXION
James Bradock gift, 1832, Sold 1931

Titian
THE WOUNDED HAND
James Bradock gift, 1832. Sold 1931

Alessandro Turchi
BACCHANTES
William Townend gift?, 1834. Destroye 1931

Paolo Veronese
A MUSIC PARTY
James Bradock gift, 1832. Sold 1931

APPENDIX 3

Pictures no longer in the collection, but which were in the 1910 'Handbook to the Permanent Collection'

The Handbook entry numbers are given first. Signatures were not recorded in the Handbook.

18 **Berghem (attrib. to)**

LANDSCAPE WITH FIGURES AND SHIPPING

Oil on canvas
1ft 1in × 1ft 5ins
Mrs. Robert Hatton gift (1908.33)
Destroyed 1934

83 **after Correggio**

MADONNA AND CHILD

Oil on canvas
diameter: 2ft 5ins
Mrs. Elizabeth Wood bequest (1908.22)
Sold 1931

380 **Teniers (attrib. to)**

STRIKING A BARGAIN

Oil on canvas
1ft 6ins × 1ft $10\frac{1}{2}$ins
Mrs. Robert Hatton gift (1908.32)
Destroyed 1934

APPENDIX 4

Index of Portraits

APPENDIX 5

Index of Donors

Index of Artists by Schools

Francken, Hieronimus II
Master of Frankfurt
Master of the Magdalene Legend
Michau, Theobald
Ommeganck, Balthasar Paul
Peeters, Bonaventura
Pourbus, Frans the Elder
Rysbrack, Pieter Andries
Snyders, Frans
Teniers, David the Younger

French
Aved, Jacques-André-Joseph
Bidlingmeyer, Jules
Blanche, Jacques-Émile
Boudin, Eugène-Louis
Bouguereau, William-Adolphe
Browne, Henriette
Caille, Léon-Émile
Cavailles, Jean-Jules-Louis
Cazin, Jean Charles
Chaigneau, Jean-Ferdinand
Challié, Jean-Laurent
Chéron, Louis
Compard, Émile-François-Jacques
Corot, Jean-Baptiste-Camille
Courbet, Gustave
Degas, Hilaire-Germain-Edgar
Derain, André
Dubufe, Claude Marie
Dufy, Raoul
Dughet, Gaspard
Ernst, Max
Espagnat, Georges de
Fantin-Latour, Henri
Feyen, Jacques-Eugène
Forain, Jacques-Louis
Fragonard, Jean-Honoré
Fraye, André
Frère, Pierre Edouard
Gauffier, Louis
Gauguin, Paul
Harpignies, Henri
Hervier, Louis-Adolphe
Isabey, Eugène
Jacquet, Gustave Jean
La Fosse, Charles de
Lascaux, Elie
Léger, Fernand
Legros, Alphonse
Le Sidaner, Henri-Eugène-Augustin
Lhermitte, Léon-Augustin
Loiseau, Gustave
Marchand, Jean
Marcoussis, Louis
Maufra, Maxime
Maze, Paul
Meissonnier, Jean-Louis-Ernest
Mengin, Charles-Auguste
Michel, Georges
Millet, Jean-François
Monticelli, Adolphe
Moret, Henry
Mura, Frank
Perrault, Léon Bazile
Piot, Antoine
Pissarro, Camille
Pissarro, Felix
Renoir, Pierre-Auguste
Salanson, Eugénie Marie
Scheffer, Ary
Semenowsky, Émile Eisman
Sisley, Alfred
Soyer, Paul Constant
Tal-coat, Pierre
Troyon, Constant
Utrillo, Maurice
Venard, Claude
Vernet, Claude-Joseph
Veyrassat, Jules Jacques
Vlaminck, Maurice de
Vollon, Antoine
Vouet, Simon
Yvon, Adolphe

German
Eitner, Ernst
Freyse, Albert
Kiesel, Conrad
Mengs, Anton Raphael
Morgenstern, Christian Ernst Bernhard
Schreyer, Adolphe
Schweitzer, Adolf
Siefert, Arthur
Voltz, Friedrich Johann
Weber, Philip
Zick, Januarius

Hungarian
Wagner, Alexander von

Israeli
Kohn, Elias
Rubin, Reuven
Simon, J.

Italian
Balducci, Matteo
Batoni, Pompeo

Berrettini, Pietro da Cortona
Boccaccino, Boccaccio
Bonzi, Pietro Paolo
Bordone, Paris
Carlone, Carlo Innocenzo
Caroselli, Angelo
Conca, Sebastiano
Corsi, Niccolò di
Crespi, Giuseppe Maria
Daddi, Bernardo
Gardini, Théophile
Gaulli, Giovanni Battista
Ghirlandaio, Ridolfo
Giordano, Luca
Guardi, Francesco
Guardi, Giacomo
Guerrieri, Giovanni Francesco
Matteo di Giovanni
Monti, Francesco
Mura, Francesco de
Pannini, Giovanni Paolo
Pasini, Alberto
Passerotti, Bartolommeo
Reni, Guido
Ricci, Marco
Ricci, Sebastiano
Romiti, Gino
Santoro, Rubens
Siciolante, Girolamo, da Sermoneta
Stanzioni, Massimo
Strozzi, Bernardo
Turchi, Alessandro
Zuccarelli, Francesco

Japanese
Oguiss, Takanori

Polish
Karlowska, Stanislawa de
Luyten-Behnisch, Jadwiga

Russian
Gluckmann, Grigory

Swiss
Erni, Hans
Giacometti, Alberto
Kauffmann, Angelica